Although born in Easington, County Durham, **Les**
P___ _le spent his first eight years in Ratho, south-west of
_____urgh. His father's subsequent career moves led Les
a__ _is family on a whistle-stop tour of England before
th_ _ventually settled in Birmingham when Les was in
hi_ _d-teens.

joined Birmingham's Metropolitan Ambulance
Se__ _e in 1977, for little more reason than that it seemed
a g__ d idea at the time. That good idea led to three
unk__ _en decades of round-the-clock emergency work.

_ Pringle is the holder of the Queen's Medal for
Lo_ _and Exemplary Service.

*Also by Les Pringle*

Blue Lights and Long Nights

*and published by Corgi Books*

# Call the Ambulance!

## Les Pringle

**CORGI BOOKS**

TRANSWORLD PUBLISHERS
61–63 Uxbridge Road, London W5 5SA
A Random House Group Company
www.rbooks.co.uk

**CALL THE AMBULANCE
A CORGI BOOK: 9780552158534**

First publication in Great Britain
Corgi edition published 2010

This book is a work of non-fiction based on the life, experiences and
recollections of Les Pringle. In some limited cases names of people,
places, dates, sequences or the detail of events have been changed to
protect the privacy of others. The author has stated to the publishers
that, except in such minor respects, the contents of this book are true.

A CIP catalogue record for this book
is available from the British Library.

Addresses for Random House Group Ltd companies outside the UK
can be found at: www.randomhouse.co.uk
The Random House Group Ltd Reg. No. 954009

The Random House Group Limited supports The Forest Stewardship Council (FSC),
the leading international forest certification organization. All our titles that are
printed on Greenpeace-approved FSC-certified paper carry the FSC logo. Our
paper procurement policy can be found at www.rbooks.co.uk/environment

Typeset in 12/15pt Times New Roman by
Falcon Oast Graphic Art Ltd.
Printed in the UK by CPI Cox & Wyman, Reading, RG1 8EX.

2 4 6 8 10 9 7 5 3 1

*For all those who ever have worked or ever will work at Henrietta Street Ambulance Station*

# Chapter One

'You mustn't push!'

'Sorry, but I must.'

'Can't you hang on? We're almost there.'

She let out a stifled moan. 'Sorry. Oh God!'

When Mike and I collected the mother-to-be from her home I hadn't suspected for a moment that the birth might be imminent. Her waters were intact and the contractions were nicely spaced at four-minute intervals. She was quite relaxed as we walked out to the ambulance and once on board chatted comfortably about this and that until a contraction pulled her up short. I glanced idly at my watch as Mike pulled on to the main road to begin the three-mile drive to hospital.

When a second contraction came along fast on the heels of the first, I looked down at my watch again and sat bolt upright. Only a minute since the previous one! How could that be? I moved to the edge of the seat and tried to work out how much longer the journey would take. No more than six minutes, eight at the outside; we might just make it. And we almost did. The contractions continued fast and furious and then, with the hospital gates no more than a thousand yards away, her cheeks puffed up and that concentrated, faraway look I'd come to know so well settled on her features. She was starting to push. I knew nothing was going to stop the inevitable, but that didn't prevent me making my heartfelt, if futile, plea for her to hang on a little longer.

'Sorry . . . my waters have just gone.' She hoisted up her smock in time for me to watch the bed linen hungrily soak up the fluid and what it couldn't cope with slosh down the stretcher frame to the floor, where it found its way into every nook and cranny. I was on my feet now and didn't even have time to consider the unfairness of it all as another contraction brought the baby's wrinkled, hairy scalp into view. The next contraction would surely herald its entrance into the world.

I shouted through to Mike and asked him to pull over, while doing my best to guide the little body into the world as gently as I could. The cord was tight round its neck, but I managed to slip a finger underneath and hook it out of harm's way when the shoulders appeared a few moments later. Other than that it was a textbook birth. The baby girl sucked in air, screwed up her face and let out a cry that was music to my ears. I bundled her up in a sheet and was congratulating the mother when she pointed at the window with a shout of surprise.

'Look!'

I glanced up and found myself staring into a pair of eyes pressed up against the glass.

Then Mike's voice boomed out.

'Oi! You! Clear off unless you want my boot up your arse!'

The eyes vanished, only to be quickly replaced by another pair. Mike was outside the ambulance and still remonstrating loudly. The second set of eyes lingered a while longer, then they too disappeared. Mike opened the back doors and climbed in, looking flushed. He glanced down at the mother and baby.

'Everything OK?'

'Yes,' I replied. 'What's going on outside?'

'Oh, it was just a couple of yobs. I parked near a bus stop and they wandered down to see what was going on. You can't believe the cheek of youngsters these days.'

The new mother gazed down at her baby contentedly.

'Oh well, it will be something to tell Becky when she grows up I suppose.' She stroked a little cheek and smiled at the gurning face. 'One day you'll be thrilled to hear you were delivered by someone just out of school while everyone off the number twenty-six bus was watching, won't you?'

A slight exaggeration perhaps, but you can't let the facts get in the way of a good story, especially one that will last a lifetime.

I sat back in my seat and took a moment to bask in the self-satisfied glow that always comes after successfully delivering a baby. Mike, however, saw to it that the glow was short-lived.

'Have you seen the state of your shirt?'

I looked down. At some point my tie had dipped into fluids on the stretcher and then gone on to smear the unpleasant residue of amniotic fluid, mucus and blood across the front of my shirt. The woman followed my gaze.

'Goodness, you are a mess.'

It was an understatement, but I made light of it.

'Not to worry, I've got plenty of shirts back on station.'

'What about your tie?' She hesitated for a moment before continuing. 'This might sound like a strange question, but will you be throwing it away?'

It was a strange question, which I answered without much thought. 'Well, yes. I suppose so.'

'In that case, do you mind if I have it?'

'What?'

'I know it sounds a bit weird, it's just that I thought it might be a nice memento for Becky when she grows up. You know what I mean – the tie of the ambulance man who delivered her and all that.'

I unclipped it and handed it to her.

'If you really want it, be my guest.'

She folded it up and tucked it carefully into her overnight bag.

'Thanks. What's your name, by the way?'

'Les.'

'Well, Les, thanks again. I'm sure Becky will treasure it.'

Mike and I wandered back outside after dropping

mother and daughter off in the maternity department. I'd picked up a mop and bucket from the sluice room and got to work mopping the ambulance floor. Mike didn't seem inclined to help, preferring to draw contentedly on a cigarette and study the evening sky. He broke the silence after a minute or two of contemplation.

'You know, some people get the baby named after them . . . It's got to be a queer fish that gets a tie named after him.'

I squeezed out the mop. 'Very funny.'

'I tell you what though,' Mike continued. 'If you keep giving away ties there's going to be a national shortage. How many deliveries does that make it now?'

I carried on mopping. 'I don't know, I haven't been keeping count.' Of course, that was a lie. It was six, and six in just over a year and a half was at least four too many in most people's book. I picked up the sodden linen and dropped it into a plastic bag before starting the laborious task of cleaning the stretcher frame. I couldn't resist getting in a jibe when Mike flicked away his cigarette and yawned.

'Would you like me to see if I can find you a chair so you can watch me clean this mess up in comfort?'

He looked at me over the top of his glasses.

'Now, now, no need to be sarky; it doesn't become you. Anyway, it's your mess, not mine.'

'My mess? How do you figure that?'

'You must be encouraging these women, or you're a jinx. Either way, it's down to you.'

Mike was the shift patriarch while I still languished depressingly close to the bottom of the pecking order. I'd been in awe of him since arriving at Henrietta Street Ambulance Station as a new recruit just over eighteen months earlier. In his mid-fifties and built like a bull, he was a tough, charismatic individual who, in common with a lot of people working at the Street, had spent many years in the forces before joining the ambulance service. His army days had taken him to the D-Day beaches and then on to see active service in Malaya and Korea. Heaven knows what he must have thought when I and others of my generation started walking through the door with our long hair and less-than-focused view of discipline. He mostly kept his thoughts to himself, only occasionally going off on a rant about the shortcomings of the younger generation. It was all a front though; behind the scary exterior was a man of compassion, wit and fierce loyalty. You needed friends like Mike at the Street. Despite having qualified six months or so earlier, I was still finding my feet in an ambulance depot every bit as tough as the inner city it did its best to care for.

When everything had dried out we loaded the stretcher and set off back to the Street. We couldn't think about taking on another job before I got cleaned up and sorted out a fresh shirt. Twenty minutes later I wandered into the messroom buttoning a crisp new shirt taken straight from the packaging and hoping I hadn't missed any pins. Mike was sitting at the communal table sharing a pot of tea with Jack and Larry, two of our shift mates. Jack was the newest member of the shift, despite being in his mid-thirties, and still had three months to go before being fully qualified. Larry, an irreverent character, was a couple of years younger but had ten years' experience under his belt. He looked up when he noticed me.

'I hear you've been at it again.'

I feigned puzzlement. 'At it?'

'Yes, at it. That's got to be at least eight. I'm going to start painting storks on the side of your ambulance.'

'Ties might be a better idea,' Mike suggested.

I sat down and squeezed half a cup from the all but empty teapot.

'Very amusing. Anyway, it's six, not eight.'

'I thought you weren't counting,' Mike said.

'I'm not. It's just that it happens to be six.'

I'd already delivered more babies than some might in an entire career. It's strange how these things pan out, but at the time it was given as read that if a baby was to be born during our time on duty, then it would be me and whoever I was working with who would end up delivering it. In a similar way, others found themselves attending every nasty road accident that came along, while for the next crew it might be cardiac arrests. The whole business, irrational as it might sound, was a fact none the less, and I was beginning to think that all I had to do to send a pregnant woman into labour was to wish her the time of day. Larry had the dubious reputation of attracting every hopeless drunk in Birmingham like a moth to the flame. As we sat around drinking tea and chewing the fat, it didn't take long for him to come up with a story that combined alcohol and childbirth.

'I think I was working with Ian Williams from "D" shift when we were called to a drunken woman in labour at a social club. It was just about closing time and when we got there she was lying outside on the grass verge, flat on her back with her knees in the air.' He looked round at the rest of us. 'You know that bloody horrible sinking feeling you get sometimes even before you get out of the cab?' We all nodded. 'Well, I had it big time. She was a hefty piece, eighteen stone at least, and howling with each contraction like someone was jabbing her with a cattle prod. When I suggested that it might be an idea to get in the ambulance, she refused point blank. She said she was comfortable where she was and wasn't moving. Even when I pointed out to her that it was dark, starting to rain and that she had an audience of at least twelve drunks, she still wouldn't budge.'

'You never did have much of a way with women,' Mike observed.

Larry gave him a sanctimonious smile and took a sip of tea.

'So what was it all about?' Mike asked. 'Was she a bit simple or something?'

'Heaven knows. I suppose she couldn't have been that bright if she thought spending the evening boozing in a social club was a good idea when she was full term. But even so, drunk or not, what was going on in her head?' Larry put down his cup. 'That's not all. There was a chip shop on the corner and most of the people coming out of the club got themselves a fish supper and then wandered over to watch the show. Some even brought their pints out as well – quite a little party. So there we were, crouching in the rain trying to help her, with the smell of chips, vinegar and beer wafting over us. Not that she gave a monkey's. She just parted her legs even wider and after about three pushes out comes the baby – just like shelling peas. I've never been able to drive past that club since without a picture of her coming into my head. And that poor baby, I hope it never finds out that it was born on a grass verge in the rain surrounded by ogling drunks stuffing chips down their throats, especially when it could all have been done neat and tidy in the back of the ambulance.' Larry rested his case and surveyed his audience while we battled to shake off the images he'd planted in our heads.

His story only served to underline what I'd been learning for the past eighteen months: no amount of training can prepare you for the realities of life on the road. The idiosyncrasies of the public are legion, if not limitless. I mean, what training officer would dream up a practice scenario the like of which Larry had just described? And if it had been dreamt up, would any new recruit have taken it seriously? I doubt it; I know I wouldn't have. Even putting the eccentrics to one side, the truth is that real patients tend to be less compliant than the plastic mannequins we practise on and, unlike training school, their symptoms never seem to be laid out on a sheet of paper to be ticked off one by one. Some may argue that it all adds spice to a job that by its very nature is unpredictable anyway. And, if I'm honest, part of me agrees with them – which is just as well, because I was to see plenty of it.

# Chapter Two

Henrietta Street was, and still is for that matter, the largest ambulance station in Birmingham, if not the country. It sits anonymously amidst drab warehouses and disused factories on the edge of Newtown, just half a mile from the city centre. Close by are the deprived districts of Handsworth, Lozells and Aston. Perhaps not a prime location for a luxury development, but as good a spot as any to base emergency ambulances covering the inner city. It was staffed by a wonderful bunch of people, but my goodness – they were an intimidating lot in the eyes of a new recruit. If you imagine starting halfway through the term at a new school where everyone is older and cleverer than you, where friendships are firmly established and every desk is already taken, you might get an inkling of what I mean. I'd stepped into this world some eighteen months earlier, in 1977, as a nervous twenty-three-year-old after making the fateful decision to join the ambulance service on little more than a whim.

I'd slowly integrated myself into life at the Street by keeping my head down and my mouth shut – a piece of advice given in training school that had stood me in good stead. It was wise advice for two reasons. Firstly, cocky youngsters simply weren't tolerated by the 'old hands'. Their military backgrounds had ingrained in them a strict sense of hierarchy that did not brook challenge. Secondly, and perhaps more importantly, coming fresh from training school with the latest theoretical knowledge doesn't prepare you for the harsh reality of life in the ambulance service. Only help and encouragement from your shift mates coupled with hard-won experience turn you into the finished product. I had been lucky to be placed on 'C' shift. There wasn't a bad bone amongst them. Mike and Steve were ex-army and in their fifties. Below them in the pecking order came Larry and Howard, and quite a long way below them came Jack and me.

Jack Turner had arrived on the shift nine months after me. I had looked forward to his arrival in the belief that he would take up the position I currently held of general dogsbody to the shift, allowing me to move on to a higher plane. Sadly, my hopes were to be dashed. Where I'd struggled to find my feet, he'd slipped effortlessly into the ways of depot life from the very start. It wasn't an easy trick to pull off, and the ease with which he managed it caused me envy and admiration in equal measure. The extra ten years he had on me, plus his seemingly ingrained understanding of the ways of the world, meant he could sit back with an appealing air of self-assurance while I was still creeping round the place trying to be all things to all men. That said, he still had three months of his probationary period to run while I had become fully qualified six months earlier. This gave us the grand total of just over two years' experience between us and, while management did their best to avoid crewing in-experienced people together, there were times when it was unavoidable. When it happened, Jack and I were left to face the world on our own. Run-of-the-mill cases didn't present us with many problems, but I was never quite able to shake off the worry that the next job would be the one to expose our collective naivety. That feeling came over me for the umpteenth time one morning when we were sent to a bungalow in Bearwood where the caller feared the patient to be deceased.

Despite my forebodings, I couldn't help but appreciate the warm, cosy feel of the bungalow as Jack and I followed the dapper little man. Bypassing the lounge and study, he turned into a softly lit corridor with three closed doors to the left. He approached the second and took hold of the ornate handle before seeming to lose confidence. After a moment's hesitation, he turned to us.

'She's at peace now. If nothing else . . . at least she's at peace.'

The solemnity of the moment weighed heavy on me. I still felt hopelessly inadequate when it came to dealing with bereaved relatives, despite having faced it quite a few times. I always seemed to be groping for the right words without ever really finding them. On this occasion

I settled for extending what I hoped was a sympathetic look. He, in turn, let out a small sigh and pushed open the door.

He'd met us a couple of minutes earlier on the doorstep, wearing an air of melancholy that only increased my feeling of foreboding. Immaculately turned out in a tweed jacket, grey flannel trousers and highly polished brown brogues, I put him in his late fifties. His face was round and ruddy; the kind of face that under normal circumstances probably broke into an easy smile. There was no suggestion of a smile now, and after a perfunctory greeting he came straight to the point.

'I'm sorry about this, but it's too late to do anything for her. I'm afraid she's passed away.' Jack and I glanced at each other as we stepped into the entrance hall. Relatives are loath to accept the sudden death of a loved one and rarely abandon even the slightest glimmer of hope.

'If you'd like to follow me,' he said, as he turned into the hall. 'I found her when I came in from walking the dogs. She's in the bedroom. It's this way.'

She lay on the bed like a waxwork mannequin. In death, her smooth, unlined face had taken on a faintly yellow pallor, emphasized all the more by her tumble of grey hair. I guessed she was in her late fifties or early sixties. She was cold and her pupils were fixed and dilated. It was plain she'd passed away some time ago.

'I'm sorry,' I said. 'But you're right – if there was anything we could do, you know we would do it. I'm ever so sorry.'

'Yes, I know. I was sure she'd been gone for some time when I found her.' He spoke without looking away from the woman. 'She was a wonderful person, you know. I'm going to miss her so much.'

We stood respectfully for what I thought to be a suitable length of time before tackling the delicate business of getting a little information about the woman. I never feel comfortable about pulling out a notepad and pen at times like these, but it has to be done. He answered my questions mechanically, only looking up when I explained the need for her doctor to attend.

'We have to make arrangements for her GP to come out. Only a doctor can certify death and we have to wait for—'

He interrupted me quietly.

'You don't need to worry about that. I've already phoned her private doctor. He should be here soon.'

Jack slipped out of the room to radio our Control and keep them up to speed, leaving us to wait for the doctor. I took care to tread softly and allowed the conversation to roam over whatever aspect of the woman's life he wanted to talk about. Talking, even to strangers, helps at times like these. Perhaps sharing anecdotes about the dead person pushes back the stark reality of their passing for a short while and allows the enormity of what's happened time to penetrate. At one point he drifted on to the subject of her medical history. It seems the only ailment she ever complained of was a chronic stomach condition. This had caused her pain and discomfort from time to time, but wouldn't have proved fatal. As we talked, I found myself admiring his quiet fortitude. Which made it all the more curious that I would shortly be possessed with the urge to grab him by his tweed lapels and shake him.

When initially examining the lady, I'd noticed a blotchy mark, or what could have been an old scar, on the front of her neck about two inches below her jaw. It was a faded purple, which probably wouldn't have stood out too much in life. Out of curiosity, and as a means to keep the conversation going, I asked how she'd come to pick up a scar in such an unlikely spot.

'Ah, that,' he said. 'It was there after I cut her down.'

I repeated the words in my head. Surely I'd misunderstood. He was still looking at his wife when I spoke to him again, slowly.

'When you cut her down? What do you mean by "cut her down"?'

He didn't avert his gaze from the woman.

'The rope was too tight. I couldn't undo it. I had to cut it with a hacksaw blade and—'

Jack came back into the room and caught the last few words.

'What's this about a rope?'

The man looked at him sharply. 'I was just telling your friend that I had to saw through it with an old hacksaw blade.'

We listened closely as he worked his way through the story. He'd come back from walking the dogs to find the house empty. Having no reason to be worried by her absence, he went into the kitchen and made himself a coffee. After drinking the coffee and reading the sports pages, he began to wonder where she'd got to. He mooched round the bungalow thinking she might have left a note. Failing to find one, he checked the garage to see if her car was there. Perhaps she'd gone for a drive. This was where he found her. She'd tied a rope to the up-and-over garage-door mechanism and fashioned a noose at the other end. After placing the noose round her neck, she must have climbed on to the car bonnet and stepped off.

Why had he waited so long to tell us? He appeared to be a normal, rational man. How could he have failed to blurt out the whole story the moment he opened the door to us? We'd stood in the bedroom calmly talking about his wife and her life and there hadn't been so much as a hint. That was a point: why was she on the bed if this had all happened some distance away in the garage? Jack started to fidget.

'I'd better get back on the radio and ask them to send the police.' He'd reported earlier that we were dealing with a sudden death at home. Now he was going to have to explain that we'd somehow managed to overlook the fact that she'd hanged herself. Rather him than me. I was left looking at the woman, wondering why I hadn't realized something traumatic had happened to her. I'd seen my fair share of people either hanging from makeshift nooses, or shortly after they'd been cut down. Most had the manner of their death etched on their faces. Not this woman; her expression was serene.

I turned back to her husband with the intention of posing some pertinent questions, but he spoke first.

'Would you like to see the garage?'

'Yes,' I said, 'I think I would.' Seeing the evidence for myself might wipe away the doubts I had about his story.

Once again I followed him through the bungalow until we came to the internal garage door, where he stopped.

'Let me switch on the light,' he said. 'The first switch operates the doors; it's the second one for the lights – bit of a silly arrangement, really.' He groped for the switch and illuminated the garage with a click. Straightaway my eyes fell on the rope hanging limply from the door mechanism, just as he'd described it. The severed noose lay on the floor. Everything else was as she'd created it in preparation to end her life. After a few moments of silent reflection I stepped back into the corridor. On the way out he switched off the light and closed the door, obviously a man of ingrained habits.

'Why didn't you tell us about this sooner?' I asked in a tone that must have betrayed some of the exasperation I felt.

He bit back defensively. 'I wasn't hiding anything, young man . . . I assumed you knew.'

This was too much.

'And how was I supposed to know if nobody told me?' I was tempted to continue along this line, but thought better of it and instead asked the next obvious question. 'Anyway, leaving that aside . . . how did she end up in the bedroom?'

He wore a pained expression as he drifted into an explanation. After cutting her down, he'd dragged her into the kitchen and tried to revive her. Eventually he accepted that she'd been dead for some time and that his efforts were futile. Leaving her on the kitchen floor was an affront to her dignity, so he decided to take her on through to the bedroom. He noticed the phone when he stopped to catch his breath in the living room and phoned her doctor. The doctor told him to dial 999 and said he was leaving immediately. With the second call made, and with some of his strength restored, he resumed the process of hauling the corpse through the house. It had been at rest on the bed some ten minutes before our arrival.

I gazed absently through the window, trying to digest this latest turn. It's no easy matter moving a dead body on your own, and I was trying to figure out how he'd managed it when a Jaguar pulled up outside.

'It looks like the doctor's turned up,' I said.

He looked over my shoulder. 'Yes, that's his car. I'd better let him in.'

We reached the front door as a police car, its blue lights still revolving, swung through the gates and crunched to a halt on the gravel drive. The doctor, who bore a striking resemblance to the patient's husband, was reaching for his bag on the back seat of the Jag. With it safely retrieved, he smoothed down his suit and walked purposefully towards us. His expression was suitably grave as he extended an arm to shake hands with the man at my side.

'Bad business, Hugh. Where is she?'

Unlike us, he'd been given the full story over the phone.

As the doctor headed off to the bedroom, one of the police officers drew me aside and asked to see the garage. He'd picked up the gist of what had happened over his radio but was keen to establish the accuracy of the story before calling his sergeant out. I was happy enough to oblige and when we reached the internal door I waved him inside with a word of warning.

'Now, don't touch the first switch. The second one's for the lights—'

The rumble of the garage doors opening drowned out anything else I had to say. As daylight flooded in I looked resignedly over his shoulder in time to watch the evidence being tangled up in the mechanism of the up-and-over doors. The constable was standing by the light switch, staring at the door as if willing time to reverse itself. When it didn't, he gave me a beseeching look and uttered the only word that came to mind.

'Shit!'

Oh well, at least it wasn't just the ambulance service messing up this morning.

Thinking it perhaps best to make myself scarce, I made my way back through the house and found the others in the living room. I perched on the edge of the settee next to the doctor to finish off my paperwork. When that was done there was nothing to keep us, so I stood up to say my goodbyes and in passing pointed out to the woman's husband that he would probably have to get clearance from the Coroner's office before contacting a funeral director.

'A funeral director? I don't understand. That surely isn't my job.'

I looked at him carefully. He couldn't be making a joke at a time like this, surely.

'At some point you're going to have to make arrangements for a funeral director to come out,' I said.

He seemed perplexed. 'Sorry, but I don't see how that falls into my lap. I want to help of course, but . . .'

He wanted to help? I continued to watch him carefully, and I tried again.

'It's the relative's task to sort out the undertaker, and as it's your wife—'

'My wife? She's not my wife, for heaven's sake. I just walk her dogs. She's a neighbour – a very good one, admittedly, but just a neighbour.'

A sense of unreality settled over me for a second time. Though it hadn't been stated, I'd been working on the assumption they were man and wife. Given his familiarity with the woman, and the free run he seemed to have of the house, I'd certainly not been given any reason to think otherwise. I opened my mouth to say something, goodness knows what, when a shriek came from the bedroom. The home help had arrived unnoticed and, alarmed at the presence of a police car and ambulance, had rushed into the house. I can't say why, but she'd gone straight to the bedroom where she found the unattended body on the bed.

The subdued atmosphere in the cab as we made our way back to Henrietta Street was eventually broken by Jack.

'I suppose that could have gone better.'

I glanced at him to see if the irony was intended and was met by a grin. Jack was good at defusing the tension I sometimes felt, but he couldn't alter the fact that we were a raw and inexperienced crew. Everyone else on the shift knew it too. Whenever the rota demanded Jack and I work together, Mike, our shift leader, would shake his head and mutter, 'Here we go again. The blind leading the bloody blind. Heaven help the bloody patients.' I would do my best to feign an air of self-confidence and point-edly ignore such remarks, but I knew he was right. Having become at ease dealing with routine jobs hadn't fooled me into thinking I was ready for all that might come my way. If anything, the opposite was true. Jack was right about this case though – it could have gone better. But the more I thought about it, the more con-vinced I became that this time it was more a matter of events conspiring against us than anything else.

The rest of the shift was on station when we got back and while Jack made the tea I recounted the case to them as a martyr might describe life's tribulations.

Larry flicked over a page of his newspaper and said, 'That bloke must have thought you were a right idiot.'

'Which bloke?'

'The neighbour!'

I was taken by surprise. I'd thought everyone would

have taken my side and seen the neighbour as being 'the right idiot'.

'How was I to know he was her dog-walker?' I said, indignantly.

'Didn't you ask him?' Mike said.

I wondered whose side they were on.

'No, actually, I didn't. What was I supposed to say – "Good morning, sir, I presume you're the dog-walker?"' I regretted the words before I'd closed my mouth. Sarcasm aimed directly at the shift patriarch wasn't just bad form, it was a bad mistake. Mike was someone I respected above anyone else and, perhaps more importantly, someone I relied on to pull me out of the holes I regularly dug for myself. I looked at him contritely, but he said nothing.

'I think what Mike meant,' Larry interjected with exaggerated patience, 'was why didn't you say something simple like, "Excuse me for asking, but are you related to the lady?"'

'I thought it was obvious,' I replied. 'He treated the place as if it were his own. He was even on first name terms with her doctor, for Christ's sake.'

'He could have been her brother,' Howard said.

I was on the defensive now.

'I didn't think of that. I suppose he could have been.'

'Or he might have been a lodger,' Howard continued.

'Yes, true, but . . .'

'Or her lover, even.'

I admitted defeat. 'Yes, OK, I get the point. But you

can't deny that it was a bloody weird situation. You can't blame me for the fact that he said nothing about her hanging herself.'

'No, you're right about that. That would have stumped a lot of people,' Mike said.

I relaxed. Mike's endorsement hard on the heels of my sarcasm was more than I deserved. He took a sip of tea.

'Of course, that's not the way the court might see it.'

My stomach gave a little lurch.

'Court?'

Mike settled back in his seat and looked at me in a kindly, grandfatherly sort of way.

'I don't want to alarm you, but I see it like this. One way or the other you're going to end up in court. It might be the Crown Court, or it might be the Coroner's Court. Personally, I'm not sure which is worse.'

'Crown Court! Why? I mean—'

'This dog-walker of yours might have bumped her off . . . Didn't that possibility cross your mind?'

'Murder.' I felt rather than heard the hush in my voice. 'No – it didn't.'

'I mean,' Mike accepted a cigarette from Larry, 'there's only the two of them in the house and she met a violent end.'

'Yes, but he explained everything eventually.'

'He could have rigged up that rope himself. Maybe it was guilt that prevented him mentioning it sooner.'

I was feeling hot, uncomfortable and riddled with doubt.

'Even if all you say was true, what's it got to do with me? I'm not a copper.'

'I suppose that's a fact, but it doesn't excuse the careless destruction of evidence . . . does it?'

I felt on firmer ground. 'You can't blame me for that. It was the policeman who—'

'That's not how the court will see it, Les.' Mike blew out some smoke. 'You shouldn't have let the policeman go into the garage knowing there was a chance he'd mix up the switches. I can just hear the barrister . . . "I suggest to you, Mr Pringle, that you failed to take appropriate action to protect the evidence. As a trained emergency-service worker, your lack of awareness can, at best, be described as incompetence and, at worst, a dereliction of duty."'

I squirmed in my seat during the ensuing silence. Giving evidence in court would be bad enough, but being tarred as a bumbling halfwit at the same time didn't bear thinking about. I glanced at the others in the vain hope that someone would offer a smidgen of reassurance. They regarded me with serious expressions while all the time seeing what I couldn't see: Mike was deliberately toying with me as retribution for my earlier disrespect. They played their parts well. Larry was particularly good. When he spoke he wore the mournful face of someone watching a friend being led to the gallows.

'I think this murder thing's a bit far-fetched, Mike. The whole idea is ridiculous. The worst thing Les has coming is a grilling in Coroner's Court.'

Mike thought about it as he stubbed out his cigarette.

'You're probably right. Mind you, facing the Coroner might be worse.'

I looked from one to the other in exasperation before addressing Mike. 'How could it be worse?'

'If you've messed up in some way or other, the Coroner always finds out. He's like a dog with a bone, and when he thinks someone's in the wrong he doesn't pull any punches in his summing up.' Then, for good measure, he added, 'And our lot always send an officer along to take notes and report back.' He smiled grimly. 'Being blasted by the Coroner doesn't exactly advance your career.'

I felt ill and thoroughly confused.

'I didn't really do anything wrong, did I? It was just a series of misunderstandings.'

'You don't need to have done anything wrong to come out of that place punch-drunk.' Mike turned in his seat looking for Steve. 'Do you remember what happened to poor old Ian Tansy?'

'Bloody hell, yes. That was awful, wasn't it?' Steve said with a shake of the head.

My eyes flicked between the pair of them.

'So, what happened?' I asked, not really wanting to know.

'It was six or seven years ago,' Mike explained. 'He'd been called out to someone collapsed in the street and when he got there the patient was in cardiac arrest. So he and his mate started working on the bloke. They made a dash for the hospital with Ian keeping up chest compressions all the way, but it didn't do any good in the end. Some time later he got a letter telling him to attend Coroner's Court. The cause of death wasn't clear, and at the autopsy they discovered the patient had several rib fractures and a punctured lung. According to the Coroner, the damage was consistent with brutal cardiac compressions and may have contributed to the eventual outcome.' Mike looked round the room. 'Can you imagine having to take the stand and defend yourself after hearing something like that? And, as if things weren't bad enough, when he was giving evidence the dead man's wife stood up in court and pointed at Ian, shouting, "That's the man who killed my husband!" '

Larry whistled softly. 'What a nightmare. Is it really true? You're not making it up?'

'It's true all right,' Mike said. 'Steve will tell you.'

'So how did it all turn out?' Larry asked. 'What happened to him?'

'Nothing. He was exonerated of any blame when all the evidence came out.'

'I don't understand,' Larry said. 'How did he get away with it?'

'It wasn't a matter of him getting away with it. He'd done nothing wrong. It turns out that an eighteen-stone police sergeant with no training in resuscitation had been doing chest compressions before the ambulance arrived. He'd done the damage, but the finger was pointed at poor old Ian. And that brings me back to what we were talking about . . . Even when you've done nothing wrong, you can still be in for a mauling. Ian made light of it afterwards, but you could tell it really got to him. He left about six months later, went on the buses I think.'

My confidence was fragile enough without hearing stuff like this, and as another silence descended I contemplated life as a bus driver.

'Anyway,' Mike eventually continued. 'If you don't hear anything from the Coroner's office in the next couple of months you'll be in the clear.'

'Gee, thanks for that, Mike,' I said gloomily. 'That makes me feel a lot better.'

He smiled at me. 'That's the spirit. Now,' he held his mug in my direction, 'how about another cup of tea?' I took the mug without demur and as I shuffled off to the kitchen Mike had his final say. 'By the way, I don't expect to hear any more sarky comments from you in the future. I've told you before that it doesn't become you.'

# Chapter Three

I spent the next few weeks on tenterhooks, convinced it was only a matter of time before a letter arrived inviting me to come and make a fool of myself in Coroner's Court. Jack didn't lose any sleep over it; he was still a trainee, which meant it was my job to carry the can for any blunders. But in the end I needn't have worried. The letter failed to materialize and in the meantime I'd found plenty of other things to worry about anyway.

All I hoped was that Jack and I wouldn't be crewed together again for a while. Don't misunderstand me: I liked Jack, and we spent a lot of off-duty time together. He was great company and shone in conversation no matter what the topic. He did have an odd side to him, though, and in many ways was an enigma. Despite having left Handsworth Grammar with a respectable assortment of O-levels, he, for reasons even he couldn't explain, had taken up an apprenticeship in ladies' hairdressing. I don't want to denigrate hairdressers but, physically, Jack didn't

begin to fit the bill. He was built like a prizefighter –
heavy-shouldered, with hands like shovels and a temper
to match. As things worked out, his choice of career
proved to be an inspired one, as he went on to win a host
of styling competitions, finishing up as the youngest college
instructor in the country. Flushed with success and acclaim,
he dropped everything to become a long-distance lorry
driver specializing in continental work. An odd career
change by any standards, but at least one more fitting his
appearance. When that eventually began to pall, he
gravitated back to Birmingham and worked as a night-club
doorman before joining the ambulance service in his
mid-thirties. It was Larry who pointed out Jack's
resemblance to Fred Flintstone, probably inspired by his
worrisome beer belly, large fleshy nose and shock of black
hair.

When Jack and I next worked together, I laughed off
the usual comments about the blind leading the blind
while inwardly surrendering to a feeling of fatalism.
Coping with our comparative lack of experience was hard
enough, but it would have been a lot easier if the patients
had played their parts as well. Most did, but not all.
Getting information from some of them was like pulling
teeth. In an ideal world everybody tells the truth, is
neither evasive nor forgetful and has a modicum of
common sense. Alas, it's not an ideal world. Sometimes
people set out deliberately to fool us for reasons only they
can explain. Sometimes we are misled by a patient
who may be under stress or has temporary amnesia

due to accident or illness. Sometimes people are just so woolly-minded that you fear for them.

As Jack and I discovered, there's not much you can do when a patient deliberately withholds vital information. One particular patient, a middle-aged man, carelessly allowed ten inches of broken broom handle to be sucked from his grasp and vanish up his rectum. He'd probably expected it to reappear when it was good and ready and must have been mortified at its failure to do so. The decision to call an ambulance a couple of hours later was probably a tough one, but perhaps made easier when he decided to keep his dark secret to himself. We found him rolling about on the bed, clutching his stomach, complaining of increasingly intense abdominal pain and not offering a word of explanation. Jack worked his way through the usual questions and was told by the patient that he'd never had such a pain before and hadn't suffered any kind of injury. He'd not eaten anything since the day before and wasn't on any medications; the pain had simply come 'out of the blue' a few hours before. His colour and pulse were good, but there was no getting away from the fact that he was in a lot of discomfort, so we took him into Casualty and thought no more of it. It wasn't until the next day we discovered he'd died. He had persisted in hiding the truth even from the doctors and as a result had been shunted into a side-room to await further tests. It wasn't until his condition suddenly deteriorated with the onset of peritonitis that staff realized there was more to this case than had at first met the eye, and by then it was too late.

I don't think there had been anything Jack or I could have said or done to wheedle the truth from the man. When Mike heard the story later, he suggested that I put it down to experience and in future always ask patients with unexplained abdominal pain if they had by chance pushed ten inches of broomstick up their bottom. His advice was usually good, but on this occasion I decided it was perhaps best not to act on it.

Dealing with patients suffering from short-term memory loss can be just as tricky. They're not trying to mislead you, but they can make you look foolish all the same – especially at eight in the morning when the old grey cells have yet to get into gear. The villain of the piece had been out bright and early cleaning the ground-floor windows of his house when he'd toppled from the small stepladder. His legs were spotted protruding from the greenery by a neighbour, who went over to find him conscious but dazed. He'd recovered somewhat by the time we arrived, but was still trying to figure out why he should find himself sitting in a clump of Michaelmas daisies. A quick check didn't reveal any physical injuries, but the vagueness of his replies made me cautious and I asked if he could remember falling off the steps.

'That's the funny thing,' he said. 'One minute I'm cleaning the windows and then the next minute I'm sitting here.' He looked about him. 'The wife's going to give me hell when she sees what I've done to her flowers. She's always out here pruning and—'

I had to interrupt him. 'So you don't remember falling?'

'No – did I fall, then?'

I went on to ask him a few stock questions like his name, date of birth and phone number to test his recall. His name was Sam and, albeit with a bit of effort, he managed all the questions. Vagueness regarding time and place is pretty typical of someone with a head injury or, commonly, someone recovering after an epileptic fit. There was no evidence of a head injury and, as he'd fallen only a short distance on to soft earth, I ruled it out.

'Have you ever had an epileptic fit, Sam?' I asked.

He smiled and shook his head. 'No. At least, if I have, nobody's told me about it.'

I regarded him dubiously, but was pleased to see that his clarity of thought was fast returning. He was surprised when I suggested that a trip to hospital for a check-up might be a good idea.

On the journey in we ran over the events without finding a suitable explanation for his fall. His health was good and he wasn't on any medication. He seemed as mystified as me.

'Honest, I'm perfectly healthy. I haven't seen a doctor in years.'

'So you've never had a fit? You're not epileptic and you're not on any medications?' I persisted.

'No! Look, I'm wasting everybody's time. Can't you just take me home?'

'I think it's best that we get you checked over,' I said.

'If you have had a fit, just imagine what could have happened if you'd been driving.'

'Why do you keep saying that I might have had a fit, for Christ's sake? Why on earth should I have had a fit?' He was confident now and beginning to wonder why he'd agreed to come to hospital. Weighing it all up, I came to the conclusion that it had probably been a simple faint after all and I'd been barking up the wrong tree.

The triage nurse listened to my version of events and I felt confident enough to finish by telling her that Sam was not an epileptic and had probably fainted.

'Seems a bit odd that he can't remember falling, doesn't it?'

'Yes,' I said. 'But he's thinking clearly. He can even remember last week's football results.'

She turned to Sam. 'Are you sure you're not on tablets for anything?'

He didn't need any time to think. 'Just the ones for epilepsy.'

'What!' I spluttered. I looked at the nurse, who was regarding me with folded arms and a raised eyebrow. 'Honest, I asked him over and over if he—'

'Cubicle four, please,' were her parting words as she turned away to attend another patient, happy in the knowledge that she'd solved a problem in five seconds that had defeated me for the past twenty minutes. Feeling stupid, I watched her go before turning to Sam, who was lying on the stretcher looking the very picture of innocence.

'We went through everything over and over. Why didn't you tell me about your medications?'

He seemed surprised by the question. 'You never asked!'

We did a couple more jobs before eventually being sent back to the Street. Jack deposited himself in a chair and shook out the *Telegraph* while I moodily watched Mike and Howard play a game of snooker. I was still smarting at the memory of being made to look a chump in front of the hospital staff. These things hit hard when you're young and desperately trying to prove yourself. I still had to learn that you can't afford the luxury of an ego when working for the ambulance service. If you do develop one, then you can be sure that there's always someone or something round the corner waiting to stick a pin in it. Jack was altogether more sensible than me and laughed the whole thing off. Not much seemed to bother him; or, if it did, he didn't show it.

'That nurse,' I said. 'She was a bit snotty, wasn't she?'

Jack looked up from the crossword. 'What?'

'That nurse. She didn't need to walk off with her nose in the air like that.'

He returned his attention to the crossword. 'Will you shut up about that bloody job? You're like an old woman.' He plucked at his lower lip and lost himself in the crossword for a few minutes. ' "A hit for Paris". Two words, eight and four letters, starts with an A . . . "A hit for Paris" . . . Any ideas?' It wasn't often he asked for help with the *Telegraph* crossword, especially from me.

I shrugged. 'You know me and crosswords.'

'Yeah, silly me, I was forgetting that you still find the *Beano* hard work.'

I was trying to come up with a snappy retort when the emergency phone interrupted the process. I took the call and looked at Jack, still poring over the paper.

'Come on, then. We've got a man behaving strangely.'

It's just as well I didn't know that my ego was about to be deflated even further. This time I would have a woolly-minded relative and a very annoying red herring to blame.

We were shown into the bedroom by the patient's wife and paused a moment at the foot of the double bed to watch the antics of the middle-aged man. His head was wrapped in a large, professional-looking bandage and, true to the description we'd been given, he was acting very strangely. Languidly moving about in the bed, he pulled randomly at the blankets as if looking for something that was constantly eluding him. He hadn't seemed to notice our entrance, so I tried to attract his attention.

'Hello, sir.'

He glanced up and absently mumbled through an expression of incomprehension, 'Harrumph.'

His wife shrugged when I glanced enquiringly at her.

'He's been like this for the last twenty minutes. I can't get any sense out of him. That's why I called you.'

I had another crack at trying to establish some kind of dialogue with the man.

'It's the ambulance service. Your wife's called us because she thinks you might not be very well.' I waited a moment or two and then spoke in a slightly louder voice. 'Hello, can you hear me? What's your name?'

He stopped moving and seemed to think before replying. 'Erm – grafft slongenbut.' Apparently happy with his response, he resumed his careful inspection of the bed sheets, smoothing them out with his hand only to crumple them up suddenly in annoyance when whatever it was he was searching for remained hidden.

He didn't seem to notice Jack taking his pulse, and didn't pay any heed as I quizzed his wife in an attempt to get some background information. Apparently her husband had gone to bed the previous evening feeling well. No, he'd never behaved like this before. No, he didn't suffer from any illness. No, he didn't take any pills. In short, he was a fit and healthy man, until now. With the routine questions out of the way, I was left with the obvious one.

'Why's he got that bandage on his head?'

She told us about the car accident he'd been involved in a couple of days earlier and the nasty blow to the head he'd received. He'd spent the best part of two days in hospital as a result, mainly under observation. He'd arrived home late the previous afternoon with a clean bill of health despite the rather theatrical bandage. So, the facts spoke for themselves. He was a fit and healthy man who'd recently suffered a head injury and was now showing clear signs of cerebral irritation. The conclusion that he probably had a bleed to the brain wasn't difficult to reach; after all, two plus two makes four. He was able neither to consent to nor to refuse our offer to take him to hospital, making it our duty to get him there one way or the other for his own good.

After trying in vain to reason with him, we were left with no choice but to manhandle him off the bed and on to our carry-chair. He had no notion of what we were trying to do and started flailing about the moment we laid hands on him. He managed to grab the bedstead with one hand and clung tight while I tried to prise his fingers free. When I succeeded in that, it was to find he'd latched on to the wardrobe with the other hand and was hanging on for dear life while it swayed back and forth, threatening to tip over at any moment. My clip-on tie was the next target and ended up being flung across the room, and at some point in the struggle Jack lost most of the buttons from his shirt. It's hard work restraining someone while making sure you don't hurt them, and the whole business became a battle of attrition that we couldn't afford to lose. His wife didn't help matters by dancing around the edge of the melee giving advice and warning us to take care. By the time we had him tightly wrapped in a blanket and on our chair, all four of us had worked ourselves into quite a lather.

With phase one accomplished, Jack and I took a breather in preparation for what was going to be a precarious trip downstairs. The patient, who was no lightweight, gurned, groaned and grunted as he sought to kick himself free of the blanket's tight embrace. Fortunately for us all, the blanket did its job and we got to the bottom without mishap; from there it was a clear run to the ambulance and then on to the stretcher. It was probably the comforting presence of sheets and blankets that helped calm him. He was quietly searching through them when Jack, still breathing heavily, leaned round from the driver's seat.

'Do you think we should alert the hospital?'

I didn't have to consider the question for too long.

'Yes. Tell them we have a forty-year-old man with a suspected intracranial bleed. He's conscious but behaving irrationally.'

Forewarning the hospital of the imminent arrival of a seriously ill or injured patient was expected of us. Making the correct judgement was our problem. No one wanted to gain the reputation of being a 'panicker', causing nurses and doctors to leave what they were doing and come running when it wasn't warranted. On the other hand, turning up unannounced with a life-threatening case didn't win you many friends either.

After passing the message, Jack gunned the engine and we set off on the short trip to hospital. The patient wouldn't let me near him with an oxygen mask and I had little choice but to leave him to his own devices. He was still preoccupied with the blankets, and as I watched him the thought came to mind of how similar his behaviour was to that of a diabetic with low sugar levels. I'd come across quite a few diabetics by now and had picked up my fair share of bumps and bruises when some tried to kick me or pull my hair on the way out to the ambulance. I called through to Jack.

'Funny, isn't it? If we didn't know better we'd have thought he was a diabetic, wouldn't we? He's acting just like one.'

It was an idle comment at which I only expected Jack to grunt. The patient's wife, sitting quietly behind me, responded before Jack had chance.

'He is a diabetic, actually.'

I turned and looked at her.

'You told us he didn't have any medical problems! You told us—'

She interrupted. 'He doesn't have any medical problems, unless you count diabetes. And that's not really medical, is it?'

I didn't bother answering that.

'I asked you if he was on any medications—' I was cut off again.

'You asked me if he took any pills. Well he doesn't, he only has the injections!'

All was clear. The head injury – the red herring – had diverted me from the obvious. Couple that with the inexplicable lack of information from someone so close to him – his wife, for goodness sake – and the way I saw it we never stood a chance.

Of course, the way I saw it wasn't necessarily the way someone else might have seen it. A more experienced member of the shift would not have been fooled so easily. Mike was forever telling me not to take things at face value and to keep an open mind, while I listened attentively and nodded in agreement. He wouldn't have relied on the woman to volunteer the information as I had. If his suspicions had been roused he would have asked her directly if her husband was a diabetic and received a direct answer. If there had been no one else home he would have gone to the fridge, where diabetics usually store their insulin vials, and found the evidence for himself. These days we check blood-sugar levels as a matter of course. The necessary kits were readily available in the late seventies but, for reasons I will never understand, the powers-that-be didn't see fit to issue us with them; it baffles me to this day.

There was no time to cancel the hospital alert – we were only two minutes from the gates and would be there before the message got through. Waiting for us with two doctors at the Casualty entrance was the very same nurse to whom I'd handed over the epileptic patient earlier. She stepped forward, wanting to know if the patient's condition had deteriorated during the journey and what my overall assessment was. I had no choice but to come clean immediately.

'Well, it's like this. It doesn't look as if it's a brain haemorrhage after all. It seems that he's a diabetic.'

She frowned. 'Seems?'

'Well, to be more precise – he is a diabetic.'

Her frown deepened. 'You mean you've got us to drop everything and wait around here for you to turn up with a gentleman with low sugar levels?' She gestured towards one of the doctors. 'Dr Jenkins has left her patients and come down from ward twenty-one.'

I glanced at Dr Jenkins, who was gracious enough to smile politely.

'I'm really sorry about that. It's just that everything pointed to—'

The nurse, wanting to emphasize her displeasure, spoke curtly. 'OK, no point crying over spilt milk. Take him to cubicle four, please.' With that she turned on her heel.

We dropped the patient off in cubicle four and left him scrabbling at the blankets while a nurse tried to take a reading of his sugar level. I was mortified by the whole business and said as much to Jack.

'I can't believe it was the same nurse who came out to meet us. She's going to have me down as being a right moron.'

He smiled and patted me on the shoulder. 'Well she won't be far wrong then, will she?'

'Thanks for nothing.'

Jack looked at me and shook his head. 'Lighten up, for heaven's sake. At least something good came out of it.'

'Oh yes?' I said warily.

'Yes. That crossword clue, "a hit for Paris". The answer came to me on the way down the stairs. I was mulling it over and it just popped into my head . . . "Achilles heel"! Weird the way these things happen, isn't it?'

I stared at him. 'Are you serious?'

'Absolutely. It was Paris who fired the arrow—'

'No, I don't mean that! You were thinking about bloody crosswords when the three of us could have ended up in a heap at the bottom of the stairs?'

He looked disappointed. 'I can do two things at once, you know. Anyway, let's get back to the Street and have something to eat. And I don't want to hear another word about diabetics or nurses.'

And the patient? Minutes after receiving a syringe of glucose he was sitting up asking how long he had to wait for an ambulance home.

Of course when you come down to it, experience means repetition. If you deal with the same thing often enough, and see it in all its guises, you are less likely to get it wrong. I filed away the cases of the epileptic and the diabetic, determined not to be caught out again. That said, no amount of experience can prepare you for the completely unexpected. Jack and I were working through the last day of our stint together when we were called to a man suspected of having had a stroke.

His wife had been pale and trembling when she met us on the doorstep and, finding it almost impossible to talk, had simply ushered us inside. The few words she did manage to force out when we reached the living room were breathless and halting.

'He's going to be all right, isn't he? Tell me he's going to be all right.' She paused for breath. 'He's had a stroke, hasn't he?'

Her husband, a slightly overweight, balding man in his late sixties, was slumped in an armchair on the opposite side of the room, snoring loudly. His head leaned to one side, nestling in the wing of the chair. Saliva from the corner of his open mouth formed a trail down his chin and pooled in a dark stain on his shirt. Moisture glistened in the corners of half-opened eyes, which stared sightlessly through the window. One arm, devoid of any muscle tone, dangled to the floor where the hand rested on the carpet, the fingers a blotchy purple. A pink flush had spread about his face and neck and a hint of blue tinted his lips.

We didn't waste any time. Jack inserted an airway into the patient's mouth to prevent his tongue falling back while I wrestled with the oxygen cylinder, wondering why, when you're in a hurry, simple things seem to take so long.* With the oxygen mask eventually in place, I snatched a glance over my shoulder at his wife. She was standing by the door, clasping and unclasping her hands, her chest heaving as she tried to control her breathing.

'Is it a stroke? Has he had a stroke?' she repeated.

'That's possible,' I said, knowing that it almost certainly was. 'Try not to worry; we're going to look after him.'

With the words ringing hollow in my ears, Jack and I began the business of lowering her husband on to the floor before placing him in the recovery position.

We were on our knees supporting the limp body when

---

*Throughout my career it was constantly reiterated that oxygen therapy was the priority treatment for anyone suspected of having had a stroke, as it would help minimize further damage to the brain. In 2008 this advice was reversed and we are now told that oxygen should be avoided, as it could in fact be detrimental . . . Makes you think, doesn't it?

the unthinkable happened. From behind came a sudden, resounding bang, accompanied by a violent tremor running through the floorboards and up into our legs. It felt and sounded as though a shelf of heavy books had crashed to the floor. We flinched, and swung round in alarm to be confronted by the sight of the woman prone on the carpet. She was on her stomach with her head turned away from us and lying deathly still. Frozen for a moment, our burden still in our arms, we gaped at her, not just in surprise but in the certainty that this was no simple faint.

Jack broke the silence. 'Christ! Here, take his weight. I'll check her out.'

He disentangled himself from our patient and moved across to the woman, leaving me struggling to heave the man into the recovery position alone. With that done, I left him with the oxygen mask clamped to his face and joined Jack. His fingers were at the woman's neck searching for a pulse and for the first time I saw stress written on his features. He looked at me and shook his head.

'Nothing.'

We turned her on to her back and, after selecting another airway, Jack placed it into her mouth. Her husband's tortured breathing and the hiss of the oxygen cylinder were all that broke the silence as we started to try to resuscitate the woman. Jack was rhythmically inflating the rubber bag attached to the mask covering her face while I counted out the cardiac compressions. Now occupied by the physical routine, we had chance to think and try to come to terms with what had happened. Jack cast a worried glance at our original patient.

'What the hell are we going to do? We need help; we can't cope with this on our own.'

The man was still greedily sucking in the oxygen, but there was little doubt that the rate of his snoring was slowing down. The room had suddenly become hot and stuffy and keeping up the cardiac compressions was draining work. I wiped away a droplet of sweat that had run down my forehead and made its way to the end of my nose. We were in a classic catch-22 scenario. We couldn't make a dash for the ambulance with the woman and leave her husband; on the other hand, we couldn't do anything for him while all our efforts were for her. Were we to try to save someone who looked as if they were about to die, or try to revive someone who had already died? There was only one way to get help, so I broke off the compressions again, went over to the telephone and dialled 999. I had just got through when there was a new and altogether unwanted development.

'Mum! Dad! What in the name of heaven has happened?'

The voice came from behind me and I turned to see a tall woman in her mid-thirties standing in the doorway. On one side of the room her father lay unconscious, and a few feet away lay her mother. She watched mesmerized as Jack worked, methodically alternating between cardiac compressions and forcing air into the lifeless body. Then she turned to me. I was by the window holding the phone and experiencing a sudden rush of irrational guilt, almost like a burglar caught red-handed. What explanation could I offer? Thirty minutes ago her parents had been going about their normal, quiet routine and then in the blink of an eye everything had been irrevocably shattered. The metallic voice of the operator sounded a million miles away as she asked which emergency service I wanted.

'Ambulance!' I snapped back, then, with my hand over the mouthpiece, I looked at the woman and searched for some appropriate words. After a moment, I heard myself say, 'I'm calling for an ambulance.'

She didn't seem to understand.

'But aren't you . . .' The sentence was left unfinished as she dropped to her knees by her mother and began speaking to her through a sudden flood of tears. Still holding the phone, I watched helplessly as Jack continued his work while trying to explain to her the sequence of events that had led up to this nightmare. She listened silently.

Assured that an ambulance was on its way, and after checking on the man, I returned to help Jack. We worked on in silence, stopping from time to time to check for any signs of life, but to no avail. The daughter moved across to be with her father and sat holding his hand while slowly coming to grips with the enormity of what had happened. In the time we waited for the second ambulance, I came to appreciate why relatives sometimes berate us for taking so long to arrive when only a few minutes may actually have passed. When Larry and Howard came through the door I could have hugged them. They'd been informed of the situation and brought the stretcher from our ambulance as far into the house as they could manage. Together we loaded the woman on to it and then out to the ambulance. They then returned inside with their own equipment to help her husband.

The dash to hospital took a matter of minutes, but there was to be no happy outcome; she was pronounced dead shortly afterwards. Her husband arrived five minutes later but the prognosis for him was poor. He had indeed suffered a massive stroke and was still deeply unconscious. As so often happens, I'm afraid I lost track of his progress over the next few days. So for us the story ended there.

Ambulance work can be very rewarding, but not always. Sometimes we are swept along by events which then spiral out of our control in the most tragic way. If I were to search for anything positive to bring from such an experience, it would only be that we did our best.

# Chapter Four

Larry had worked in the jewellery quarter before throwing his lot in with the ambulance service in his twenties. Over six feet tall and stick-thin with tombstone teeth, he came across as a comical figure even before you noticed the mischievous twinkle in his eye. He was known for being an irreverent joker who seldom took anything seriously, least of all his job or his workmates. Yet despite his light-hearted, devil-may-care manner, it was quite clear that he was as dedicated as anyone else at the Street, with the added bonus of possessing a natural affinity for people. Curiously, the level of his commitment was something he did his best to obscure behind a cultivated air of indifference. We were all guilty of this to one degree or another, but Larry had it down to perfection.

It was helping an elderly couple in what many might describe as a routine job that allowed me a glimpse of Larry's caring side. It can't be denied that Henrietta Street's catchment area was plagued by hopeless individuals down on their luck and reliant on alcohol or drugs to get them through the day. They kept us busy enough, but by no means constituted the bulk of our work. Most of our patients were decent folk living in the nearby terraced streets of Handsworth and Aston. Many were elderly and had spent their lives in honest, if meagrely rewarded, toil. But they were true Brummies: pragmatic to the core and endowed with a wry humour that belied their dour surroundings. Sadly, the trend was for their offspring to move on to greener pastures, leaving them lonely and marooned in a fast-changing society. With the passing years it was inevitable that they should find themselves increasingly dependent on our services and, to be truthful, they constituted the part of our work that often proved the most rewarding.

The couple in question were in their eighties and when he'd fallen at their terraced home in Aston his wife was left with little choice but to call an ambulance. A delighted smile illuminated her aged face when she opened the door to Larry.

'Oh, you got here quickly, and they've sent two of you, how nice. Come in.' She shuffled back against the door to make space for us to squeeze past. She couldn't have been more than five feet tall and so frail that a sudden draught might have carried her off. 'I didn't want to bother you, but I'm in such an awful pickle and didn't know what to do for the best.' She closed the door and slid the bolt. 'I knew it was going to be one of those days as soon as I got up this morning. You'll have to excuse the place – I've not had chance to get anything done yet.' All was spick and span, but no amount of dusting and polishing could disguise the ancient furniture and threadbare carpets. Dominating the room was an oversized oak sideboard dotted with knick-knacks and on the wall behind were half a dozen framed photos of grinning children.

'It looks tidy enough to me. You should see my place,' Larry said, without condescension. And then to the matter in hand. 'I hear someone's had a bit of a fall.'

'That's right – it's Cyril, my husband. He falls a lot these days and it's a right job to get him up again. He's in the downstairs toilet.' She led us into the back parlour and on through a tiny kitchen to a closed door at the opposite end. 'I heard this big bang, you see, and now I can't get him to speak to me. I think he's gone to sleep.'

It was easy to understand why she thought that. But the snores reverberating through the door weren't from somebody asleep; they were coming too fast and too deep. Larry listened for a moment and then tapped sharply on the door.

'Hello . . . Cyril. Can you hear me?' The gurgling snores continued and Larry tried the doorhandle only to find it locked. He turned to the lady. 'I'm sorry, I didn't catch your name.'

'Grace Stubbs.'

'Well, Mrs Stubbs, it doesn't look as if Cyril's going to be able to open the door for us. I'm afraid we're going to have to force our way in. It will mean breaking the lock. Is that OK with you?'

Concern spread over her face. 'Yes, of course dear, you know best.'

Larry turned the handle and delivered the door a measured blow with his shoulder. There was a crack as the screws holding the small bolt broke free and the door opened a fraction. Larry pushed cautiously and met resistance when the gap was about twelve inches.

'That's as far as we get, I'm afraid. Cyril's in the way.' Larry gauged the space available. 'I should be able to squeeze through.'

I didn't doubt it. He was so thin that I swear he could have gone up a drainpipe if he put his mind to it.

We watched him slither in and listened to his muffled mumblings and exclamations as he manoeuvred into position to access Cyril. When he eventually addressed me, his voice dropped to little more than a whisper.

'He's in a bad way. It looks like he's had a stroke, and a big one at that. Pass the oxygen through, will you?' I slid the cylinder through the gap and a moment later the hiss of oxygen mingled with the snores. Grunts and heavy breathing from Larry interspersed his commentary. 'Geez, he's a bloody big bloke . . . There! I've managed to move him a bit and get him on his side, but there's still no way we're going to get the door open. There's not enough room in here to swing a bloody mouse, never mind a cat.'

I was trying to think of something to suggest when Mrs Stubbs piped up from over my shoulder.

'How is he? Is he going to be all right?'

Larry heard her and raised his voice in reply.

'I have to be blunt with you, Mrs Stubbs. He's unconscious.'

'Oh dear. Can't you wake him?'

'I'm afraid not – he's out for the count. But I don't want you to worry. We'll soon have him out.'

'Oh dear.'

Larry added a bit of levity to his voice. 'There's one thing for sure – you certainly feed him well!'

She smiled. 'Oh yes, he's always been a man who enjoys his food.'

I pressed closer to the gap and expressed my concern at a low pitch. 'We'll soon have him out? How?'

Larry's face appeared uncomfortably close on the other side.

'We've got to get rid of the door. If I pull on it as much as I can from this side you might just be able to get at the hinges. You'll find a screwdriver and crowbar in our emergency kit on the motor. To be honest, I don't give much for his chances whatever happens.'

Less than a minute later I was working on the screws securing the hinges. The heads were encrusted with paint, which had to be chipped away first. I was making steady progress when the screwdriver skidded and made a neat hole in the palm of my free hand. I yelped and hurriedly pulled a bandage from the first-aid bag to quell the eruption of blood. Mrs Stubbs's face clouded with concern.

'Oh dear, I am sorry.'

'No, no, it's my fault. I was clumsy.'

She looked doubtful. 'I tell you what. How about if I make you a nice cup of tea?'

I felt a sudden upsurge of affection for her. She either didn't understand how serious things were or was refusing to accept it.

'No, we won't bother with tea.' I started again on the screws. 'Do you have any relatives you can telephone?'

'I've got two daughters. Jean lives in Bournemouth and Alice is in New Zealand. Cyril and I are going over to visit her in a couple of months.'

'Is there anyone else who could come with you to the hospital? Are there any friends nearby?'

'There's only Dorothy at fifty-one, but she's not good for much since she broke her hip.'

'What about your neighbours?' I asked, hopefully.

'The couple next door are lovely. They always say hello, but I hardly ever see them. Young people are so busy these days.'

The final screw came free and I manoeuvred the door from the frame and carried it through to the living room. When I returned she was bending over her husband, gently stroking his face. Larry laid a hand on her shoulder.

'What I want you to do now, Mrs Stubbs, is to sort out your coat, handbag and door keys while we get Cyril out to the ambulance.' Her eyes were moist and her bones creaked as she straightened up and made her way back through the kitchen.

Larry hadn't exaggerated Cyril's size. He was a tall man of about sixteen stone and all but filled the tiny toilet. It's difficult to appreciate how hard it is to move an unconscious person unless you've tried it for yourself. Lack of muscle tone means the body becomes like a huge beanbag on which it's impossible to get any solid purchase. Limbs flop wherever gravity cares to take them and the heavier the person, the greater the problems. Just edging him from the confined space and on to our carry-sheet was an ungainly and exhausting procedure that wouldn't have been any easier even if we'd had assistance; there simply wasn't room for an extra pair of hands. Squeezing him past the sideboard in the front room entailed re-arranging the furniture by piling the three-piece suite on top of itself. By the time we reached the front door Larry and I were puffing like a couple of old men, while Cyril lay hungrily sucking in the oxygen, oblivious to everything.

I'd been forced to position the stretcher outside on the path for lack of room inside, which meant having to man-handle Cyril's dead weight over the threshold. Mike liked to describe my muscles as sparrow's kneecaps whenever he got the chance, and, even though I'd built up a fair bit of strength over the past eighteen months, I was beginning to see his point. The final hurdle was the three steps up into the ambulance; only when they were safely negotiated could we take a breather and do another check of our patient. Nothing had changed for him and as Larry connected up a new oxygen cylinder I went looking for

Mrs Stubbs. I found her in the front room buttoning up her coat.

'We really must get going, Mrs Stubbs.'

'Yes, dear, I'm all ready. Oh no, silly me.' She looked down in mock horror at the hem of her apron protruding from under her coat. 'I've still got my pinny on.'

'Don't worry about that. No one's going to notice.'

'I can't go to the hospital looking like a skivvy!'

I moved anxiously from foot to foot as the coat came off, followed by the apron, and then back on with the coat. 'Now, all I need is my hat.'

I tried to keep the impatience from my voice. 'Please, Mrs Stubbs, we haven't got time. You don't need a hat.'

'Will you be a dear and fetch it for me? It's in the big wardrobe in the front bedroom.'

I took the stairs two at a time and when I got back she was in the kitchen putting the butter and milk in the fridge.

'Cyril's waiting, Mrs Stubbs. We really must get a move on.'

'Yes, I know. But if you rush me I'll just get all flustered. Will you check that the television's unplugged for me while I find my handbag?'

I was tempted to pick her up and carry her out, but settled for linking an arm in hers and more or less propelling her through the house, picking her handbag off the sideboard on the way.

'She's a darling, isn't she?' Larry observed as he waved at Mrs Stubbs through the Casualty window. She was on her feet in the waiting area, smiling broadly at us as we made our way to the ambulance. Cyril was in the safe care of the hospital staff and we were about to relax with a cup of tea. Larry winced as he settled himself into the driver's seat. 'I've pulled something in my bloody back.' He stretched and tentatively flexed his shoulder blades. 'I felt it go when we were getting him on to the stretcher.' I had my own concern. My injured hand was throbbing like the dickens and just extending my fingers was an effort. Larry leaned back into his seat. 'We're a couple of crocks, aren't we? At least it was a genuine case and I suppose, when all's said and done, that's what we're here for.' He didn't often express such thoughts, but I agreed. Medically, there hadn't been much we could do for Cyril, and in all honesty I doubt there was much the hospital could do either. But that wasn't the point. We represented the only avenue of hope for an elderly and vulnerable couple with nowhere else to turn. At the risk of sounding sanctimonious, I saw it as a privilege to be in a position to help.

Cyril's plight crossed my mind the following morning in the messroom and when I casually wondered aloud how he might be doing, Larry surprised me.

'He was in intensive care last night. It was like we thought – he'd had a massive stroke.'

'How do you know that?'

Larry seemed uncomfortable and spoke in a low voice to avoid being overheard.

'I called round at the house yesterday evening after work and the old girl told me.'

'You what?'

'I went to put the toilet door back on its hinges and sort out the three-piece for her.' He was almost defensive. 'She couldn't have done it herself and there was nobody else to help her.'

I was impressed. 'You're a dark horse.'

He glanced furtively round the room. 'That's between you and me. Don't tell the others.'

'Why on earth not?'

'They'll think I've gone soft. You know what they're like. The sarcastic bastards will be asking me to do all their DIY jobs from now until kingdom come. I'll never hear the end of it.'

His reply would have confused me eighteen months earlier, but not now. I'd come to understand that an attitude of aloof detachment towards every aspect of the job was a prerequisite for survival. More than half the people at the Street were ex-military and had no time for sentimentality, not least because it might be mis-construed as weakness. An outsider would have been perplexed, not to say dismayed, at our apparent callous lack of concern for everything and anything. But there was something ever-present that few people were allowed to see: dedication. It was there in abundance but rarely alluded to, and certainly never in the messroom where brickbats, sarcasm and banter were seen as perfectly normal means of communication.

This had been brought home to me, if it needed to be, a couple of months earlier when Simon Kennedy from 'A' shift saved a patient's life. He and his partner had forced their way into the woman's house to find her unconscious and quite literally at death's door. They assisted her feeble breathing with a bag and mask, and when she went into cardiac arrest halfway to hospital Simon's skilled intervention won back a faint pulse. He was justifiably pleased with himself, especially when the woman went on to make a recovery and the Casualty consultant sent a letter of commendation. His shift mates happily listened to the story and no doubt learned from his experience. The problem was that Simon didn't know when to stop beating his own drum. Instead of playing down the incident and waving away praise as etiquette required, he actively encouraged it, and in the process became a bit of a bore. A week later his shift clubbed together and bought him a nurse's kit from Woolworths. The centrepiece was a white plastic apron stamped with a big red cross. Accompanying this was everything an enthusiastic seven-year-old would need to start out on a career in medicine: plastic tweezers and dish, plastic stethoscope, plastic thermometer and, most impressive of all, a fully operational plastic syringe, albeit with a rubber needle. Everything was neatly contained in a plastic box with handle. It might not have been a particularly subtle message, but Simon had to live with it and could only mutter to himself on hearing his partner call for the nurse's box when they were dealing with a tricky case out on the road. Over time, and unbeknown to the patients, calling for the nurse's box became a kind of coded message that things were serious. But I digress.

Our conversation came to an end with the ring of the emergency phone. Howard picked it up, jotted down a few notes, then looked over at Larry.

'There you go – a job for you. It's only round the corner.'

Larry stared at him. 'We're not next out!'

Howard allowed himself a resigned smile. He and Larry enjoyed bickering so much that it had become their normal form of communication.

'Don't try that one on me. You know full well you are.' He lobbed the case sheet in Larry's direction. 'There's been an *incident* in Buxton Road.'

Larry picked up the sheet. 'What kind of incident?'

'Don't know. I didn't ask.'

'Well, thanks for nothing.'

Howard returned to his newspaper. 'You're welcome. Don't rush back on our account.'

Buxton Road was less than half a mile away and when we pulled up outside the address it was clear that something very violent had occurred inside. A downstairs window had been shattered with most of the glass strewn on the lawn along with pieces of the frame. The curtains, which had billowed through the gap, flapped idly in the breeze, as if beckoning us forward to investigate. Neither of us was very keen to do that. It was a job for the fire brigade, but as our journey time had taken under a minute we were there well before them.

'Looks like there's been an explosion,' I said to Larry from the safety of my seat.

'Really? What makes you think that?'

I ignored the sarcasm. 'What are we going to do?'

'Not much. If there's been one explosion, who's to say there won't be another? The zombies will be along soon – they don't mind being blown up.'

I was distracted by an urgent tapping on the glass by my ear and turned to be confronted by a stout woman in her mid-sixties, complete with curlers and jutting lower lip. I wound down the window.

'Well?' Her tone was belligerent.

'Well what?' I asked.

'Why aren't you doing anything?'

'We—'

Larry leaned across me. 'We are doing something. We're waiting for the fire brigade.'

She bridled. 'You're not going in?'

'No.'

'You're a disgrace. Someone's probably hurt in there. If you're too scared to find out, I'm not!' She strode off towards the house without waiting for our reaction.

Larry groaned and opened his door. 'Shit. Come on, we'll have to stop her.'

I grabbed the first-aid bag.

We caught up with her at the gate, where she turned a gimlet eye on us. 'Changed your minds then?'

'Yes,' Larry said, resignedly, and gestured towards a group of neighbours watching disapprovingly from across the street. 'You go back to your friends and we'll find out what's happened.'

We watched her go, then gingerly edged across the lawn towards the broken window, our noses twitching for any hint of gas. The first thing we saw on peering over the sill was a man of about twenty-five sitting on a stool looking as if he'd been pulled from the village stocks after a particularly enthusiastic pelting. The small kitchen lay in ruins around him. Broken crockery and pots and pans were scattered over the floor and the contents of containers were strewn over work surfaces. The walls looked as if Jackson Pollock had been set loose with food instead of paint, the occasional glutinous blob still dripping from the ceiling. Chunks of gouged plaster mingled with the mess on the floor.

After taking in the scene, Larry broke the stillness by loudly addressing the figure on the stool.

'You OK, mate? What's happened?'

The figure didn't respond and, as there was too much broken glass to risk climbing in, we walked round to the front door, which was on the latch. Inside we were met by the rather pleasant waft of beef stew and followed it through to the kitchen. The figure still hadn't moved. He seemed oblivious to everything, including the puréed tomatoes, carrots, onions and pieces of meat oozing down his face. The greasy mixture covered every inch of him, leaving his splattered T-shirt and jeans hanging wet and limp.

I tentatively repeated Larry's question. 'Are you OK?'

'What?'

'Are you OK?' I said again.

'Yeah, of course I am. Something's happened, that's all.' He didn't seem to notice the piece of carrot easing down his neck, or the gravy droplet obstinately clinging to the end of his nose.

Larry intervened. 'Are you hurt, mate?'

'No, I'm not hurt, just a bit, well, you know . . .'

Larry glanced at me, then back at the patient.

'Come on then. Let's take you through to the bathroom and get you cleaned up.'

As he guided the dazed man back through the door, I scanned what was left of the kitchen and was drawn to the cooker by a faint smell of gas hiding in the aroma of beef stew. One of the burners was hissing gently at low level. As I switched it off I noticed the mangled remains of an aluminium pressure cooker on the work surface close by. Some feet away in a corner lay the twisted and torn remains of the lid. Looking upwards, I wasn't surprised to see a hole in the ceiling the size of a cannonball. It was pretty clear what had happened and, with the mystery explained, I went on through to find Larry.

He was wiping the last of the vegetables from the patient's face while trying to coax him into conversation.

'So, what's your name?'

'Dave.'

'Dave what?'

Dave ran a hand through his hair and dislodged a few onions. 'Bradbury, Dave Bradbury.'

'Do you remember what happened, Dave?' Larry asked.

'Yes. I wanted a sandwich. I'd just reached the bread bin when the world went mad. I don't know what happened then.' He gazed down at his jeans and absently flicked a piece of meat off his thigh. 'Just look at the state of me.'

He proved to have a good memory of events when Larry pressed him further. It seems his wife had put a stew in the pressure cooker and then nipped out, leaving him dozing on the settee. He woke from his nap half an hour later feeling peckish and the image of a cheese sandwich popped into his mind. After mulling it over for some time, he reluctantly came to the conclusion that the sandwich wasn't going to make itself. Mohammed was going to have to go to the mountain.

He entered the kitchen at the precise moment the pressure cooker blew up. If he ever cares to look back on events, he might judge himself to have been the victim of outrageous bad fortune. On the other hand, a fatalist would argue that the pot was patiently waiting for him to make an appearance before exploding. The truth is less esoteric: he'd been incredibly lucky. To have escaped unscathed when the pot exploded only three feet away, and in such a confined space, was little short of miraculous. If he wanted confirmation of the fact, he need only take a look at the kitchen, which had been all but destroyed around his ears.

His only obvious injury was a red, stinging face caused by the hot food, but he adamantly refused our offer of hospital treatment.

'I'll put some cream on it when I've had a shower. Then I've got to try to get the kitchen cleaned up before the wife gets home.'

Larry looked at him dubiously. 'It'll take more than a dustpan and brush.'

'Yeah, I know. I don't suppose you'd give us a hand, would you?'

The expression on Larry's face in response to the request made me wince, but whatever he was going to say remained unsaid. The sound of sirens in the street made us all look up.

'That's the fire brigade,' I said hurriedly. A few moments later the peace was broken by squawking radios and the all-too-familiar smell of burnt carpets that follows firemen everywhere they go.

'We'll leave you to it then, Dave,' Larry said. 'These blokes will help you clean up if you ask them nicely.'

Five minutes later we were back in the messroom. Howard looked up from his paper.

'That was quick!'

'It's called efficiency, H. Something you wouldn't know much about.'

Howard gave him a wry look. 'More likely the patient scarpered when he saw you coming.'

Larry grinned and looked at me. 'The smell of that casserole's made me hungry. Fancy a sausage sandwich, Les?'

'Yeah, good idea.' It wasn't really a good idea, but I felt that I should show willing.

Larry placed an elbow on the kitchen serving hatch and smiled ingratiatingly at Phyllis. Phyllis had been the depot cook for about a hundred years. She was a lovely, warm-hearted Welsh woman of indeterminate age who knew as much about cooking as I know about taxidermy. Everything she touched was reduced to a cinder in the blink of an eye. If rumour was to be believed, and I never heard it disputed, her greatest culinary achievement was once to have set fire to an egg. In saying that, we wouldn't have changed her for the world.

'Two charcoal sandwiches with a hint of sausage please, my good woman. And go heavy on the brown sauce. We don't want to taste anything.'

She threw a few sausages into the pan and wiped her hands down her apron.

'You're a cheeky bleeder. You'll get this frying pan somewhere you don't want it one of these days.'

Larry pretended to be affronted. 'Hey! I'll see to it that you lose one of your Michelin stars if you go about talking to customers like that.'

Her eyes narrowed. 'I'll Michelin star you if you don't sit down and shut up.'

When the sandwich arrived I crunched into it, half listening as Larry related the story of the pressure cooker to the others. He missed out the bit about the old lady shaming us into action. Technically, he'd been perfectly correct in wanting to wait for the fire brigade. It was drummed into us not to run the risk of ending up as casualties ourselves by blundering about in situations beyond our expertise. I doubt that Mike would have followed the rules so keenly, though. His view was that rules were there only to be broken, and the idea of waiting for the fire brigade to go in first would have been complete anathema anyway. With the story told, Larry uncoiled himself from his chair and wandered over to the kitchen counter with his empty plate.

'Thank you, Phyllis. That was bloody horrible.'

It was the nearest thing to a compliment she could hope for from Larry, but she always gave as good as she got.

'I'm glad you enjoyed it. It took ages to grind the glass.'

'Is that what those gritty bits were? And there was me thinking I'd lost a few fillings.' He stopped and made a show of scanning the kitchen surfaces behind her while she regarded him suspiciously.

'What are you looking for?'

'I was just wondering if you'd got a pressure cooker in there.'

'No.'

'Really?'

'Why are you asking?'

'Oh, nothing really. I just thought that I might get the shift to club together and buy you one as a token of our appreciation.'

# Chapter Five

Howard Hallam, or H as he was commonly known, was a rare and particularly likeable character. Slightly over-weight and not particularly tall, with unruly sandy-blond hair, he was a gentle, easy-going thirty-five-year-old who gave little heed to life's tribulations. His demeanour seldom varied and his patience was inexhaustible. Everybody liked him and he liked everyone. He even liked the patients. He even liked Larry, despite the pair of them having been engaged in a running battle of tit-for-tat practical jokes since long before I joined the shift. It was an odd relationship. They were firm friends, but any chance either had of putting the other down was eagerly grasped. It was typical of Larry that, after deciding Jack was a dead ringer for Fred Flintstone, he should dub Howard Barney Rubble. What with Howard's hair colour and build, there was definitely a passing resemblance and from then on they were known as the Flintstones when-ever they worked together. Larry was all for cutting a hole in the bottom of their ambulance to allow their feet out to do the running.

Mornings were usually tranquil at the Street. We came on duty at seven and more often than not had time to laze around and read the paper before the work started trickling in. Even though we were considered a busy station by the standards of the day, there were plenty of quiet periods when the place would take on the feel of an exclusive social club rather than a place of work. It was a big room, big enough to accommodate a full-size snooker table and leave plenty of space for armchairs and a large communal table.

On one such lazy morning, Howard and I had nipped out to a local café and returned with sausage and bacon baps for the shift. We had to get them eaten quickly and dispose of the wrappers before Phyllis arrived to open the kitchen. She didn't take kindly to us frequenting the local competition and could be quite feisty when she found out. In her eyes, the local café was a filthy hole that should have been closed down years ago. We took her comments to be nothing more than sour grapes, so it came as quite a shock when her suspicions were proved to be well founded. The shop she constantly lambasted was closed down by the health inspectors a year later. One was quoted in the evening paper as saying that it was by far the worst case he'd seen in twenty years. The roof space and top floor were groaning under the weight of pigeon droppings, while the first floor was alive with rats' nests. These rats had full run of the building, including the kitchen, where they battled it out with mice and cock-roaches for the choicest morsels of rotting food that was apparently left festering in every corner. I think the quote ended by stating that the kitchen was a place of such squalor and filth, with rat urine and droppings on every work surface, that it beggared belief that there hadn't been a serious outbreak of food poisoning.

Of course, we weren't to know any of this until much later, and tucked into the tasty sandwiches with relish. Howard scrunched up the tinfoil wrapping and licked his fingers in appreciation.

'Bloody marvellous! Wouldn't life be perfect if Phyllis could knock out sarnies as good as that?' We all agreed, in the sad knowledge that Phyllis would never be able to raise her game so high.

For once the phone waited for us all to finish eating before squawking into life. I answered it and was given an address in Handsworth where a baby had been born at home. H was driving, and as I helpfully found the page for him in the A–Z, he gunned up the engine and depressed the clutch. I didn't see it happen, but I certainly heard Howard's sudden yelp of surprise and looked up sharply from the A–Z to see water dripping from his face and shirt. For a moment I was totally confused. Howard stared straight ahead and seemed to be struggling to compose himself before pulling a handkerchief from his pocket.

'Bloody Larry! The man's certifiable!' He dabbed the hankie round his face. 'If a five-year-old had done this, I'd tell him to grow up.'

I was still confused. 'What's he done? What's happened?'

H pointed towards the clutch. 'The silly sod's tied a syringe full of water to the side of the clutch pedal. When I pushed on the clutch, I also pushed on the syringe.' He ran the hankie under the collar of his shirt. 'I'll have a chat with him later. I suppose in the meantime we'd better go and sort this baby out.'

We had just come off the Hockley flyover and were heading up the hill towards Handsworth when H let out a groan and switched on the wipers.

'That's all I need. First Larry, now Declan bloody Heneghan!'

I'd spotted him at the same moment, standing on the pavement a hundred yards ahead. As usual, he was swaying back and forth like a scarecrow in the breeze while judging our approach with mathematical precision. For reasons I never did discover, this modern-day village idiot hated ambulances with a passion and would spend the day in one spot just waiting for one to come along. He expressed his dislike by spitting at us as we passed. And it wasn't just ordinary spit. When he saw us coming in the distance he would drag it up from somewhere deep in his chest and masticate it into a huge sticky lump that would eventually splatter over our windscreen and stick like glue. His aim was nothing short of remarkable. It didn't matter what speed we were doing, or what evasive actions we took; he simply never missed. Howard pressed the washer button as we came into range. Declan, chewing furiously, leaned his head back before throwing it forward as if he were trying to launch it from his shoulders. Splat! Direct hit, as usual. The wipers spread the mess across the windscreen as Howard let out a sigh.

'I don't know which one's worse, Larry or Declan. Either way, I've got a feeling it's going to be one of those days.'

All but the last trace of Declan's phlegm had been coaxed off the windscreen by the time we reached the address five minutes later. A woman of about forty opened the door still in her dressing gown. Her face was pale and tearstained. Howard looked at her with concern.

'Are you OK, love?'

She leaned against the doorframe and tried to smile through quivering lips.

'No, I'm bloody well not. Imagine waking up and finding out you're a grandmother.' She gave a nervous laugh and wiped away a tear. 'Not that it's ever likely to happen to you.'

'If it does I'll make a fortune selling my story to the *Sun*,' Howard said. 'Where's the baby?'

She moved towards the stairs. 'In my daughter's room. It's this way.'

We followed her upstairs and into the back bedroom, where a girl of not much more than fourteen was sitting up in bed cradling a baby. She looked utterly miserable, with a tearstained face matching her mother's. My first thoughts were that all wasn't well with the baby, but a quick examination showed it to be a bundle of health. The placenta had also been delivered without any problems.

'Well,' H said, with forced joviality as he spoke to the downcast pair. 'Everything's fine.' He looked at the new grandmother. 'Congratulations. Have you delivered a baby before?'

She glanced at her daughter and shook her head.

'I didn't deliver the baby – she managed it all on her own. I don't know how her father's going to deal with this.'

Howard, seemingly as perplexed as me, glanced from one to the other. The girl was far too young to start having babies, but surely the family had had plenty of time to get used to the idea.

The girl on the bed gave her mother a beseeching look and started to cry.

'I'm sorry, Mum, I'm really sorry. I was frightened of what Dad would do when he found out. I thought he'd throw me out. Have you phoned him?'

'Of course I've phoned him, you stupid girl! He's on his way back from work right now. I just hope he doesn't crash the car.' She folded her arms and moved to the window. 'It's all such a shock, my head's spinning. I can't believe I'm awake.'

The picture being painted was too improbable to be true. You read about things like this in the newspapers without ever quite believing it possible.

'You didn't know she was going to have the baby?' Howard asked tentatively.

'I didn't have a clue! I didn't know she was pregnant.

When she said she didn't want to go to school today because she'd got stomach pains, I actually brought her up a cup of tea to see if it would make her feel better. Can you believe that, when all the time she had the baby hidden under the bedclothes? If he hadn't started crying I probably still wouldn't know she'd had him. Can you imagine how stupid that makes me feel?'

I looked afresh at her daughter. She might have been slightly on the plump side, but I wouldn't have thought she was carrying enough weight to conceal a pregnancy. But what did I know? One thing I did know was that we were a couple of strangers in the middle of a domestic situation that had absolutely nothing to do with us. Howard made an effort to divert attention back to the baby, sleeping peacefully in his mother's arms.

'Well, whatever's been going on, at least he's a healthy little—'

'I still can't take it in.' The mother turned back from the window and confronted her daughter once again. 'You must have thought I was daft. It's been staring me in the face all the while and I was too stupid to see. Losing interest in your appearance, taking to wearing shapeless old smocks and not bothering with your mates. To think that I even tried to get you on a diet!'

'I tell you what,' Howard said. 'We'll go and wait in the ambulance until the midwife turns up. That way you can have a little time to yourselves.'

We bumped into the midwife on the pavement and gave her the story before she went in. A few minutes later a car roared up and a man in his early forties leapt out and made his way up the path at a trot. We figured we were best off where we were and waited out the fifteen minutes it took for the midwife to prepare the girl for hospital. Everyone was very tight-lipped as they trooped out of the house, and I was relieved when the new grandfather decided to follow in his car. After dropping them off at the maternity department, Howard shook his head in wonderment.

'It's one thing to keep the pregnancy secret, though I don't know how she managed it. What I can't get my head round is the way she kept quiet even after it was born. Did she think it was just going to vanish? They won't believe a word of it when we tell them back at the Street.'

We had to wait a while before putting it to the test.

I booked clear and we were given a case just round the corner in Winson Green.

'Man bitten by a cat?' I repeated the controller's words, feeling something approaching disbelief. 'How on earth can a cat bite warrant calling an ambulance?'

The sight that greeted us when we pulled up outside the house answered my question. An elderly man was sitting on a kitchen chair by the front door looking for all the world like an apparition in red. I couldn't reconcile a call to a cat bite with what I was looking at. Confused, I tucked the first-aid bag under my arm and we headed up the path for a closer inspection. The apparition was indeed flesh and blood, though at first glance more blood than flesh. He was wearing pyjamas, and from his hair to his toes he was saturated in blood. The vivid red turned to pink at his feet, which faded to a washed-out white as it drained down the path. A woman of about sixty had her arm round his shoulder to prevent him toppling off the chair.

'Oh, poor Mr Frith, he's in a right state and it's all my fault.'

I couldn't argue with the first part of her statement, but Mr Frith contradicted the second part in a surprisingly firm voice.

'It wasn't her fault. It was Sammy – I must have frightened him.'

'Sammy?' I asked, as I started looking for the source of the bleeding by tentatively probing here and there at the congealing blood. 'Who's Sammy? Did he use a Stanley knife or something?'

'No!' the woman said in surprise. 'Sammy's my cat.'

I had forgotten all about cats.

Between them, they pieced together a picture of what had happened. Sidney, Mr Frith, had gone to the front door to collect the milk. As he straightened up with the bottle in his hand, Sammy leapt on to his head from a nearby bush. The bottle slipped from his grasp and smashed on the ground as he raised both hands in an attempt to dislodge his assailant. Only Sammy could say what his intentions were, but it could be that the breaking bottle and flailing arms frightened him into further action and he set about the old man with a vengeance. He clawed and bit him about the head, face and neck and then started to work his way down the body, scratching and biting as he went. It had been a sustained attack from what we could see through Sidney's torn pyjamas; there were bites and claw marks all over him. His skin, being old and fragile, had parted easily and the blood had flowed, running down his body before eventually mingling with the spilt milk on the path. To make matters worse, he had trodden on the broken glass and had several nasty cuts to his feet. Sammy was last seen making his escape over the garden fence at high speed.

We settled for wrapping Sidney from head to foot in a sterile burns sheet – it would have been futile and time-consuming to start messing with bandages. The hospital was only round the corner, and a few minutes later he was in Casualty having his wounds tended and being treated for shock. Despite his ordeal, he wouldn't have a word said against Sammy.

'When all's said and done, he was only defending himself. You can't blame him.'

'But all you were doing was fetching in the milk,' the nurse pointed out, as she dabbed at him with a lint swab. 'He could have had your eyes out. Something will have to be done with him.'

'No. He's always been a good cat. He's bloody fast though. I don't think I'd want to take him on again.'

Sidney's stoicism said much about his generation. I've treated plenty of dog bites over the years, some of them quite nasty, but never have I seen so much blood as a result of an animal attack.

After an obligatory cup of tea, we headed back to the Street for a meal break. Phyllis was making noises in the kitchen with pots and pans while Larry lay sprawled across a chair with a newspaper over his head, sleeping the sleep of the innocent. Howard leaned over the counter and interrupted Phyllis with a smile.

'Can I have two bangers and mash, please, my little Welsh dragon.'

Howard's attention wandered from her to Larry and he gave his chair a sharp kick.

'That was a funny trick you played with the syringe. I looked a right idiot walking into someone's house with a soaking-wet shirt!'

Larry pulled away the newspaper and sat up.

'And what makes you think it was me?'

'Oh, let me think. Maybe because you're the only five-year-old on the shift?'

Larry was affronted. 'Five-year-old? No five-year-old could have set that up. Have you got any idea how long it took to work out all the angles?'

Howard sat down and reached for the abandoned newspaper.

'You ought to transfer to Bristol Road. There are plenty of people working there you'd get on well with.'

'Oh yes? And what makes you say that?'

'I did a shift there on overtime a couple of nights ago. It was like being in a mad house – they made you look like an amateur. Stink bombs . . . can you believe grown men would actually go into a shop and buy stink bombs?'

Howard looked reflective. 'Mind you, if I'd had my wits about me I'd have snaffled one to put under your brake pedal.'

'So what were they doing with the stink bombs?' Larry asked.

'As you would imagine; letting them off all over the place. Then they made a big mistake. You know that the ambulance station at Bristol Road has a fire station next door?'

'Yes, of course.'

'It must have been about three in the morning when one of the bright sparks decided it would be a hoot to lob a few into the firemen's dormitory. They always sleep with the windows open to let out the stink that occurs in there naturally.' H turned a page of his paper and scanned the headlines before continuing. 'I warned them not to do it. Past experience has taught me that you take on firemen at your peril. I was wasting my time. A couple of them crept up to the building and dropped their bombs through every open window they could find and then came scuttling back. An hour later there still hadn't been a reaction from next door and everyone relaxed and assumed the firemen hadn't noticed the extra smell.'

'But you knew better,' Larry said.

'Oh yes. And it didn't occur to any of them that our windows were also open just like the firemen's. Some time after four there was a thump against the metal window frame above my head and the nozzle of a bloody great hose appeared. Everybody but me was dozing and I just about had time to get out of my seat before it was switched on. I learned one thing that night: it only takes a fireman let loose with a hose four seconds to destroy a messroom. The jet knocked over chairs, took down the notice board and reduced all the crockery to shrapnel. Everybody and everything was soaked. It took until the morning shift came on duty at seven to get the place looking half respectable.'

Phyllis leaned across the serving hatch. 'Two sausage and mash.'

Howard regarded the plates with suspicion and, after scraping away some shreds of soggy onion, prodded a blackened sausage with his fork. It failed to penetrate the skin and he looked up to see Phyllis eyeing him defiantly.

'Something wrong?'

'No, Phyllis. It looks almost good enough to eat.'

'Well, I suggest you do just that, unless you want it over your head.'

Phyllis always had the last say, and Howard and I went to work on the food without further comment. Unknown to us, at the very same time a building-site labourer was starting his lunch in a pub three miles away.

We got the call half an hour later as 'man fallen down a hole'. How big a hole could it be? Birmingham was short on big holes at the time but, as the location was a building site, we thought it best to keep an open mind. A workman waiting for us at the site entrance flicked away his cigarette as we pulled up.

'Just carry on in and stay to your left. You won't miss the fire engine.'

A fire engine? Perhaps it was a decent-sized hole after all. H slowly edged the ambulance forward along the rutted, muddy track and parked next to the big red machine. There had been a lot of rain in the preceding days which had reduced the place to a quagmire. My feet sank into three inches of mud and we squelched over to the nearest group of workmen, who were standing with folded arms on the rim of what we assumed was the hole in question. We followed their gaze downward and two things struck us immediately. Firstly, with a circumference of at least twenty yards and anything up to fifteen feet deep, it was the mother of all holes. Secondly, at its centre was an upturned dumper truck with its wheels pointing at the sky. Several firemen in bright yellow leggings were crowded round it and, if I wasn't mistaken, one of them was engaged in conversation with a head lying on the ground near the front of the truck.

I spoke to the workman nearest me. 'Am I looking at what I think I'm looking at?'

He turned and, recognizing the uniform, said, 'Yes, mate. It's that daft bastard Mick. He downs eight pints of Guinness in his lunchbreak and then spends the afternoon racing around on his dumper truck like he's Stirling Moss. It was only a matter of time before something like this happened.'

The far side of the hole had a gentler incline and, as we trudged round with all the equipment we might need, our guide explained that Mick's job that day was to start filling in the hole with waste from around the site. He had been going at it hammer and tongs until a momentary lack of judgement sent him and his truck over the edge. Somehow, he'd contrived to hit the ground first, with the truck following close behind. He was trapped from the waist down but had been saved from an unpleasant death by sinking into the mud. The fire officer straightened up at our approach and, as was usual, got straight to the point.

'His breathing seems to be fine and he isn't complaining of any specific pain. The problem is that he's trapped below the waist. We're going to dig him out and shore up the truck as we go along. That OK with you?'

'Er, yes, but we'll just have a word with him first.' Howard and I squatted on our haunches and spoke to the head. Actually, closer inspection revealed that his arms and chest were exposed, but were so covered in mud that they blended into the surroundings.

'Hello, Mick.'

He smiled broadly. 'Hello there, boys. And how are you both?' The question didn't come as the surprise you might think: there are always people who, no matter what their own circumstances might be, will enquire after our health before we get chance to ask about theirs.

'We're fine, thanks,' I replied. 'Shame I can't say the same about you. You've landed yourself in a fine mess, haven't you?'

'That I have, sir. There's no denying it, so there isn't.'

We chatted for a bit and pieced together the facts. The truck had him pinned down at waist level and, though he couldn't move, he had full sensation in his legs and could wiggle his toes. His colour was good and he had a strong pulse. We couldn't see any reason to delay his extraction and handed over to the firemen.

It didn't take them long to remove enough soil and mud to be able to slide Mick back out into the land of the living. We kept him flat and soon had him bound up in our Neil Robinson stretcher. This was a handy piece of kit, made of wooden slats attached to stout canvas that conformed to the body shape while still keeping the patient thoroughly immobilized – the kind of thing mountain rescue teams use. The next step was to get him up to the ambulance. A rope was attached to the stretcher, the plan being to pull from the top while pushing from below. Howard went off to prepare the ambulance and I stayed with the patient, occasionally taking his pulse to give the firemen the impression I was doing something while they worked. They grunted, slithered and cursed all the way to the top, and by the time they got there their yellow leggings weren't quite so yellow any more. In fact, they looked as if they had been engaged in some ghastly homo-erotic mud-wrestling competition.

Howard had covered the interior of the ambulance in sheets to protect it from the worst of the mud. And it was just as well. Four firemen carried the stretcher on board and managed to smear mud in places you wouldn't have thought it possible to smear mud – the ceiling, for example. Despite carrying out what we considered to be a thorough cleaning afterwards, we were still finding traces of it days later. Mick, maybe aided by the Guinness slopping about inside him, proved to be a model patient and grinned cheerfully throughout his rescue, despite the fact that X-rays later proved that he had a fractured pelvis. A very nasty injury, but one I'd have happily settled for if I'd been told that a three-tonne dumper truck was going to land on top of me.

With Mick safely in the care of the Casualty staff, we wandered out and surveyed the state of the ambulance. It was filthy, inside and out. The Neil Robinson stretcher was caked in fast-drying mud, as were we. Howard explained our plight to Control over the radio and, with a suspiciously amused tone to his voice, the officer of the day sent us back to the Street to get cleaned up. We had a long, boring job ahead of us, and things took a turn for the worse when we turned into Warstone Lane and spotted a scarecrow swaying back and forth on the pavement a hundred yards ahead.

'Heneghan!' Howard almost shouted as he switched on the wipers. 'Twice in one day! I've a mind to run the bastard over.'

Oblivious to the danger he was in, Declan's head went back as he calculated our speed, wind veer and, for all I know, the relative position of the moon. Splat! Bull's eye, as ever.

# Chapter Six

Everyone had been delighted when the latest Ford Transits began to replace our outdated fleet of Bedfords. And it wasn't just because they were lighter and nimbler than their forerunners; they had the novel feature of sliding cab doors. A lack of even the most rudimentary ventilation system in the old Bedford's cab meant that on hot days we gently stewed in our seats. Now we could leave the sweaty past behind and drive about with the doors open when the sun was shining. Management, of course, frowned on the practice and sent out a steady stream of directives demanding that the doors be kept closed for health and safety reasons. We appreciated their concern but, like so many other things, we universally ignored their entreaties and the doors stayed open. So it was that I relaxed back into the driver's seat with my cup of tea and savoured the cool breeze wafting through the cab.

My feeling of well-being was tinged with a little

sadness. There wasn't much doubt that the elderly gentleman we'd just dropped off at Casualty had been on a one-way trip to hospital. Howard obviously felt it as well.

'Shame, isn't it?' he said. 'He was a fascinating old boy.'

I should point out that Howard found most people fascinating, all the more so if they were elderly. He loved getting them to talk about the past and always listened attentively to anything they had to say. Most were surprised and flattered that he should show an interest, but Howard saw it as a way of adding to the picture of a Birmingham long gone. Any wartime memories were particularly relished.

'So what did he have to say for himself?' I asked. 'The pair of you were going at it ten to the dozen all the way in.'

'Oh, this and that, but mainly it was about the time he spent in a Bavarian prisoner-of-war camp during the First World War.'

'The *First* World War?' I said in surprise.

'That's right. He and his mate were snatched from a forward trench in the middle of the night. Apparently both sides captured prisoners when they could for interrogation. Especially officers.'

Howard broke off to inform Control over the radio that we'd completed our case, leaving me trying to reconcile the image of a teenage soldier foraging in a prisoner-of-war camp with the wizened old man about to face his final battle.

'He was captured in 1916,' H continued. 'He reckons he wouldn't have stood a chance of surviving the war if he hadn't been taken prisoner—' The radio came to life and a disembodied voice instructed us to return to station. H carried on talking as I started the engine and headed for the exit. 'It just goes to show, if you make the effort with these old 'uns, it can be like stepping into a time machine. I just wish I'd had longer to chat with him.' He held his hand into the slipstream as we gathered pace. 'It's funny really, isn't it?'

'What is?' I asked.

'An English Tommy having his life saved by the Germans—' He stopped talking abruptly and stared through the windscreen. 'Hang on – who's that in front?'

A few hundred yards ahead another ambulance was approaching a set of red traffic lights. H craned forward in an effort to make out the registration number.

'Great! It's Larry and Jack.' He reached behind his seat, pulled the fire extinguisher from its retaining clip and placed it between his legs. 'OK, pull up beside them and let's hope he's got his door open – and try to act casual.'

'Act casual?'

'Yeah, like nothing's going to happen.'

I glanced down at the fire extinguisher, then back at him.

'Tell me you're not going to do what I think you're going to do.'

'I certainly am. He's got it coming, and this is too good

an opportunity to miss. I've been waiting days to get the bastard.'

'Suppose they've got a patient on board?' I said, in the forlorn hope of dissuading him.

'If they're both sitting in the front it means there's no one in the back, and we're in the clear.'

'We?'

H tugged the safety clip from the canister as I drew up to the right of Larry's ambulance.

Larry looked across from the driver's seat and smiled at Howard in mild surprise.

'All right, mate? Where did you come from?'

Howard smiled back and raised the extinguisher. The only discernible movement from Larry as H pulled the trigger was a slight widening of the eyes. Any subsequent movement was lost as his cab was instantly engulfed in a powerful blast of compressed powder. Howard kept his finger hard down on the trigger until the lights changed and I could accelerate away from the scene like a mob driver in a Jimmy Cagney movie. A hundred yards up the road I stole a glance in the wing mirror. The traffic lights were still on green but Larry's ambulance, not to mention the queue of cars trapped behind it, hadn't moved. An impenetrable grey fog behind the windscreen obscured any sight of the occupants.

H put the extinguisher back in its cradle and smiled contentedly.

'I'm surprised Larry fell for that – he's either getting old, or stupid. Bit of both probably.'

I didn't feel quite so sanguine.

The unwelcome spin-off from these practical jokes was that sometimes completely innocent bystanders got dragged in – me, for instance. And, the way I saw it, Larry would now have me down as a legitimate target for a retaliatory strike.

'Why do you goad Larry when you know full well he's only going to do something worse in return?' I asked.

'I don't goad him, I respond. What you just witnessed was nothing more than a measured response.'

This was the kind of answer I'd get from either one of them.

'So I presume that was your response to the syringe?'

'Amongst other things. He pulled another trick on me the other week – only worse. He lobbed a jumping-jack into my cab! Can you believe it?'

Jumping-jacks are banned these days, but were readily available in the late seventies. They were fireworks made from tubes of cardboard concertinaed into a zigzag shape and filled every few centimetres with small charges of gunpowder. When lit, each charge went off separately, causing the whole explosive mix to leap around in a totally unpredictable manner. Despite myself, I had to smile at the thought of H scrabbling around trying to kick it out of the cab. He caught my look.

'It wasn't funny! I was doing thirty miles an hour in the Queensway tunnel at the time!'

H was interrupted by Control repeating our call sign

over the radio. Unperturbed, he carried on talking as he picked up the microphone.

'And when you bear in mind the oxygen we carry on board, well, he could have blown us to kingdom come.' He broke off to jot down the details of a fresh case and signed off. 'I tell you, the bloke's certifiable.' He shook his head and dragged himself back to the moment. 'So, what have we got – "man with a cut face".' He didn't sound too impressed. 'Yet another big emergency.'

I looked up the Erdington address in the A–Z and eased out into the traffic.

A woman was waiting by the garden gate as we pulled into the cul-de-sac. Despite being well into her fifties, she had the ramrod stance of someone poised for action and the instant her eyes fell on us she threw both arms into the air and leapt out on to the pavement, furiously beckoning at us as if guiding a jet on to the flight deck of an aircraft carrier.

'Nice to be wanted, isn't it?' H said, as I pulled up and switched off the engine.

She'd sprinted to the front door of the house in the time it took us to get out of the ambulance and waited impatiently, knotting and unknotting her hands.

'Do hurry, please!' she begged. 'He's in an awful state.' Then she was off into the house with us trying to catch up. When we reached the hallway she was halfway up the stairs and bent double in an effort to catch her breath.

'Come on – I don't know if he's still alive!' Then, as if she'd reminded herself of what was going on upstairs, she let out a whimper and was on the move again. We were close behind now and almost collided with her as she halted abruptly at the open bathroom door. For a moment she looked into the room and, as she stepped aside for us to pass, said quietly, 'Oh Dad, what have you done?'

'Bloody hell,' Howard muttered to himself as we stood shoulder to shoulder in the doorway, gazing in at what looked to be a ghost sitting on the closed toilet. His left arm was resting on the adjacent wash basin for support while his right clutched the edge of the bath. His upper body was leaning forward slightly and, as he became aware of our presence, his head turned slowly in our direction. There wasn't a hint of colour in his face save the two watery blue smudges that were his eyes. The chalky whiteness of his complexion and the shock of unruly white hair served as a perfect backdrop to emphasize the great red splash of blood that drenched his pyjamas. If he was indeed a ghost, then he'd certainly come to a violent end before passing over.

He wasn't a ghost. He was an old man who had gone into the bathroom, locked the door and cut his throat from ear to ear with a razor blade. It was a ragged gash rather than a clean cut. To the accompaniment of his daughter banging on the door, he'd spent several minutes hacking away at his neck, making a series of small cuts which linked up to form a huge wound. He'd somehow avoided severing an artery and his windpipe was still intact. The bleeding had stopped, leaving large, glutinous clots hanging from his neck, some curving down in thick strands where they had attached themselves to his chest. When the blood had been running freely, droplets had spattered the floor like ruby raindrops. The tiled walls were daubed with bloody handprints, as were the sink and bath. A blood-sodden towel, which I presume his daughter had used to try to stem the bleeding, lay at his feet. It's always alarming to see the effects of extreme violence on a person, but when it's self-inflicted it's even more unnerving.

That he was conscious was little short of amazing. His eyes followed us as we approached him. He tried to nod a greeting with grotesque effect. The movement was accompanied by squelching sounds from the gaping wound and the strands of congealing blood wobbled and swayed slightly. I stared down into the gash and felt I could see into his stomach. My toes curled in revulsion. Why wasn't he unconscious or, at the very least, collapsed on the floor? His blood pressure must have been in his boots judging by his colour and the amount of blood he'd lost. Howard fished three of the largest bandages from our bag and wrapped them round the wound while I supported the old man. We then stripped off the sodden pyjamas and cocooned him in a blanket.

We didn't have the means to increase his blood volume by giving fluids in those days, so it was vital to keep him as flat as possible. We did this by placing him on our carry-chair and then raising it in such a way that his feet were kept at a higher level than his head. It wasn't particularly elegant, but it was quick, and we made it to the ambulance with a minimum of delay. When we had him flat on the stretcher and connected up to the oxygen I relaxed a little and found a moment to look into those little blue eyes. They looked back, but said absolutely nothing.

After delivering him into the care of the hospital staff, Howard and I sat in the ambulance discussing the case over another cup of tea. It wasn't a long conversation. We would never know what had driven the old man to take such desperate action, and pontificating on the whys and wherefores would have been pretty pointless. One thing we did know: the fewer cases like that we had to deal with the better. It's a popular misconception that ambulance crews spend half their lives wading around in blood. It does happen, but not nearly as often as most people would believe.

With our tea finished, Howard booked clear on the radio and sat back.

'He must have been an old soldier too.'

'Yes, he'd got to be a pretty similar age to the chap we brought in earlier,' I said.

'Eighty-four,' H responded. 'They were both eighty-four. It makes you think, doesn't it? He's gone through two world wars, and God knows what kind of hardships in between, and then ends up cutting his—' He stopped in mid-sentence and listened intently as Control passed over our next case.

'This has to be some kind of joke,' H said when they'd finished. If it was a joke, then it would be the first

Ambulance Control had ever cracked. We were being sent to an elderly woman who'd cut her throat. I checked the address and pulled out of the hospital drive into the morning traffic.

Once again a middle-aged woman was waiting outside when we arrived. Once again we found ourselves trying to keep up as she furiously beckoned and then fled inside. Once again we tumbled upstairs and stopped at the bathroom door. Here we were met with a sight almost identical to the one we'd witnessed just half an hour before. The only difference was that the patient was a woman. She'd been discovered by her daughter bending over the sink sawing away at her throat with a razor blade. Again, I couldn't understand how the patient had remained conscious. Nothing vital had been cut, but she'd still lost a river of blood. Her clothing was saturated and just about everything round her was smeared red.

It's difficult to describe the sense of unreality I felt as I supported her and watched Howard bandage her neck. With the bulk of her sodden clothing removed, I enveloped her in a blanket as Howard set up our carry-chair. She didn't protest at, or even seem to acknowledge, our presence as we carried her out to the ambulance with her feet in the air. When she was on the stretcher I looked down at her just as I had the old man. She was cocooned in the blanket with the oxygen mask covering most of her face. For the second time, a pair of expressionless, watery blue eyes stared back at me. Once again there was no communication. Why had she done it? I would never know.

Despite its being commonly referred to, very few people actually get round to cutting their own throats, or anyone else's for that matter. Howard, with more than ten years' experience, had never seen it attempted before. I certainly hadn't and, not that I knew it at the time, I would never come across it again. Which makes being called out to two such cases, one after the other, all the more extraordinary. But what really sent my head spinning were all the coincidences bound up within a coincidence. To all intents and purposes, the two cases were identical in every detail of their execution; the only essential difference was the gender of the patients. Even their ages – he was eighty-four and she was eighty-two – were nigh on the same.

Howard and I talked it through for a while and when he rubbed his chin in a thoughtful manner I assumed he was going to wrap up the conversation with a profound comment on the vagaries of life.

'I suppose I'll have to apologize to Jack for the fire-extinguisher thing. It was bad luck he was working with Larry today.'

His change of tack threw me.

'Er, yes. I suppose it was,' I replied, for want of anything better to say.

'It's not as if he'd done anything to deserve getting blasted along with Larry.'

'No, that's true,' I said, still trying to readjust.

'The thing is,' H looked at me with an aggrieved expression, 'I was working with Jack when Larry lobbed the jumping-jack into the cab. And, from what I remember, he didn't see the funny side. In fact, he was quite put out by it.'

'Poor old Jack,' I said. 'So he was on the receiving end both times?'

'I'm afraid so.' Howard looked contemplative, then brightened up. 'Oh well, these things happen I suppose. I'll buy him a drink next time we're in the pub.'

# Chapter Seven

Jack got his apology and a free pint in due course. We
hadn't been crewed together for quite a while but still saw
plenty of each other on station and at parties organized by
the Henrietta Street Social Club. It might seem a bit sad
to have spent our leisure time in each other's company,
but such was the spirit of the place that we genuinely
looked forward to these nights out. Mike seldom attended
as he drank little and socialized even less. Jack was just
the opposite. He drank a lot and thrived on the kind of
loud banter these alcohol-enhanced evenings generated.
He usually commandeered a stool at the bar, where he
would wait for people to gravitate towards him and then
regale them with stories of his life as a lorry driver and
night-club bouncer. I didn't have a clue at the time that he
had an ulterior motive for staying close to the bar: it gave
him chance to top up surreptitiously with vodka shots in
between rounds.

The true extent of his reliance on alcohol only emerged

over time. We all drank too much on these nights out and as far as we were concerned Jack fitted in very nicely with the requirements of the day. So well, in fact, that when he didn't show up he was missed by everyone. I don't want to give the impression that all our nights out ended in drunkenness, just that it was known to happen and, when it did, Jack was always in the thick of it. On the occasion of Gerard Lynch's stag night he was enjoying himself so much that he almost started a fight.

Gerard was on 'D' shift and had more or less exploded into my consciousness a few months earlier when the messroom was crowded at shift changeover time. I was sitting at the long communal table with a few others finishing a cup of tea and idly scanning the sports pages when Gerard heaved himself out of an armchair and made his way over. I was only vaguely aware of the little skip and hop before he launched himself on to the table in a shallow dive. Arms outstretched as if cutting through water, he slid virtually its whole length, scattering everything in his wake. We reared back to avoid his flailing boots and the cups of hot tea clattering to the floor around us before regaining enough composure to watch him casually swing his legs off the table and saunter out through the door. Mystified, I looked round at the others, expecting there to be a general hue and cry, but not a word was said. Someone went off to get a broom to sweep up the broken crockery while the rest resumed their seats and began putting their newspapers back together as if nothing had happened.

The only person to catch my eye was Howard. He looked at me enquiringly and then, as if suddenly realizing an explanation was needed, said, 'He was in the Navy.'

'The Navy?'

'Submarines, I think. You know what submariners are like.'

'No, I can't say I do. I don't think I've met one.'

'Well, you have now. They're as mad as hatters, every last one of them.'

Howard was right – Gerard was as mad as a hatter. He was perfectly good at his job, but as mad as a hatter none the less. I found myself working with him on an overtime shift a few weeks after the table incident and it proved to be a day that would stick in my memory, not for the cases we attended, but for his sheer eccentricity. For example, try to imagine what it might be like to spend the best part of eight hours sitting beside someone wearing an antique gas mask. He'd pulled it from his kit bag and slid it over his head as I was approaching a set of red traffic lights. When I brought the ambulance to a halt, he turned slowly in my direction. I, aware of the movement, and aware that he was up to something, looked round to be confronted by a pair of opaque, goggle eyes set in black rubber not twelve inches from my face. That kind of experience gives you a bit of a fright and the effect wasn't lessened by the moth-eaten breathing hose dangling limply against his chest like a geriatric elephant's trunk. The lights changed, and as I pulled away my smile was tempered by the knowledge that we still had most of the shift left to do.

As things panned out, I was right to be concerned. I suppose I should be thankful that he at least took the mask off when dealing with patients, but that was the only concession he made. He wore it at every other opportunity, revelling in the bewildered stares and pointing fingers his appearance drew from other road-users whenever we were in slow-moving traffic. The sight of a gas mask didn't have the sinister implications it would today; all it said was that the person behind it had lost grip of his senses. I think my worst moments came in the queue at the local chip shop. He engaged as many customers as would come near him in muffled conversation, ranging from the weather to Aston Villa's chances of beating Arsenal on Saturday. It really tickled him that, with true British reserve, no one made reference to the mask and instead either moved away or found something interesting to gaze at through the window, as you might if you found yourself sitting next to an oddball on the bus. The uniform, not to mention the ambulance parked outside, meant that I couldn't dissociate myself from him and had to endure more questioning looks than he did. I was tempted to tap my temple as some kind of explanation, but decided that it wasn't really necessary.

Later in the day he proved that, when it came to acting the fool, he could use anything as a prop. We'd been called to a block of flats to check out reports of an unconscious man on the fifth-floor landing. When the lift doors opened, Gerard was first to respond to the sight of our patient sprawled against a door opposite.

'Billy bloody Bunger! I'll swing for you one day!'

Billy was well known in the area as an incorrigible drunk. There was no malice in the man and, to be fair, he never actually called for an ambulance himself. Other people did that for him. Middle-aged, unkempt and smelly, his habit was to fall asleep wherever the fancy took him, descending into such a deep state of oblivion that passers-by assumed him to be dead or dying. Gerard chewed his lip as he considered the scene. I think he was regretting leaving the gas mask in the ambulance but, being nothing if not resourceful, he used what he had to hand. He unfolded the blanket we always carry and draped it over his head. It reached his feet and, when it was adjusted to his satisfaction, he crossed the landing and towered over Billy. The weave of the blanket was loose enough for him to see through comfortably and, raising his voice to a shout, he prodded the slumbering body with his foot.

'Billy! Wake up, you smelly reprobate!'

The response wasn't immediate, but Billy eventually opened a bleary eye and, regarding the blanket with no outward show of surprise, said, 'Hello, mate. What can I do for you?'

'You can get up and clear off for a start! You can't go around sleeping on people's doorsteps. You're lucky we're not the police.'

If Billy was fazed by finding himself conversing with a blanket, he didn't let on.

'It's my doorstep. I couldn't get in. The lock's broken or something. I was trying to work out what to do next and must have dropped off. Then you turn up out of the blue shouting at me.'

'Your flat? You don't live here, do you?'

Billy thought about it. 'Yes, mate.'

A bulge in the shape of a hand appeared in the blanket. 'Give me the key.'

Billy dipped into his pocket and after a bit of rummaging produced the key and thrust it at the waiting blanket, which, in turn, fitted it into the lock.

Gerard fiddled for a few seconds then gave up.

'This isn't the right key! No wonder you couldn't get in.'

Billy, who'd been on the verge of drifting off again, squinted at him.

'It's the only key I've got.' He leaned round to get a better look at the door. 'Ah, that explains it. It's the right key, but that's the wrong door. I live at number twenty; you're trying to get into twenty-two. Don't blame yourself, mate. It's an easy mistake to make; I do it all the time.'

Gerard stared at him – at least I think he did – then strode across the landing and opened the door of flat twenty.

'OK Billy. Disappear! And don't, even if the place catches fire, ever come out again. You got that?'

Billy struggled to his feet, weaving unsteadily across the threshold.

'Yes, mate, got it. And I want to thank you.' He held out his hand for the inevitable drunken handshake, which Gerard reluctantly responded to through the blanket. 'You blokes are great,' Billy continued. 'I don't know what we'd do without you, I really don't. It was you that helped me last week when I fell off that wall in Handsworth, wasn't it?'

Gerard, still clasping Billy's hand, and still hidden under the blanket, stiffened.

'I might have done.' Then he gave the game away by saying, 'How did you know it was me?'

Billy tried to focus in the general direction of Gerard's head under the blanket.

'My memory might be shit, but I never forget a face.'

Gerard was silent for a moment, then burst out laughing. A puzzled smile crept briefly over Billy's face before his head went back and he joined in the laughter with a wheezy roar. I watched them from the sidelines in wonderment. Gerard's sense of humour thrived on the ridiculous, and this was about as ridiculous as it got.

I was still recovering from my day with Gerard when the shift received its invitation to join him on his stag night. We met the request with mixed emotions. No one wanted to miss out on a good booze-up, but agreeing to an evening with Gerard and his shift mates required a pause for thought. We mulled it over and were on the point of agreement when Howard idly asked, 'Who would be daft enough to marry Gerard?' It was a good question. Steve thought about it.

'There's only one answer to that . . . someone even dafter than him, obviously. The real question is, where on earth did he find someone like that?'

'I bet it's that bird he brought to Jim's retirement do a couple of months ago,' Larry said. 'Remember? The one who looked like the Elephant Man in drag.'

'She wasn't that bad,' Steve said.

Larry looked at him askance. 'You're joking! Not even the tide would take her out.'

'Well, just in case it is her, I'd keep it buttoned when you're around Gerard.' Steve looked at us. He was in his early fifties but was always up for a night out. 'So, we're going then?'

Everyone agreed that we were, save Mike, who pulled out his diary.

'What date was it?'

Larry told him and watched as he flicked through the pages.

'Oh, that's a shame – I'm planning on watching TV that night.'

More than twenty of us were crowded into the lounge of a local pub on the big night. Gerard went at it hammer and tongs from the off. We did our best to keep up, but the only person capable was Jack and, if truth be told, he didn't find it difficult. The drunker Gerard got, the more gregarious he became and, instead of just amusing himself as was his wont, he entertained everybody with slapstick comedy I assume he'd perfected during long months spent under the Atlantic. Unfortunately, I could only dredge up fragments the following morning, but I did remember laughing more than I had ever done before at the way he animated each routine by shoving himself round the room on his stool while talking to imaginary people like a drunken and very profane Joyce Grenfell. His timing and delivery were so perfect that our ribs were still aching when he got up to visit the toilet.

When he failed to return after twenty minutes, Jack organized a search. The first sign we had of anything being amiss was when one of the searchers came back into the lounge and asked the manager to call an ambulance. We looked at each other in that drink-befuddled way we saw all too often in some of our patients.

'An ambulance?' Larry exclaimed. 'I've got to watch this. I've never seen anyone actually calling for an ambulance before.' As he got unsteadily to his feet there was a commotion on the other side of the lounge as Jack and his helpers barged into the room carrying Gerard face down on what looked like a toilet door.

'What the hell's going on?' Steve was the first to react.

'We found him spark out in one of the cubicles. I don't know what's wrong with him,' Jack gasped.

'It could be that he's as drunk as a skunk,' Steve said.

'Oh no,' Jack was indignant. 'He's had no more to drink than me, and I've only had about eight pints and a few vodkas, so it can't be the booze.'

Gerard was sliding about on the Formica door like a wet fish on a plate, coming perilously close to the edge at one point. Howard compensated by lowering his side, but overdid it and Gerard slid back the other way, coming inches away from being deposited on to a table of drinkers.

One of them jumped to his feet and barked at Jack, 'What do you morons think you're playing at?'

Jack's eyes narrowed as he regarded the heavily built man. 'Take my advice, pal, and zip it before I get annoyed.'

The man took a step closer and I feared the worst. Jack loved to tell of the bar-room brawls he'd been involved in when he was a continental lorry driver and was particularly proud of a night he spent in a Yugoslav jail as a result. I'd taken these stories with a pinch of salt, but now, with the drink in him, Jack had taken on a menacing air that left me feeling very uncomfortable. Luckily, he was diverted by the manager shouting at him from behind the bar.

'Oi! Is that one of my toilet fucking doors?'

Jack swung round and again came close to tipping Gerard on to the floor.

'Er, yes. Don't worry – we're only borrowing it.'

'Borrowing it?' The manager put his hands on his hips. 'I've been in this game twenty years and I reckoned I'd seen everything, but this takes the biscuit.'

'We're just taking him out the front so it will be easier for the ambulance crew when they get here.' Jack was trying to sound conciliatory, which was a good thing because we'd booked the upstairs function room for an after-hours' knees-up, including a buffet and two strippers. It didn't seem likely that Gerard would make it, but it would have been a shame if the rest of us missed it by being thrown out. Jack's explanation incensed his burly protagonist, who rounded on him.

'You've never called out an ambulance for that oaf. Hasn't it crossed your mind that they might have better things to do with their time than waste it on drunks?'

Jack did his best to restrain himself. 'He's not drunk.'

'Not drunk? Are you insane? Look at him, for Christ's sake . . . Don't you know a drunk when you see one?'

We all looked at Gerard sleeping contentedly on the door, and saw a drunk. His face had taken on a babyish expression, made all the more convincing by the occasional smacking of lips and the gentle drool running down his cheek. Jack wasn't to be put off though.

'I know what I'm talking about. I happen to be an ambulance man, so, for the last time, zip it before I'm tempted to give you a slap.'

The man gaped at him. 'Christ! If that's true, then remind me never to get sick in this fucking city.'

Jack eyed him disdainfully. 'For your information, we're all ambulance men, and we know what we're doing. Don't we, lads?'

Steve put his head in his hands and groaned quietly. 'Oh God. I knew I should have stayed in and watched telly with Mike.'

Gerard was eventually whisked off in an ambulance and we staggered upstairs to the function room, glad to escape the thunderous looks and barely concealed comments of our fellow drinkers. The rest of the evening is all but lost in the fog of my memory. I don't even remember a great deal about the strippers, other than that they threw an awful lot of talcum powder about, which left me with a bit of explaining to do the next morning.

We were back on duty the following evening to start the night shift and, even though our hangovers had been shaken off, there was a subdued atmosphere in the mess-room, especially when it came to Jack, who must have looked back on the night before with some embarrassment. He'd even managed to upset the crew that came to collect Gerard. They had about thirty years' experience between them but that didn't stop Jack carefully explaining exactly what was expected of them in the care of their patient. Not a tactic designed to win yourself friends, especially when you're still a probationer yourself. I was crewed up with Howard and we both took an oath never to touch alcohol again. We didn't want to taste or smell any booze again for the rest of our lives. A night of nursing little old ladies with chest infections or similarly worthy complaints would do us just fine.

The early signs were promising, and then at about midnight we were called to a man reported to have fallen in a city-centre toilet. The first question we always want to ask when toilets are involved is: was the patient on his way in, or on his way out? It matters, and it doesn't take much imagination to figure out why. In this instance, as is usually the way, he was on his way in. He'd been with two mates wandering between clubs when they noticed the public toilet and decided to make use of it. Two factors conspired against them. Firstly, they'd been on an all-day drinking binge and were barely able to put one foot in front of the other; and, secondly, the toilet they spotted was something akin to a Second World War air-raid shelter buried deep below street level. Anyone driven to venture inside this profoundly uninviting place had to be desperate, or drunk. As it happened, they fell into both categories. From what I learned later it seems the leader managed only one of the concrete steps before losing his balance and pitching head first into the gloom below.

A police car pulled up behind us as we arrived outside the toilets, and Sid and his partner got out. We couldn't help but be on first-name terms with most of the policemen on our patch, as they treated Henrietta Street like a second home and were forever there drinking tea or taking shelter when the weather closed in. Even the mounted officers dropped in from time to time for a cup of tea and polo mints for their horses. One we saw a lot was Sid, a rather reticent, subdued character, whose shift pattern mirrored ours. He wandered over, adjusting his cap, and spoke to Howard.

'Hello, H. What have we got here, then?'

'Seems like some bloke's fallen over down there. Are you going to give us a hand?'

'Well, seeing as we're here I suppose we might as well.'

Sid was one of these characters who rarely showed any interest in police work, giving the impression that his sole aim was to get the shift over and head off home. As it turned out, he would have been doing himself a favour if he'd just left us to it.

Our patient was face down on the floor. His deep, regular snores reverberated round the tiled walls like a ghostly river foghorn, leaving us in no doubt that he was unconscious even before we reached him. He was a big, beefy chap, but thankfully he'd rolled into a position that made it relatively easy for us to give him an all-over body check. The nasty bruises welling up on his face and forehead made it painfully clear that his head had bounced off quite a few steps on the way down. On the plus side, there was no outward evidence that anything was broken, other than his nose, which was bleeding profusely. The blood had mingled with a huge pool of beer on the floor that had presumably been inside him when he started his descent. For good measure, he'd also wet himself. There was no way of knowing just how serious his head injury was, or what unseen damage he might have done to his neck and back. This meant we were going to have to work carefully and get him back up to ground level without unnecessary delay. In view of his weight, heaving him back up the steps was going to be an operation akin to a mountain rescue. Not that we had any clear mountain air to breathe. We were drawing on an atmosphere that would have put the giraffe house at Dudley Zoo to shame.

Driven by the urge to escape the fetid stench as much as anything else, we worked quickly to immobilize him on our scoop-stretcher while taking care he didn't drown on the beer that was still dribbling from his mouth. With that done, we arranged ourselves so that H and the other officer were at the top of the stretcher, leaving Sid and me to push from below. On the count of three we heaved the stretcher off the ground and took a couple of tentative steps up the stairs. The balance seemed about right, and I was beginning to think that it wasn't going to be so difficult, when from above my head came a noise like a breaching whale. Half a second later a powerful gush of beer-laden vomit erupted from deep inside the patient and splattered horribly against the nearby wall. There was no escape for Sid or me. I cursed at the thought of allowing myself to be positioned underneath an active human volcano. If I'd had my wits about me I would have been at the top beside H and out of harm's way, even if it did mean leaving the two policemen in the line of fire. With the damage done, we rotated the stretcher so that, as those in medical circles would say, postural drainage could occur and prevent the patient from choking.

I stood for a moment waiting for my own waves of nausea to subside before making a second attempt to get him back up to street level. It was during this pause that a group of lads clattered down the stairs. Bystanders can be helpful sometimes, but seldom after closing time. This particular bunch obviously hadn't any intention of breaking with convention, and the moment they saw us they let out a cheer before launching into uninhibited, not to say obscene, conjecture about our motives for tying up a man in a public toilet. Sid was still wiping traces of vomit from his hair as he made an attempt to stamp his authority on the grinning faces.

'OK. You've had your fun, now get lost!' This didn't bring the instant obedience he'd hoped for. The lads, as if carefully rehearsed beforehand, seamlessly broke into song. It wasn't a song chosen randomly either. I looked for Sid's reaction as the chorus from 'Y.M.C.A.', the song made famous by 1970s gay icons the Village People, echoed round the toilets. It was doubtless inspired by our uniforms, and their uncompromising train of thought. The light was poor, but I'm sure Sid turned a shade of purple as he threw down his handkerchief and bellowed at them, 'You've had your last warning! Get lost! And get lost now, or you'll be arrested!'

The singing faltered and one of the lads spread his hands in supplication as he spoke.

'Hey, cool it, man. We were only having a laugh. No offence meant.' There wasn't time to tell if Sid was appeased or not because, after casting a glance at our patient, the lad continued talking. 'It's none of my business, but I'd have thought you'd have tied him face down on that stretcher. It'd give you much easier access, if you know what I mean.'

'Right! That's it!' There was no mistaking the rage in Sid's voice as he made a move towards the joker. I would have loved to see him in action, but stopped him before he could get any further by pointing out that, like it or like it not, our priority was to get the unconscious man on to the ambulance. Sid glowered at the group and gave them a final warning. 'If any of you lot are still around when we get up these steps I'll have you banged up in the back of my car before you know what's happened to you.'

'Ooh! Promises, promises!' It was said in an outrageously camp voice, but it proved to be the parting shot as the group took Sid's advice and made themselves scarce.

I checked that our man was breathing normally before we continued up the steps. He'd resumed snoring and with each exhalation a fine mist of blood sprayed from his battered nose and hung in the air before lazily drifting down towards us. A steady trickle of beer, vomit and urine flowed down the frame of the stretcher and, after warmly engulfing our hands, dripped on to our trousers and shoes. I was battling to control the anger I felt towards this stranger. If he'd been the innocent victim of an accident, or if some kind of infirmity had led him into this predicament, he would have had my complete sympathy and any personal discomfort I may have felt would have been neither here nor there. Patently, no such circumstance existed. He was a victim of his own irresponsible actions in drinking solidly for twelve hours. There's nothing quite like the self-righteous anger of a reformed sinner and I had trouble keeping my feelings to myself as we heaved and pushed. When we reached the relatively fresh air at street level I shared my thoughts with Sid.

'What on earth are we doing here at this time of the night covered in someone's piss and vomit? We must be mad.' He grunted in agreement, but the comment had been overheard by one of the patient's mates, who until now had been keeping a low profile. He took exception to it, and came out with a statement that has stuck in my mind ever since.

'If you don't like your job, why don't you get another one?'

I was momentarily lost for words. I wasn't expecting any thanks, or even an expression of regret at the state of my clothes, but equally I didn't expect to be told to get another job. I stared at him and searched for a quick response. Nothing came to mind that wouldn't have condemned me in court. Was this what my job represented to him? Did he think I was exclusively employed to scrape up drunks in the early hours of the morning? And if that's what he truly believed, was he implying that by not enjoying it I was standing in the way of someone who would? Did he imagine that as a schoolboy I sat in class, gazing out the window, dreaming of the day when I would be old enough to trawl public toilets for people pickled in alcohol who'd knocked themselves out? In the end I chose to say nothing, and contented myself with marking it down as one of the joys of being a public servant.

# Chapter Eight

When my wife, Marie-Madeleine, announced one evening that she was pregnant, it was as if the last piece of the jigsaw was in place. Our little terraced house in Erdington was ready after two years of nest-building, albeit on a tight budget. If my memory serves me well, the only item we bought new was the living-room carpet, an indulgence we thought long and hard over. Everything else came from second-hand shops or was spotted for sale in corner-shop windows. Even the smelly old paraffin heater we used to keep the landing warm was donated by a kind soul from the pub. Our car was held together by string, sticking plasters and a few pounds of body-filler from Halfords. It sounds hard by modern standards, but we certainly didn't see it that way. Life was good, and news of the baby made it better. I had settled into my new career as Marie-Madeleine had into her new country. She had arrived in England from France in 1975, and here we were nearly five years later about to produce our first Euro baby. All great stuff.

I don't remember it being much of a hardship to work round-the-clock shifts in those early days, though I dare say Marie has her own thoughts on the matter. It did impinge on our social life to some extent, and it could be frustrating to flick through my diary after receiving an invitation to some do or other and find I was on nights. In fact, I became fatalistic about it, and perhaps even a little cynical. If the occasion was a wedding, or some other event I would have been quite happy to miss, then I could be sure it would fall on my day off. Shift work throws up all kinds of annoyances, but these quibbles were as nothing when balanced against the advantages. Not being trapped in an office, being able to visit the shops on a Tuesday instead of standing in a queue on a Saturday, never being caught in rush-hour traffic jams, and always being home ten minutes after clocking off are just a few.

Then there was the work itself. Not knowing what might lie round the next corner held an allure that became almost addictive. It could be exhilarating at times, but mostly it was quietly rewarding. Helping someone who can't help themselves is a basic human instinct; we got chance to do it all the time and got quite a sense of accomplishment in return. Of course, there were low points. They didn't come along often, but when they did we were affected the same way as anyone else would be. After all, when it comes down to it, we were just members of the public wearing a uniform.

On this particular day, Mike and I were going to have a bad time. Of course we weren't to know it, but the omens weren't good when our first job came through at quarter to eight. A pedestrian had been hit by a bus and was feared dead. It was a case description guaranteed to quicken the pulse of the most hard-bitten crew, and we kept our eyes on the road and our thoughts to ourselves as we sped through the city centre.

The call had been made by a police officer who'd happened on the accident five minutes earlier. He had covered the body as best he could with a tarpaulin taken from the boot of his car after a passing doctor had stepped from a group of onlookers and, after a quick examination, confirmed the patient to be deceased. He gave his details to the officer, then went on his way. The policeman's suspicions confirmed, he now had the confidence to cancel the ambulance and ask for a coroner's van to be sent instead to remove the body. He'd just finished talking into his radio when Mike and I arrived.

It was a grim sight. The tarpaulin wasn't big enough to hide the victim completely, leaving his splayed feet protruding from one end, and dark, viscous blood oozing from the other. I was only vaguely aware of the bystanders moving aside as we walked towards the body. Most people hurry away from a grisly incident after a furtive look, but there are always a few who will form into a group and see things through to the end. The policeman spoke over his shoulder as he directed the slow-moving traffic into the outside lane.

'A doctor's just certified him. I tried to cancel the ambulance and arranged for our lot to come out to deal with it.'

Mike lifted the tarpaulin as I listened to what else the officer had to say. From what witnesses had told him, it seems the victim had been standing on the corner of the busy street waiting for his chance to cross the road. He probably became impatient and was seen to step forward into the gutter just as a bus came swinging round the corner. He tried to leap from its path and almost made it, only to be struck by the side of the bus and thrown violently against the kerb. The bus driver, unaware of the accident, continued his journey. With the doctor having unofficially certified the victim, and with the coroner's van already on the way, there didn't seem much left for us to do.

I joined Mike as he carefully searched for a pulse at the patient's neck and shook his head. Everything was awash with blood. Gooey strands, which had stuck to the inside of the tarpaulin, stretched and broke, falling back on to the upturned face. His scalp had become detached from his skull and in the top of his head there was a huge mushy depression as large as my fist. The blood that had run down over his face completely obscured his features and soaked his clothes. My gaze returned to the injury. Tiny white shards of splintered bone protruded from the sea of red; it had been a frightful blow. Mike suddenly broke the silence.

'What was that?' His face had become tense with concentration.

'What?' I asked.

'There! Look – his nose!'

I stared intently, wondering what I was looking for, and then, as I watched, a small bubble of blood slowly expanded over a nostril before suddenly popping. Was it air escaping naturally from the body, or was it evidence that he was trying to breathe? A cloud of diesel fumes from a passing bus engulfed us as I tried for a carotid pulse. I felt something. It was barely discernible and very slow. It was all but inconceivable that he could have survived such an injury, and hadn't he already been declared dead by a doctor?

I grabbed our suction device and, pumping furiously, hoovered up as much blood as I could from his mouth and nose before double-checking that his airway was clear, then helping Mike secure his neck. While doing this we got our second surprise. He hadn't been scalped at all. He'd been wearing a wig, which had become detached and soaked in blood. The blood had congealed over the webbing, giving the appearance of body tissue hanging loose. If anything, though, the hole in his head looked bigger. Mike positioned the stretcher while I did my best to assist the patient's breathing with a bag and mask. The policeman was asking questions but we weren't listening. He tackled us again a few moments later as we loaded the stretcher on to the ambulance.

'What's going on? Where are you going with him? I told you the coroner's—'

'He's alive,' I said. 'We're going to the Accident Hospital.'

'Alive? But the doctor said he was dead.'

'Well, he's not,' Mike said. 'Now, stop the traffic so we can get out of here.'

The patient died less than an hour later in hospital. Everything was done for him, but there had been no possibility of his surviving such a severe head injury. When it was over, the hospital staff could only marvel at the tenacity with which he'd clung to life. For our part, and without the aid of a cardiac monitor, it had all boiled down to a little bubble of blood and an almost indiscernible pulse. A pulse, by the way, which I had great trouble in finding for a second time. And the mystery doctor in the crowd? He may have been bogus, but I rather fancy he was the genuine article. I'm sure we'd have found out soon enough if the police had followed up his status and found him to be an impostor. Either way, we heard no more of him.

The rest of the day continued without drama, the only other notable low point being Phyllis's liver and onions at lunchtime. It was about five minutes from our finishing time when we were called to a woman in labour. This kind of thing isn't guaranteed to put you in a good mood. We would be late finishing and find ourselves in the rush-hour traffic to boot. To make matters worse, our destination was a tower block in Nechells, a truly wretched part of Birmingham in the late seventies. What had once been an honest, working-class district had slowly degenerated into a dumping ground for just about every social misfit in the city. As the problem families and the unemployable moved in, the good moved out, giving the new inhabitants free rein to vent their frustration on their surroundings.

Mike and I exchanged tight-lipped glances as the lift marked its slow ascent with a series of metallic screeches and clangs. It had been against my better judgement to get in it in the first place, but as Mike hadn't seemed bothered I'd obediently followed. My worst fears were realized when it jolted to a halt at the eighth floor and, after humming and vibrating, the doors remained firmly closed. Mike raised his eyes to the ceiling.

'Great! I knew we shouldn't have got in this bloody thing. How often have I told you to steer well clear of council lifts? Now I'm stuck in a mobile urinal with only you for company.'

'It wasn't my idea!' I bleated. 'You're the one who—'

He ignored me and stepped forward to deliver the doors a hefty blow with the flat of his hand.

'A fat lot of good that will do,' I said, and then watched as the doors shuddered open.

By the time Mike and I spilled from the lift, a familiar feeling of despondency had settled on me. Just being in the building was a dispiriting experience. Evil-smelling fumes from a rubbish chute set in the wall opposite pervaded the air and the landing itself had all the appeal of a modern-day Turner Prize exhibit. Half-hearted attempts to replace swathes of vandalized wall tiles had resulted in a jumble of mismatched colours, finished off by local kids with yards of lurid graffiti. The communicating doors hung at angles from their frames and the floor was filthy. Years of accumulated grime lay buried under piles of more transient rubbish. It wasn't a place to linger and Mike, not being much of an art lover anyway, marched off down the echoing corridor checking the doors. He stopped in front of one and leaned forward to read the imprint left by the missing numbers. Satisfied it was the flat we were looking for, he ignored the bell and knocked loudly.

The door was opened by a man of about twenty-five who, like the tower block he lived in, exuded an air of shabby neglect. Skinny and hollow-chested, he had a pinched, pasty face that wasn't done any favours by the lank black hair that framed it. There was no smile, no greeting, just a surly look and a few puzzling words.

'You've got problems!' He turned back into the flat without waiting for a response and wandered down the hall to a closed door. Gesturing towards it, he looked back at us. 'She's locked herself in the toilet.'

We joined him at the door.

'Locked herself in?' Mike didn't try to hide his irritation. 'You mean the door's jammed – she's stuck?'

'No, I mean she's locked herself in and won't come out. Like I said, you're going to have problems.'

Mike's irritation turned to bewilderment. 'Won't come out?'

'Nope.'

'I don't understand – she's got to come out. Tell her we're here and haven't got time for tantrums.'

The man leaned against the door frame and raised his voice.

'Donna, the ambulance is here. They want you to come out right now.' He waited for a response, then tried again. This time he was rewarded by a timid reply.

'Tell them to go away.'

'They're not going to go away – come out!'

'No!'

Mike stared at the door as if hoping it might offer some explanation. When it failed to do so, he returned his gaze to the shabby man.

'I don't get it. Am I missing something important here? Why won't she come out?'

He was met with a shrug of the shoulders and a single word. 'Dunno.'

'You don't know? Are you her husband?'

'Well – kind of.'

'You're her *kind of husband*?'

'Yeah, I suppose that's a way of putting it.'

Mike took a deep breath. 'Correct me if I'm wrong, but as her *kind of husband* it strikes me that you must have some tiny inkling why she's locked herself in the toilet!' His sarcasm fell on stony ground.

'I think she's a bit scared of hospitals.'

'She's had nine months to get used to the idea, for Christ's sake. Tell her she doesn't have a choice – she's got to come out.'

The young man's surly expression deepened.

'If you're so clever, you have a go. She won't listen to me.'

Mike's jaw hardened and for a moment I thought he was going to lose his temper. Instead, he turned to me.

'You speak to her. I don't trust myself.'

I wasn't sure where to start and settled for the casual approach for the want of any better ideas.

'Hello, Donna, it's the ambulance crew. We're waiting to take you to hospital if you're ready.' There was no reply. 'Are you ready? We're ever so busy. We've got other people to collect – it's not fair to keep them waiting.' This lie didn't work either; in fact, nothing I tried worked. I looked appealingly at Mike, who spoke to the man in a carefully measured tone.

'Look, I'm asking you for the last time – what the hell's going on?'

He shrugged again and said nothing. Mike took a breath and addressed Donna through the door. Although angry, he used a surprisingly conciliatory voice. He assured her there was nothing for her to fear and that she would be safe with him. He would look after her personally all the way to the hospital and even go with her to the delivery suite. Ten minutes later nothing had changed and all the time the skinny man leaned against the door like a casual spectator. I looked at my watch; I should have been home half an hour ago.

The only thing I saw clearly was the utter absurdity of the situation. Even if she came out, there wasn't much we could do. We couldn't drag her out to the ambulance if she still refused to come with us. Faced with this kind of intransigence, we would normally give up and leave the patient to it, but this was different. There was no walking away from the fact that the unborn baby was at risk. I decided to have another go.

'Think of the baby, Donna. You can't do this – you might be putting him in danger. Please come out.'

Her partner, who'd been idly picking at a spider tattoo on the back of his hand, looked up.

'The baby? The baby's in the living room. She had it before you came, and then she ran into—'

We didn't hear any more. As one, we made a dash for the living room.

What we saw made even Mike catch his breath. Chalky white and motionless, like a discarded ceramic doll, the baby lay spreadeagled on a rug in the centre of the room with the placenta lying at its side. We went over and knelt by the little body. He was perfectly formed, and looked a good weight, but he was icy-cold and lifeless. I prised apart the sticky eyelids and found the pupils to be cloudy and fixed. He'd been dead some time – there was no hope. Mike and I sat back on our haunches and exhaled. It was impossible to think clearly for a few seconds.

'It's dead, isn't it?' said the man from the doorway. We looked round at him. What kind of person was he?

Mike didn't make any attempt to control his anger, and shouted at him, 'Why in God's name didn't you tell us the baby had been born? You let us stand around for twenty minutes when we might have been able to do something. You – you brain-dead cretin!'

The man answered back defiantly, 'Now hold on! I figured that it was dead – it never did breathe. I was more worried about Donna.'

How could anyone be so crass, so insensitive, so mind-numbingly inhuman? Even the way he'd told us about the baby was casual, almost as if it was an irrelevance.

A bizarre situation had become sinister. We had no way of knowing what had caused the baby's death; anything could have happened in the flat before we arrived. As for the woman in the toilet, she might well be haemorrhaging. We needed help. Mike got to his feet and spoke to me while fixing the scrawny man with a stare that conveyed more menace than any number of words.

'We'll have to get the police here. I'll go down to the ambulance and get on the radio. If I stay here a minute longer I'll end up punching this stupid bastard into next week.'

It was still stalemate when two police officers arrived. They'd been warned what to expect, but it didn't lessen the effect the sight of the baby had on them. One turned on his heel and left the room. The other listened stony-faced as I went over the story as I knew it. When I finished he turned to the man.

'You! I want a few words with you.' The officer steered him none too gently towards a corner of the room. With his back against the wall, the man's sulky look turned defensive as he tried to fend off a barrage of questions. I went back into the hall as Mike returned to the flat with a doctor. He took him straight through to the baby and after a careful examination it was confirmed he'd been dead for some time. There was nothing obviously suspicious. Then he asked to see the mother. When he heard that she was holed up in the bathroom refusing to come out he could hardly believe it.

'But this is nonsense. Does she think she can stay in there for ever? Maybe if I have a word with her and explain things – make her see that nobody blames her for any of this.'

'That might be an idea.' Mike's voice didn't carry any real conviction. 'Please, have a go.'

It didn't take long for the doctor's calm, rational voice to develop an increasingly exasperated tone. Eventually he shrugged his shoulders and quietly addressed the police officer.

'I can't see we have any choice but to force the door.' He looked round at us. 'It's in her own interest. She's got to come out one way or the other.'

The policeman didn't offer any objections and was getting into position to launch a hefty kick at the door when the skinny man intervened.

'I already thought of doing that, but it's a big bolt that I put on myself. The original one fell off and the council couldn't be bothered to come out and fix it. You know how long it takes them to get off their arses . . .'

Mike spoke to the officer. 'That means it might take a fair few kicks.'

'So?' said the policeman.

'So,' Mike said, 'her baby's dead and she's obviously unbalanced and may be in shock. If we start battering at the door she could do anything.' He looked at us. 'I mean, we are on the eighth floor after all.'

His words hung in the air and the policeman, still balancing on one leg, slowly lowered his foot.

'You don't think she'd jump out the window, do you? She wouldn't do that, surely?'

'Probably not,' Mike said, 'but it's a possibility.'

It was an unwelcome suggestion that forced the officer to reach for his radio.

Some twenty minutes later a police inspector, a sergeant and two plainclothes negotiators came through the door. An ambulance officer followed shortly after and made straight for Mike. He told him that another ambulance had been sent and we could go when it arrived. Mike made a half-hearted protest, but the officer was adamant that we should get off home. It was strange to think we would never lay eyes on Donna, but – and I'm sure I speak for Mike too – it was a relief to get away from that wretched block of flats. Word later filtered through that the negotiators had taken half an hour to get Donna out of the bathroom, and then a bit longer to persuade her to go to hospital for a check-up. The inquest followed in due course and found that the baby had been stillborn. His only chance of survival would have been expert help at the time of birth.

When we got back to the Street, Mike threw his bag in

his locker and left without a word. I made myself a cup of tea and slumped into a chair. It had been a good week up until today. We hadn't dealt with anything too taxing; we'd applied bandages here and there, and dished out our quota of comfort and sympathy where it was needed. In our 'down time' we'd lolled around station drinking tea, reading or playing Scrabble. Life was good. And then everything was turned on its head. The senseless death of the pedestrian and then the baby. I'd never seen a dead baby before. I'd never even thought of such an eventuality. It hit me pretty hard, especially when I considered I would soon be a father myself. I knew it was futile, but I wanted to sort out the case in my head and somehow find answers. I was coming to the reluctant conclusion that there weren't any when Stan Phillips from 'D' shift wandered into the room.

'What are you doing sitting around here? Haven't you got a home to go to?'

I stood up and put my cup on the counter.

'Yeah, I suppose I'd better be off.'

He looked at me quizzically. 'You all right?'

'Yeah, of course. See you tomorrow.'

# Chapter Nine

*House fire; persons reported.* Four words guaranteed to send a chill of apprehension through me in my early days. My over-active imagination threw up images of victims huddled on window ledges crying for help or, even worse, trapped behind glass from where there was no escape. What else could the dread, unfinished sentence *persons reported* mean other than that people were trapped inside the burning house? It took repeated false alarms for it eventually to dawn on me that the phrase didn't mean anything, and was used as a matter of course whenever we were sent to a fire, even if it was just a toaster run amuck. It's still used to this day, and for the life of me I don't know why. So, when we responded one morning to a house fire tagged with the usual caveat of *persons reported*, it didn't raise the feeling of trepidation that it might have done a year earlier.

The fire engines were scattered around belching greasy diesel fumes into the air by the time Larry and I turned up.

They had the situation under control, but even so firemen were dodging here and there, careful not to trip on the hoses criss-crossing the road. Firemen always seem to be going somewhere, or returning from somewhere. Seldom do you see one standing still unless he's drinking a cup of tea. So when we spotted the officer's white helmet in the melee we set off after him on foot and caught up only when he stopped moving to bark instructions into his hand-held radio. On seeing us, he got to the point without any preamble.

'We've got one for you. She's inhaled a lot of smoke by the look of it. She's in that appliance over there.' He waved an arm towards a fire engine parked a few yards away, then finished by saying, almost casually, 'The other one's dead.'

'Oh!' Larry was clearly startled. 'We'd better take a look.'

'No, I'm afraid I can't let you do that.' The officer seemed impatient to be somewhere else. 'The body's still upstairs in the bedsit and the floor's unsafe, so you can't go in.'

Larry looked doubtful.

'You know I can't just drive away without confirming it for myself.'

The officer cast him a less than tolerant glance.

'I'm not an idiot. You're just going to have to trust me. The bloke's burnt to a crisp. Oh, and by the way, he's the woman's husband, so you'd better go easy with her.'

Our patient sat draped in a blanket with a fireman

holding an oxygen mask to her face, which she pushed away from time to time to cough sooty phlegm into a handful of paper towels. She'd lost her eyebrows and what was left of her hair was frizzed into little bundles. Sooty residue was spread over her face, but it didn't obscure the reddened skin beneath. There wasn't any sign of blistering, so my initial conclusion was that she'd been very close to the heat but probably not in contact with the flames. We guided her to the ambulance and sat her on the stretcher, where she breathed more oxygen while I sponged down her exposed skin. Every now and then she would sit up and cough more blackened phlegm into the bowl I'd given her.

After one of these bouts she looked at me and croaked, 'I've lost everything, haven't I? Everything's gone!' She coughed again and looked about her. 'Where's Jim? Why's Jim not here with me?'

'Jim's your husband?' I asked.

'Yes. Where is he?'

Despite anticipating the question, I still hadn't worked out a response. I felt desperately sorry for her and didn't want to deceive her into thinking he was still alive, but the back of an ambulance didn't seem the place to break the news. It would be better done at hospital, where they could give her the support she would need. I evaded the subject by telling her that I hadn't seen Jim and that another ambulance would be sent to bring him to the hospital.

Life can sometimes be so cruel that it shakes you to the

foundations. To me, this woman had suffered more than anyone should. She'd lost her husband, her home and all her possessions at a stroke. Her world wasn't just in pieces; it had ceased to exist. Even the clothes on her back would have to be thrown away. I tried not to, but after dropping her off I brooded on the fragility of life and how everything, no matter how solid it may seem, can be torn down and laid waste in moments. Larry caught my sombre mood as we sat on a wall outside Casualty, kicking our heels as we waited for the pungent aftermath of the smoke to clear from the back of the ambulance. Even with all the doors and windows open it was going to take a good thirty minutes. There's no smell more invasive than that left after a fire. It had impregnated the woman's clothes and hair, not to mention the very air in her lungs. While we waited, Larry tried to cheer me up by reminiscing on fatal fires he'd attended over the years. It was nice of him, but I can't say it helped much, and only got me thinking back to the only other serious fire I'd been party to.

It had happened in an old folks' home a few months earlier. Part of the building had caught light at about midnight and several ambulances had been sent to help evacuate the residents. It was an eight-mile trip from the Street and we were the last to arrive. The fire had claimed three lives and, as is often the case, it was the smoke, not the flames that did for the victims. They were still in their beds when I saw them – three small, grey-haired ladies, each looking tranquil and untroubled. There was nothing to suggest they'd been aware of their impending fate. The bedclothes were undisturbed and their room was un-damaged. They had simply fallen into a sleep from which they would never wake.

One of the Casualty porters wandered over and joined us. After lighting a cigarette, he leaned back against the wall and blew out the smoke.

'That woman you brought in is making a hell of a racket in there. She's shouting for her husband even though they've told her he's been fried.'

Larry looked at him. 'I hope they put it a bit more gently than that.' Then, abruptly changing the subject, he pointed at a load of wooden panelling and glass stacked against the side of a building opposite. 'Is that a greenhouse?'

The porter followed his gaze.

'Yeah, it's waiting to be collected and taken to the dump. It was round the back but they need the space for a Portakabin.'

'They're going to dump it?' Larry's eyes had lit up. 'Are you sure?'

The porter nodded. 'Definite, mate. It's a crying shame, because there's nothing wrong with it. Do you want it?'

'Bloody right I do. I've been after one for ages.'

The porter flicked his nub-end into a bush.

'Help yourself then. It's a sin just to chuck it away. You'd better hurry up though – it'll be gone by the end of the day.'

Larry turned to me. 'What do you think?'

'Think? Think about what?'

'The Street's only a couple of miles away. We could drop it off and be back here in twenty minutes.'

I sighed. 'Larry, if you think we're going to load that pile of junk on to the ambulance you're even madder than I thought you were . . . and that's saying something, believe me.'

He looked pained. 'Come on, what's the problem?'

I wasn't the easy touch I'd been twelve months earlier. I'd learned to stand up for myself, and I like to think that my resistance could be stern and to the point when it needed to be.

'What's the problem?' I repeated. 'The problem is that if we get caught with that on the back we'll be sacked on the spot! That's what the problem is. Forget all about it!'

He rolled his eyes as if he were dealing with a truculent child.

'Who's to know? We've already told them that it's going to take half an hour before the ambulance is usable again. We'll be back well before then.'

In an effort to end the conversation, I tried to give him one of those hard looks Mike was so good at.

'Supposing we break down? Have you thought of that? How would we explain away a greenhouse to the tow-truck driver?'

Losing the job I treasured would be bad enough, but there were other, even more pressing reasons to stay in work. Unemployment in the country was high and joining the dole queue would have been a disaster, especially

141

when Marie was expecting our first child and interest rates were climbing steadily towards 15 per cent. It was disconcerting to see Larry give the porter a knowing wink while I painstakingly pressed home these points.

It didn't take much more than five minutes to get the greenhouse loaded on to the ambulance with the help of the porter. All my previous concerns for our bereaved patient were submerged beneath a sea of anxiety as I drove carefully back to the Street while Larry sat next to me without a care in the world. Then it happened. And it was something I hadn't foreseen: a passing call. Very occasionally we get flagged down in the street by someone who's just witnessed something they think is worthy of our attention. In this instance it was a small, middle-aged man out in the gutter, frantically waving in our direction. Behind him on the pavement sat an Asian child of about five, crying his eyes out. Larry pulled his feet from the dashboard and sat bolt upright.

'Shit!'

I braked and pulled up a few yards past the man, then turned on Larry.

'I knew it! You and your stupid ideas. What are we going to do now?'

Larry looked tense, but told me to relax.

'Relax! Are you mad? How do you think it's going to go down when we open the back doors and a bloody greenhouse falls out?'

Larry wasn't listening. He'd picked up the first-aid bag and was already out of the cab.

He was bending over the child when I joined him. At a glance there was nothing obviously wrong with the lad, and I listened keenly as the man described to Larry how the little boy had run into the road and bounced off the side of his car.

'So it wasn't a case of you hitting him,' Larry said, deliberately. 'It was more a case of him hitting the car?'

'Yes. Thank God it wasn't the other way round.'

Larry carried on with his checks and finished with a very careful examination of the boy's head. One of the great dangers for a pedestrian in collision with a car is being flung to the ground and hitting their head on the concrete. It hadn't happened in this case and there was relief all round. The driver wiped a hanky over his forehead.

'So he's going to be all right?'

'Yes, he's fine, other than a sore bottom when he sat down too quickly. In fact, I've a feeling he might not even have touched the car.' Larry looked about him. 'Who's he with? Where are his parents?'

As if in answer to his question, a shriek of extraordinary intensity came from a house nearby, closely followed by a blur of multi-coloured sari. The boy's mother had noticed him missing and, spotting the ambulance through the window, now came running towards us as if the hounds of hell were on her heels. She collapsed on to him, kissing him and whimpering through her tears before looking up at me beseechingly. I tried to reassure her that all was well, but it was immediately apparent that she didn't speak English. A neighbour translated and the mother, still on her knees, grabbed my hand and kissed it. But she didn't finish there. She kissed my wrist and then moved up my forearm, placing kisses every couple of inches. I didn't know how to react, but when she reached my elbow and seemed intent on continuing, I was spurred into gently shaking her off. The car driver was equally effusive, if in a more English way, and shook Larry's hand vigorously.

'You got here so quickly. It couldn't have been a couple of minutes after I made the call.'

Larry was modest in return. 'Thanks. We do our best.'

As he spoke, the sound of sirens was growing in the distance and we turned to watch the rightful ambulance make its final approach and pull up behind ours. Larry spoke in a low voice.

'Let's hope it's a crew from the Street, otherwise we've got a bit of explaining—' He broke off when he recognized Howard and Jack. 'Thank Christ for that. It's the Flintstones. I never thought I'd be happy to see that pair.'

They listened attentively as Larry explained what had happened. When he finished by telling them it was their decision whether or not they took the child to hospital for a check-up, Howard looked at him sharply.

'What do you mean? You were here first. This is your case, not ours.'

Larry moved a little closer and spoke from the side of his mouth.

'Strictly speaking, we shouldn't really be here at all. We were just passing.'

'Where should you be?' Howard asked, not unreasonably.

'That doesn't matter. The point is that we've got a greenhouse on the back of the truck and time's of the essence for us at the moment.'

Howard looked at our ambulance as if expecting it to confirm or deny the statement.

'A greenhouse?'

'Yeah. I'll explain when I get the chance. See you.' And with that we made our escape.

I had time to dwell on the events of the day at my leisure, as we weren't due back on duty for forty-eight hours. Even though I was learning not to brood or worry about work-related issues, there were times when it was difficult not to. People often want to know how we deal with the memory of harrowing sights. Well, in my case it's not really a secret. I package them up and relegate them to a dusty corner in the attic of my mind. What's harder to banish is the emotional impact of some of the cases we have to deal with. The woman whose husband burned to death is a good example. I hadn't seen him, and as I wasn't really involved in his fate I didn't give it a great deal of thought. What did play on my mind was how his wife might be managing. How had she spent the last couple of days? How was she going to go about rebuilding her life? Who was going to help her? I didn't brood on it, but her plight was never far from my thoughts. Then there was the greenhouse. I did brood on that. What if we'd been spotted loading it on to the ambulance? The more I dwelt on the subject, the worse it got. Maybe the porter was wrong and it wasn't going to be scrapped. Maybe the hospital chief executive had it earmarked for his back garden and a full investigation was under way concerning its theft. By day I dismissed these worries as silly. It was at night, a time when little worries become big worries, that they came back to bother me as I tried to drop off to sleep.

They were more or less banished by the time I clocked on for the afternoon shift two days later. In fact, I was in quite good fettle until I ran into Bill Eastwood, the station manager. He was waiting for me in the corridor and what he had to say set off alarm bells.

'Two coppers are waiting to interview you and Larry in the top office.'

'Police? Why?'

'That's not for me to say.' He started to turn away, but thought of something else. 'When they've gone I want to see the pair of you in my office.' Then he softened a little. 'Larry's in the messroom. It might be an idea if the two of you get your story straight before you go in.'

'Our story? What story?'

He looked at me over his reading glasses.

'I think you know what I'm talking about.' Bill loved this kind of game. He was in his late fifties and had been on the service for about fifty years longer than Phyllis. Before joining he'd spent a hundred years in the Navy as a chief petty officer, where he'd honed his stern, head-masterly manner. He wasn't a bully, but he seemed determined that new members of staff should go through a rite of passage, which involved keeping them in their place by frightening them half to death every now and then. His tactics were varied, but he didn't really have to try very hard to achieve his ends. 'You gotta keep these youngsters on their toes' was his stock defence when someone like Mike observed that he could be a rotten bugger at times.

He'd managed to catch me out months earlier just when I was beginning to think I'd got his measure. I was in the messroom working my way through one of Phyllis's sausage sandwiches when he poked his head round the door and levelled his gaze at me.

'Mr Pringle, I want to see you in my office in ten minutes. If a job comes in, put your vehicle to the back of the running order.' With that, he was gone. I stopped in mid-chew. Phyllis's sandwiches needed all the lubrication they could get, and I seemed to have run out of saliva. It was Bill's tone, as much as the rather formal use of 'Mr Pringle', that convinced me I was in trouble. My state of mind wasn't helped by the fact that I, along with every ambulance worker, carry an inbuilt guilt complex, something akin to original sin. We get involved in so many situations, and meet so many people, that occasional conflict or differences of opinion are inevitable, any of which could have unwanted repercussions. Bill knew this as well as anybody else and had thoughtfully given me ten minutes to stew. By the time I knocked on his door I was convinced that just about every patient I'd dealt with in the last six months had joined forces in denouncing me as a charlatan.

He looked up from his desk and, without inviting me to sit down, leaned back in his chair and held up a letter between two fingers as if it were contaminated.

'I received this in the post today.' My eyes fixed on the piece of paper as he waved it gently to and fro. My mouth was still as dry as a bone, otherwise I'm sure I'd have blurted out that I could explain everything before even hearing what the letter was about. Unperturbed by my look of panic, Bill pushed his glasses further up his nose and continued. 'I think it might be best if I read out its contents before we go any further.' I braced myself as he cleared his throat and began to read out a torrent of thanks and appreciation from the grateful relative of a patient I'd looked after a few days earlier. When he had finished he smiled and held out his hand. 'Well done. This reflects well on you and, just as importantly, it reflects well on the service.'

My emotions came in a single bundle – relief, pleasure and anger. I resisted the urge to call him a 'rotten bugger' as I shook his hand; we both knew that a lot more water would have to pass under the bridge before I could take that kind of liberty.

It was with this encounter in mind that I now considered Bill's ambiguous warning about the police. It was quite common to give statements to the police concerning

some of the cases we attended but, as I stood there rack-
ing my brains, I couldn't think of anything in the recent
past that might have warranted this visit. Then it hit me.
The greenhouse. That was all it could be. I watched Bill
make his way back to his office and then shot into the
messroom looking for Larry. He was leaning against
the serving hatch sipping a cup of tea as if there wasn't a
guilty bone in his body. I didn't wait for him to look
up.

'Do you know the police are waiting to speak to us?'

'Yeah. So?'

'So, they haven't just dropped in for a chat, have they?'

He looked at me quizzically. 'Probably not.'

'And as we haven't done any ambulance work in the
last week that would interest them, there's only one thing
it can be about!'

He took another sip of tea. 'Oh, what's that then?'

'It's got to be that bloody greenhouse. What else could
it be?'

Larry groaned and put down his cup.

'You're not still fretting about that, are you? It could be
anything. Honestly, you'll worry yourself into an early
grave unless you stop acting like a big girl's blouse.'

'Big girl's blouse!' I retorted. 'Getting the sack is one
thing, spending a month in Winson Green Prison is
another!'

I was still fuming as we trooped into the little room and
faced the two officers. One of them greeted us.

'All right lads, your boss will have told you that we

need a couple of statements concerning the murder you attended on the twelfth.'

Larry and I looked at each other, then back at the policeman.

'Murder?' Larry said. 'You've got the wrong crew. We haven't been out to a murder for months.'

The officer looked down at the patient report form on his lap.

'Pringle and Timmins – that's you, isn't it?'

As I indulged in a silent prayer of thanks that I wasn't to have a criminal record for stealing a greenhouse, Larry leaned forward and looked at the report form.

'Yes, that's us, but . . .' He scanned the form and then glanced over at me. 'It's that bloke who died in the fire.'

The policeman looked vaguely perplexed.

'Hasn't your boss told you anything?'

'No,' Larry said, in a knowing kind of way. 'He's a busy bloke – I suppose it slipped his mind. So the fire was deliberate, was it?'

'It certainly was. What we need off you is an account of exactly what his wife had to say on the way into hospital.'

Larry smiled. 'So she's your number-one suspect, is she?'

'More than that. She's the culprit.'

Larry's smile vanished. To say that this bit of news came as a bombshell would be an understatement. Neither of us could quite believe what we were hearing. I broke the ensuing silence.

'I don't understand. She couldn't have done it. She almost ended up like her husband and she was hysterical in the hospital when they told her what had happened to him.'

The officer leaned back in his chair.

'She kept up the act for quite a long time, but when we put it to her that armchairs aren't prone to spontaneous combustion, she began to crack. It didn't take long for the fire investigators to find evidence of accelerants having been used and that she still had traces on her even after being cleaned up. I don't know how she thought she was going to get away with it.' He gave us a wry look. 'It's a funny old world, isn't it?'

I didn't think it was very funny. I'd used up precious quantities of compassion and sympathy over the weekend that could have been saved for more deserving causes. Apparently the couple were notorious for keeping their neighbourhood awake at all hours with drunken slanging matches that more often than not ended in violence. When these confrontations turned into full-blown fights, it usually ended up with one or the other of them needing medical treatment or being locked up for the night. The picture the police painted of their final altercation was this. He'd fallen asleep in an armchair after a particularly heavy drinking session and she, also well tanked up, had got it into her head to set fire to him. She had doused him and his chair with something like a litre of white spirit and thrown in a match. Maybe the resulting inferno jolted her back to some kind of sanity and, regretting what she'd done, she stayed in the room trying to put out the flames before being forced to flee.

I was forever being told by my more experienced shift mates not to jump to conclusions or pre-judge situations, but only the weariest cynic would have suspected anything in this case. Even Larry hadn't sniffed out a rat. And as for the greenhouse? As far as I'm aware, it's still sitting in Larry's back garden, and long may it stay there.

# Chapter Ten

It was a relief to find myself working alongside Steve for a few weeks. Larry could be fun in small doses, but the dose I'd just had would do me for quite a while. Steve, on the other hand, was rock steady and nothing if not predictable. He must have been in his early fifties and was, to my mind, the epitome of what an ambulance man of the day should aspire to be. Calm, self-confident, attentive, knowledgeable and, above all, permanently good-humoured, with an inexhaustible reservoir of patience. He also looked the part. His black hair was always immaculately slicked back beneath his cap, revealing a face that spoke of his good nature. Tall and broad-shouldered, he fitted into the uniform as only an ex-guardsman could. If anything, the uniform added to his persona by lending him an air of benign authority – something it never did for me, no matter how long I practised in front of the mirror. I think one of the most striking things about Steve was that, although never confrontational, he was able to convince even the most objectionable drunk that he had his interest at heart and everything would be fine if they could only sort things out together. Mike got similar results, but it was more often achieved by radiating implied menace than conciliatory overtures. Steve was a gentleman, and it was an eye-opener to see just how much his approach could accomplish. If this all sounds a bit like hero worship, then I have to hold my hand up.

He was a few years younger than Mike, but had similar life experiences. Both had served long stints in the army and, like so many others, were directed to the ambulance service as a means of employment when returning to Civvy Street. Nothing stands still, though, and as their generation approached retirement the door opened for youngsters like me, who were beginning to arrive in increasing numbers. There had always been a small percentage of women working alongside the men, but in essence the job was still seen as a male bastion, much as nursing at the time was seen as a female preserve. And it has to be said that it was still a very physical job, with little or no thought given to developing any lifting aids that might have made life a little easier. Every patient unable to walk had to be carried using the ergonomics of brute strength. So it was that the messroom was essentially a male-dominated world, and as a result generated all the rivalry and lively banter you might expect. Steve and Mike were the elder statesmen of this world and treated with the respect their position demanded.

One of the great things about being crewed with Steve was that I didn't have to worry about anything. It was a bit like working with my dad; he was always in total control. This was in stark contrast to the way I felt when working with Jack. It wasn't the fault of either of us, and I loved Jack's company; it's just that our combined lack of experience made it impossible to shake off a grumbling feeling of anxiety whenever we were put together. There was no such anxiety when I was with Steve, and it was good to see him sitting in his usual chair, shrouded in pipe smoke and chatting to Mike, when I came in to start the night shift. I wafted away some of the fug and sat down next to him, feeling that all was well with the world, not knowing that it was going to be one of those nights that gave you cause to wonder if spending your working life prowling the inner city had been such a wise career move after all.

Larry answered the phone on the second ring and, after a brief conversation with Control, replaced the receiver and handed me the case sheet with a few words delivered in a deliberately deadpan voice.

'Man unconscious in a wheelbarrow outside Higgins Tower in Nechells.'

I read down the sheet, expecting it to reveal a little more information. It didn't, and I looked at Larry. He'd plonked himself in front of the telly, leaving me speaking to the back of his head.

'Is that it? "Man unconscious in a wheelbarrow"?'

He didn't take his eyes off the screen.

'Yip. It happens all the time. Surely you've been out to people in wheelbarrows before?'

So much for getting any sense out of him. I didn't have the statistics at my fingertips, but I was pretty sure that there weren't many wheelbarrows in the middle of Birmingham, never mind one containing an unconscious man.

Sid was one of the two police officers waiting for us when we turned into the small service road leading to the tower block. He wore his usual woebegone look as he greeted us and led the way to the wheelbarrow. Some said that he'd suffered with depression since his wife left him and took the kids. I didn't know the truth of that, but I did know that he wasn't one of those people who shone a beacon of happiness before them.

'Someone living in the block spotted him,' Sid said as we stared into the wheelbarrow. 'Looks like he's been given a good pasting, doesn't it?'

You didn't need to be Dr Kildare to figure that out. The victim's head and face were a mass of bruises. Swelling had closed both eyes, while ugly lumps caked in dried blood had risen on his forehead. From what we could see of his torso through the rips and missing buttons of his shirt, it seemed clear that the beating hadn't been confined to his head. Deep, rasping snores accompanied each intake of air that fought its way past his battered lips and chipped teeth.

Sid looked over our shoulders as we checked for any evidence of broken bones before thinking about moving him.

'Is he going to be OK?'

It was an irritating question. Most people who ask it are looking for reassurance, and that's fair enough, but Sid's motives were less clear. Steve glanced at him.

'Sid, how do you expect me to answer that? I can't see what's going on inside his head, can I? You can see the state he's in for yourself. He's out for the count and there's every chance he's got a fractured skull.'

Sid took a long look at the patient as Steve held the lolling head still and I began fitting a rigid collar round his neck.

'It's just that if it's serious I'm going to have to get a sergeant down here.'

'Serious?' Steve repeated. 'Of course it's bloody serious.'

Sid rubbed his chin. 'So what are you trying to say?'

A hint of exasperation crept into Steve's voice.

'I'm not trying to say anything, other than it's more than just serious. At best it's very serious.'

'And at worst?'

'Very, very serious,' Steve said, as we began easing the injured man into position to extract him from the wheelbarrow.

'You don't mean he might peg it?' Sid's thin face had taken on a look of concern for the first time.

'I don't know, Sid. But for your sake, it might be an idea if you do get that sergeant here. It might just be that you're going to end up with a murder on your hands.'

Sid's eyes widened.

'I knew it!'

Sid's partner helped us lift the patient on to the ambulance while Sid busied himself radioing for a sergeant before wrapping police tape round all the lamp posts he could find. I sent through a radio alert to warn the Accident Hospital we would be with them in eight minutes. All Steve could do on the way in was to keep the patient supplied with 100 per cent oxygen and ensure that his airway remained clear. He also found time to cut away some clothing, which revealed more extensive bruising. He said later that his guess was that the victim had been beaten with something like a cricket bat. He remained unconscious throughout and we left him at the hospital in more or less the same condition as we found him. It was the worst beating I had seen to date, and it shocked me that anyone could dish out such violence to another in what appeared to be a cold-blooded, calculated fashion. All we could hope was that the victim survived the head injury.

We had almost made it back to the Street when we were called up on the radio and given another case. Our hearts sank a little when we heard the location and the job description. 'Man feeling unwell' by the phone boxes in Stevenson Place. This was a notorious little corner of the city centre which attracted every ne'er-do-well Birmingham had on its books. Wastrels, alcoholics, tramps, those suffering from a plethora of mental-health problems, and just about any other misfit you care to imagine gravitated there when the urge came on them to call an ambulance. It was like a human version of the mythical elephant's graveyard. To this day, I can't recall ever picking up a genuine patient from Stevenson Place in countless visits. Steve's experiences were similar, and as we turned off New Street and pulled up by a bank of telephone boxes he let out a groan.

'Oh God, it's bloody Neil Marshall again. This is getting beyond a joke.'

'You know him, then?' I asked, regarding the distressingly shabby little man waiting on the pavement.

'Know him? Surely you've been out to him before. The little runt gets everywhere. He's a pain in the arse, he's ... a dead bloody albatross tied round the neck of the ambulance service.' There was no mistaking the vehemence in his voice as he stared through the windscreen at the object of his displeasure. 'You can deal with him on your own. I'm not getting out of this seat!'

Witnessing the sudden evaporation of Steve's legendary poise was a new experience. He was patient, attentive, seldom swore, and very rarely so much as raised his voice, but here he was ranting at the mere sight of a harmless little man. I opened the cab door and glanced back at him uneasily.

'Are you sure?'

'Yes. And there's no need to look at me like that. He won't eat you. The worst he'll do is bore you to death.'

I stepped from the cab and addressed the shadowy figure.

'Hi, have you called for us?'

His hands were deep in his pockets and his eyes fixed on the ground.

'Yeah, I suppose so.'

'You suppose so? You are the patient, aren't you?'

'Yeah, if that's what you want to call me, I suppose that's what I am.'

'It's Neil Marshall, isn't it?' I asked, trying to show willing. 'What's the problem?'

'The problem? Well – it's everything really.'

'I'm sorry?' I said. 'I don't quite understand what you mean. Are you ill?'

'Am I ill? That's for you to decide. I might be, I don't know.'

I drew a breath and counted to ten in my head.

'What I mean is,' I persisted, 'are you unwell? Are you in pain or something?'

'In pain? No, I don't think so. I don't think you'd actually call it pain.' His voice had an unappealing nasal whine to it.

'Shall we try to meet halfway on this?' I suggested. 'Let's start with you telling me why you need an ambulance.'

'My arm's been itching like mad all evening and I've lost one of my shoes.'

'What? You've called us because you've got an itchy arm?'

He glanced up and, catching my expression, quickly dropped his gaze.

'My arm's doing my head in, and I can't get anywhere with just one shoe.'

Thirty seconds into the conversation and already I'd had enough.

'Is that what you told them when you dialled 999?'

'Not really. I told them that I didn't feel too good.'

'So, tell me how you feel.'

'Oh, I don't know. I feel kind of funny, I suppose.'

'Funny?'

'Yeah, you know . . .'

'I don't know, I'm afraid.'

He kicked a leg back and forth listlessly.

'I suppose you could say that I've been feeling a bit rough.'

'You're going to have to be a bit more specific, Neil.'

He sighed, and continued in a dreary monotone. 'Dodgy. That's probably a better word to describe it.'

It was my turn to sigh.

'Look, if I take you to hospital the nurse is going to ask me what's wrong with you. What's she going to say when I tell her you're feeling funny, rough and dodgy? Do you see my point?'

He looked at me properly for the first time.

'How about if you try and think up something better for me?'

I counted to ten again.

'Neil, if your only problems are an itchy arm and a missing shoe, then I'm getting back in that ambulance and driving off.'

'The real trouble is,' he continued, seemingly oblivious to threat, 'everything seems pointless. There must be a point. Can you tell me what it is?'

I really didn't want to go down this path at one o'clock in the morning on a street corner, but maybe it offered a means of escape.

'The point is that you're probably depressed, Neil. A hospital Casualty in the middle of the night isn't going to be able to help you.'

'Depressed?' He smiled faintly. 'No, it's not that. I've never been depressed. I know I've got more than my fair share of problems, but depression's not one of them.'

'Have you ever thought of phoning the Samaritans instead of us?' I asked, in the hope of passing the buck.

'The Samaritans? I was on the phone to them before I called you . . .' His voice trailed off.

'So, what did they say? Were they any help?'

'They hung up on me.'

'They hung up on you? You're not serious.'

I wouldn't have thought it possible, but his woeful expression deepened.

'I'm always serious. I don't make jokes when there's nothing to joke about.'

Ignoring the pall of gloom emanating from him, I pressed on.

'Are we talking about the same people? The Samaritans are the ones there to listen, and talk you through your problems. They don't hang up on people.'

He attempted another smile and then thought better of it.

'That's what I used to think. It's not the first time they've done it either. I'm not complaining, they're nice people – she said goodbye at least five times before she put the phone down.' He gave me another fleeting glance. 'I bet you're glad you're not me, aren't you?'

He wasn't far wrong in that observation and the longer the conversation continued, the more I thanked my lucky stars that I wasn't him. After ten infuriating minutes of going round in circles and listening to a litany of woes that in my opinion completely exonerated the Samaritans' course of action, I abandoned him and rejoined Steve in the cab. He looked at me ruefully.

'So, made a new friend then?'

I leaned back and exhaled.

'Bloody hell, I thought my head was going to explode.'

'He's not coming with us, then?' Steve asked.

'Bloody right he's not. I think I would have strangled him before we got to the hospital.'

Steve put the ambulance into gear and pulled away from the phone box lest Neil felt tempted to wander over and resume the conversation.

'It's strange that you've never come across him before. He's forever calling us out. What was his problem tonight? No, don't tell me – he's lost a shoe?'

'Yes, and he's got an itchy arm.'

Steve smiled. 'An itchy arm? That's a new one! He's letting his imagination run away with him.'

The others were sitting around chatting when we got back to the Street. Mike and Jack had been out to someone who had burned himself while trying to put out a chip-pan fire. Unsurprisingly, the conversation was now ranging round the subject of burns. I went through to put the kettle on while Steve sat down next to Mike at the table and began searching through his pockets for his ever-elusive pipe. When the beloved object was eventually located, the pipe-cleaning ceremony could get under way. This involved several minutes of scraping and blowing until eventually a final inspection passed it fit for a fresh plug of tobacco. I was back in with the tea by this time and placed a mug in front of him as he began patting at his pockets for his tobacco pouch. It wasn't to be found. He was getting out of his seat to check his coat pockets when a thought occurred to him.

'Talking of burns, Mike, do you remember Maurice Brent?'

'Maurice Brent? I don't think so.'

'Of course you do. I'll give you a clue – he'd got plastic ears.'

Mike laughed. 'Of course! He was a right character. I haven't thought about him for years. His ears were burned off in the war, weren't they?'

Steve returned to the table with the tobacco and began pushing a handful into his pipe.

'That's right. He lost them in the war when his plane went down in flames.'

Howard was intrigued. 'What, he was shot down?'

Steve tapped down the last of the tobacco and looked round for his matches.

'Yes. He didn't talk about it much, but I know for a fact that he won the Distinguished Flying Cross.' Steve chuckled to himself. 'He was a card, though. You know how you hear stories of someone with a false eye whipping it out as a party trick? Well, Maurice's trick was to pull his ears off. He caught out quite a few people with that one. Anyone seen my matches?'

'So he actually worked here at the Street?' Howard asked.

'Yes, he was here a good few years.'

'When did he retire?'

'Oh, he's been gone about ten years.' Steve had found the matches and began puffing life into his pipe. 'He didn't retire, though – he got himself sacked.'

Howard was indignant. 'What? They sacked a war hero?'

'It was the silly sod's own fault. He was on a really cushy number ferrying old folk in and out of day centres. He didn't have to do shifts and all his work was pre-scheduled every day of the week.' Steve blew out the match and wafted at the cloud of blue smoke. 'These patients of his were ancient and eventually began to die off one by one. But, instead of letting the planners know as each one fell off the perch, Maurice kept it quiet. His work-load became less and less until he had virtually nothing to do. He would come in every morning at eight, pick up his ambulance and then bugger off home for the day.'

'Surely even our lot would have noticed?' Howard's tone had changed to one of incredulity.

'You would have thought so,' Steve continued, 'but the silly buggers didn't have a clue. He only got found out when one of his neighbours phoned in asking why there was an ambulance parked in the street every day. It had been going on for months. He even claimed overtime occasionally. DFC or not, he was on his bike.'

Larry got up to answer the phone and I collected the teacups and took them through to the kitchen to wash up. I had just started when, even from a distance, it became clear Larry was having a heated argument with the controller. I dried my hands and wandered back into the messroom to find out what it was all about. Everyone was looking at Larry as he banged the phone down.

'This job gets madder and madder!' He looked at the wall clock. 'It's gone one in the morning and they give me the daftest treble nine I've heard of in my life. I can't believe they didn't tell the caller to piss off! I might just go to the papers about it.'

Jack was Larry's partner for the night and took it upon himself to ask the obvious question.

'Well? Spit it out. What is it?'

Larry took a breath.

'They're sending us out to a man who hasn't washed for thirty years!'

There was a couple of seconds' silence as we took it in. Mike was first to respond.

'You're making it up.'

'Making it up? How could I make up something like that? I doubt Spike Milligan could have made it up.'

'Is there something else wrong with him?' Mike asked.

'Not as far as Control knows. The twit on the other end of the phone said the safest thing to do was to go and check it out. I ask you – the bloke waits thirty years, and when he decides to have a bit of a spruce up it's in the middle of the night! Why didn't our lot just tell him to jump in the bath?'

Steve and I didn't have to wait long for the phone to ring again and give us a dubious-sounding job of our own. Steve put down the receiver and looked at the case sheet as he slipped his pipe into his pocket.

'Man won't wake up. What I'd like to know is how someone discovered that this guy won't wake up. I mean, who goes round the house in the middle of the night checking to see if people will wake up or not?'

I couldn't answer that, and ten minutes later we were standing on the doorstep of a small semi in Newtown hoping to find the answer. While we waited for someone to come to the door, I noticed something that suggested all might not be well inside. A small pane of glass in the porch was broken and smeared with blood. It didn't look like an attempted break-in, but it was odd all the same. There were a few spatters of blood on the step, and when a child of about nine opened the door to let us in we could see a sprinkling of blood trailing down the hall carpet. Steve smiled at the boy.

'Hello, young man, you're up late. Is your mum or dad about?'

'My dad's pissed and—'

The lad was cut off by his mother, who had appeared in the doorway of a room further down the hall.

'Peter! Get upstairs to your room right now!'

'I was just telling them that Dad's—'

'Upstairs – now!'

She watched him moodily make his way upstairs before turning her attention to us. I would say she was about forty, thin in an unhealthy kind of way and, from her rather dowdy appearance, not one to spend too much time in front of a mirror.

'Sorry about him. He worries about his dad. So do I, for that matter. He's not well – he drinks too much. I've been trying to wake him up and get him to come upstairs to bed but I can't get anything out of him. He's in here.' She stood back for us to enter the room.

Her husband was lying on his stomach on the sofa with his head turned towards the door. Other than the shallow, fast breathing, everything else about him suggested he was dead. There wasn't a hint of colour in his face or arms and, although I could hear his breathing, I couldn't see any associated movement; his whole body conveyed a stillness rarely seen in the living. A small amount of dried blood on the side of his face failed to divert my attention from the partially open, but unseeing, eyes. I couldn't find a pulse at his wrist and it took a bit of doing for Steve to locate the carotid pulse at his neck. He was as close to death as he could be and there was no obvious reason why. Steve shone a light into each eye with barely a response from the pupils. The dried blood we'd noticed came from a glistening cut on the bulbous part of his nose, which wouldn't need more than three or four stitches. It seemed logical to assume that he'd somehow managed to do it on the glass outside. While Steve busied himself giving the patient a full body check, I questioned the woman.

'Does he suffer with any illnesses?'

'No, not really. Well, he does take something for his blood. You know, that stuff they poison rats with.'

'Warfarin?' I suggested.

'Yeah, something like that. I'm always telling him that he lives on booze and rat poison. It's the drink that's his biggest problem, though.'

Warfarin is a powerful blood-thinning drug that works wonders for those who need it, but, on the down side, it can be quite a nuisance when it hampers the natural clotting process at the site of a cut or an internal injury. Her revelation gave me food for thought.

'What about the cut on his nose? Did he do it on the porch window?'

She seemed surprised by the question.

'I've got no idea. I didn't speak to him when he came in.'

I began to build up a picture of everyday life in her home as she talked. He was an alcoholic, who would be in the pub when it opened at eleven and only make his way home to sleep it off on the sofa in the back room when it closed in the late afternoon. Anyone daring to enter once he'd taken up residence did so at their own risk, which meant he was left very much alone. The pattern had been followed the previous afternoon but, rather than emerging as usual a few hours later, he had remained ensconced behind the closed door. His wife went to bed after the ten o'clock news and woke a few hours later to find he still hadn't joined her. Worried, she gathered her courage and went down to investigate.

'Christ! What on earth's going on here?' It was Steve's tone rather than his words which made me look round sharply. His right hand was covered in blood. I was confused.

'Where's that come from?'

'The sofa.' He patted it as he spoke, and recoiled at the discovery of more blood. 'It's everywhere – the whole thing's soaked in it! It doesn't make sense. I've checked him over, he hasn't got any injuries, his mouth and nose are clear.' He prodded at the cushion where the man's head was resting. It squelched with blood that was all but invisible against the burgundy upholstery. 'You know what? It's got to have come from the cut on his nose. He's lain there, drunk and not moving, while the blood's been sucked out of him and into the sofa. It's the only answer.'

'What, like a wick?'

'Yeah, exactly like a wick. Trickle, trickle for hours without clotting.'

Steve's analysis was later proved correct. The patient

had stumbled trying to put his key in the door and in the process headbutted the pane of glass, gashing his nose. If he'd noticed, it hadn't bothered him, and thirty seconds later he was asleep on the sofa with his nose pressed into the cushion and his life blood slowly draining out of him. There might be stupider ways to die, but not many that I can think of.

We were both worried and found ourselves caught in a moment of indecision.

Steve lowered his voice. 'He's at death's door. I'm scared that if we try to move him he'll peg it on the spot.'

I agreed. The patient needed fluid replacement to push up his blood pressure, but we had no means of supplying it. It was something that rankled even back then. It's not as if it's a complicated procedure, but the powers that held sway at the time denied us this potentially life-saving training, and I can only say shame on them. There was a rumour that a team of doctors could be called out from East Birmingham Hospital when we faced something too tricky for us to handle. But it was only a rumour – I hadn't seen anything official proving their existence, or met anyone who had ever seen them. Besides, that particular hospital was a good eight miles away. Steve's head was bowed in contemplation. When he looked up he'd come to a decision.

'I'm going to phone Dudley Road and see if I can get someone to come out.' This was a startling announcement. Dudley Road Hospital was relatively close by and staffed by some fine trauma doctors, but the idea of getting one to drop everything and come out to us was something I would never have thought of.

'Are you going to ask Control to arrange it?'

He looked at me and smiled.

'No, I don't think so. I'll do it myself.'

As he put the phone down a few minutes later, Steve said, 'Old Higgins will be here in ten minutes. All we can do is to keep him on oxygen and cross our fingers until he turns up.'

I was impressed and relieved. It's not something that would happen today. Not that it needs to: proper arrangements are in place to cope with most eventualities, but, even if they weren't, doctors wouldn't dare practise their skills outside the hospital environment for fear of invalidating their insurance. As it was, 'old Higgins' arrived in his own car exactly ten minutes later. He made a quick assessment before searching for a vein through which he could gain access. The patient's natural defences had diverted his remaining blood to the major organs in an effort to keep him alive, which meant robbing the peripheral areas of blood, causing the veins to disappear from sight. Not that it appeared to bother Higgins. He slipped a canula into a vein that was, as far as I could see, completely undetectable to the human eye or touch. Half an hour and three bags of fluid later, the patient's blood pressure had risen enough to allow him to be moved safely. My gut feeling was that Steve had been right in saying that the patient wouldn't have survived the journey without prior intervention. He'd made a good call and the patient survived as a result.

Jack and Larry were hanging about in Casualty when we wheeled our empty stretcher from the resuscitation room. They were keen to hear about our case, but when Steve asked about the man who hadn't washed for thirty years both their faces screwed up at the memory.

'I really, really don't want to talk about it,' Larry said, and then he told us about it. 'Control had got it wrong as usual. It wasn't thirty years he'd gone without a wash – it was at least fifty. He opened the door to us wearing a pair of underpants he must have put on in 1930. I tell you, I've never seen anything so disgusting. He made Stig of the Dump look like a pageboy.'

Jack seemed willing to elaborate.

'And his toe nails were curled—'

Larry held up a hand and cut him off. 'Enough! I'm trying to wipe it from my mind.'

'Neither of us will be able to wipe that smell from our minds until we get rid of it from the back of the ambulance,' Jack said. 'I reckon it might be an idea to burn some rope in there to cover it up.'

'So you brought him into hospital?' I asked.

Larry still wore a pained look.

'Didn't have much choice. I know it might have hurt his feelings, but I wore the oxygen mask with the flow turned up full all the way in. Heaven knows how the nurses are coping. I could never be a nurse. They're stuck with him for the next few hours. Just twenty minutes was enough for me to start to lose the will to live.'

The seamier side of Birmingham's nocturnal element hadn't finished with us quite yet. On the way back to the Street, Steve and I were diverted to a road in Aston where the police were asking for our assistance. It seemed they had a man under arrest who had suddenly collapsed at their feet. We stepped from the ambulance to find Sid and his partner waiting for us. Close by on the pavement was a raggedy youth of about twenty pretending to be un- conscious. Despite having only a couple of years on the job, I had become adept at picking out fraudsters, mainly because most of them were so inept. This particular lad was no better than the rest and was on a hiding to nothing if he thought he was going to fool us. Steve ignored him and spoke to Sid.

'Hello, Sid. What's the story?'

Sid seemed a little put out by Steve's apparent lack of concern and flicked his eyes between Steve and the patient.

'Well, we'd just placed him under arrest when he went down like a sack of spuds. There was nothing we could do and I thought it might be serious.'

'Why did you arrest him?' Steve asked.

'He's been smashing windows all the way down the street.' The street was fronted by terraced houses opening on to the pavement. A glance showed broken glass at intervals up the road and several householders standing outside following the proceedings with interest.

Steve bent over the prone youth and tried to persuade him to sit up. Predictably, it didn't work; he was determined to avoid ending up in the police station and wasn't going to give in easily. We then set about 'waking' him by using painful stimuli. This is a perfectly acceptable means of trying to gauge someone's level of consciousness and entails, as the phrase suggests, inflicting mild doses of pain by squeezing the cuticles of their nails or tweaking an ear. There are, I am told, more extreme methods, but I wouldn't know anything about that. Whether it was drink or drugs or both that seemed to make the lad immune to pain I couldn't say, but he resisted our efforts and remained obstinately 'unconscious'. The longer it went on, the more agitated Sid became.

'Don't you think you should just chuck him on the ambulance and take him to Dudley Road?'

Steve straightened up and spoke patiently.

'What would be the point in doing that when there's nothing wrong with him? We'd end up wasting our time and look stupid into the bargain.'

'Yes, but how can you be so sure? I mean, after that bloke in the wheelbarrow and everything . . .'

Steve looked at him doubtfully.

'Sid, there's no comparison between the two jobs.'

'He's dead you know, that bloke in the wheelbarrow.'

We were both taken by surprise.

'Dead?' Steve repeated. 'No.'

'Yeah, he popped his clogs ten minutes after you dropped him off at the Accident Hospital.'

'Poor bastard,' Steve said.

'It seems that he lived in the block of flats where we found him. The thinking is that he was beaten up somewhere else and whoever did it thought they would do him a favour and give him a lift home so he wouldn't have far to walk when he eventually woke up – can't get your hat on, can you? Anyway, it's made me edgy and I think you shouldn't waste any more time and take this kid in.'

Steve looked at me. We both knew without a shadow of doubt that the youth was wide awake but, having failed to prove it, we were left on the verge of admitting defeat. Then I had an idea. And it wasn't an idea someone of Steve's generation would have come up with. I wasn't much older than the lad on the floor and had a hunch that if I got on his wavelength there was a chance it might produce results. I bent over him and spoke fast and furious into his ear. Within seconds he was on his feet with a roar and trying to throw a punch that would have dropped me like a stone. Despite being taken by surprise, Sid and his mate managed to grab an arm each before the lad could make contact and dragged him backwards. Spitting venom, he tried to shake them off and get at me, but they soon had him in handcuffs. He had to content himself with verbal threats as they pushed him into their car.

'If I ever see your fucking face round here, you're fucking dead! You got that, you fucking wanker?'

Steve watched him impassively and pulled out his pipe.

'He doesn't seem to think much of you, Les. Did you tell him you were an Arsenal fan or something?'

Sid slammed shut the door of his Panda and walked over.

'What an evil little bastard.'

Steve struck a match and held the flame over the waiting tobacco.

'So you're convinced he's awake now, Sid?'

Sid allowed himself a rare smile.

'I should say so.' He looked at me. 'I don't know how you woke him up, but he nearly had us all fooled for a while, didn't he?'

Steve was keen to know exactly what I'd said as we headed back to the Street. I was still smiling to myself, but felt self-conscious at the idea of repeating all I'd whispered into the yob's ear.

'You don't want to know the details, Steve. Let's just say that I called him every vile name I could think of and finished up by saying that the word on the street was that his mother was the local bike, and not a very good one at that. I was pretty sure he would react—'

I was interrupted by Control calling us on the radio. Steve sighed and plucked the mike from its cradle.

'That's a pity. I just fancied a cup of tea.' His eyes narrowed when the controller passed us the new case. 'Man with a bleeding foot in Stevenson Place, city centre.' Steve pursed his lips and pressed the transmit button.

'Do you know how his foot came to be bleeding?'

There was a short pause.

'It says on the case sheet that he stepped on a piece of glass after losing his shoe earlier in the evening.

There's something wrong with his arm too, apparently.'
Steve put the mike back and groaned.

'Neil bloody Marshall again.' He rubbed the bridge of his nose and stared through the windscreen. 'You know, I once thought of writing a book, but I gave up on the idea when it struck me that people wouldn't believe a word of it.'

# Chapter Eleven

We didn't have late-night television. Nor did we have video players, computer games, the internet or mobile phones to entertain us. We had to find our own ways of whiling away the time on a quiet night shift. Not that it was a problem. Cards, snooker and Scrabble were popular, along with reading and, heaven forbid, good conversation. And, of course, there was the neverending routine of patching rust holes in the old bangers we all drove. Some pursued hobbies; I went through a phase of building wooden ships, two of which I still have today. Then there was cooking. We took it in turns to prepare a meal for the rest of the shift whenever we could.

As extra entertainment, one night Steve laid on a much-postponed slide show of his army days in Bulawayo, Rhodesia. It had been against his better judgement when he'd surrendered to Howard's constant badgering. Consequently, I didn't detect much enthusiasm on his part as he set up the projector. When he'd finished arranging a worrying quantity of slide boxes into some kind of order on the table, he addressed the room.

'Right.' He lit his pipe and shook out the match. 'Any sarcastic comments from you lot and the show's over.' He looked at Larry. 'Understood?' Larry nodded obediently and Steve flicked a switch sending a bright shaft of light through cigarette smoke and dust. 'OK then, the first few are of our barracks.' There followed a procession of grainy black-and-white images of dusty, single-storey wooden verandas surrounded by shrubs and sand. Steve talked us through each one: the mess hut, the cook house, the weapons store, the sleeping quarters . . . by the time he got to the latrines, which were just six holes in the ground with what looked like orange boxes over them, even he could sense that he was beginning to lose his audience. 'I can show you the rest of those later, if you want.' He held a slide up to the light. 'Here's one of me with Sergeant McLeod. He was a tough Jock from the Gorbals, smashing bloke but not somebody you'd want to get on the wrong side of, especially when he was drunk.' The image that flashed up drew gasps. Dwarfed beside the Glaswegian was a boy, thin as a lath and grinning with a shy confidence, proud to be photographed with his hero. He was bare-chested, wearing a pair of voluminous shorts ending just above a pair of socks that disappeared into a pair of Charlie Chaplin boots.

'That's never you?' H said.

'Of course it's me.'

'Look at those ribs! You could play a tune on them,' said Larry.

Steve ignored him and clicked through a few more slides showing his younger incarnation relaxing with the other squaddies, or sometimes playing table tennis and volleyball. We had to grin, and when Larry opened his mouth again we all had to laugh.

'That's the British Army? It's more like an *It Ain't Half Hot Mum* convention at Butlins!'

Steve stared at the ceiling and tapped a finger resignedly on the projector as the follow-up jokes played out. When allowed, he continued.

'I'll have you know that we were sent off to the war in Korea not long after those pictures were taken. And, you won't believe this, but that's the kit we were wearing when we stepped off HMS *Unicorn* and straight into a Korean winter. If it wasn't for the Yanks helping us out with some warm clothing, we'd have frozen to death.'

Mike stirred in his chair. 'Don't talk to me about the Yanks! The war would have been over a darn sight sooner if they'd stayed out of it. We would take a hill in a night assault and hand it over to them in the morning. Then, as sure as eggs, they'd be driven off by midday and we'd be back again the following night to do it all again.' Steve and Mike loved to talk about the fighting in Korea, and while they chewed the fat I looked anew at Steve. The man in front of us was in his early fifties, well built, straight-backed and quietly self-assured. It was sobering to see for myself just how young he'd been when given a gun and packed off to the other side of the world.

Steve pulled out another box of slides. People were starting to get fidgety, but perked up a little when he announced that he'd done some wildlife photography while in Rhodesia.

'I bought a colour film for the animal pictures. Cost me a fortune.'

It didn't take long to conclude that he'd wasted his money. We sat through a host of unfocused shots, albeit in colour, showing assorted herbivores grazing in the middle distance. He clicked on to another slide. 'This is one I managed to get of a lion. It took a bit of doing. I would never have managed it if it wasn't for the African trackers.' He had our interest again, until we found ourselves gazing at an expanse of featureless yellow ochre grass fading into the horizon.

'Lion?' Howard said. 'It's just grass.'

Steve looked exasperated.

'There! A lioness!' He pointed at a slightly darker smudge in the middle of the frame. 'If you look carefully you'll see she's got a pair of cubs with her as well.'

Larry got up from his seat and inspected the screen.

'Bollocks. It's a tree stump.'

Steve raised his eyes to the ceiling and waited for Larry to sit down again.

'OK. Try this one.' He rummaged through a stack of slides on the table, selected one, and snapped it into the projector. 'There's no mistaking what this is.'

Suddenly, we were being charged by a magnificent bull elephant. Its enormous ears and raised trunk all but filled the screen. Sunlight glinted on tusks and sparkled in the little rage-filled eyes as they bore down on the viewer. Everything was in perfect focus, right down to the creases on its leathery hide. A professional would have been proud of it. Mike looked round at Steve.

'You're not trying to pretend you took that, are you?'

'Of course I took it,' Steve answered defiantly.

His response induced catcalls and hoots all round. Larry was in bits.

'I suppose you've got those African trackers to thank for helping you set it up.'

Even Howard weighed in. 'Whoever took that picture was dead two seconds later!'

Steve surveyed the room and shook his head. 'I can pack it all away right now if that's what you want.'

Mike tried to placate him. 'Don't be so touchy. What's next?'

Steve wasn't happy, but adopted an aloof air and continued against his better judgement.

'The next one's a rather nice shot of a warthog.'

And there on the screen was the young Steve, grinning out at us with a baby warthog in his arms. Larry leaned back in his seat and regarded the picture with pained tolerance.

'It's obviously a warthog – but what on earth's that it's holding?'

Steve switched off the projector as the laughter moved round the room.

'That's it! Show finished. I don't know why I bothered.'

As it happened, Larry and I wouldn't have been there to see the end of the show anyway. A few minutes later we were heading for the city centre where someone had fallen and injured their leg. Larry was still chuckling to himself as we made our way through the quiet streets.

'That shot of the elephant. How could Steve think anyone would believe that he took it? He obviously bought it in the souvenir shop.' He broke off as we approached a group of men standing in the street at the location we'd been given. At their centre a young man was lying on the pavement. Larry craned his neck as he brought the ambulance to a halt. 'What the hell have we got here? That fat kid on the ground looks like he's wearing a tutu.'

And indeed he was – a yellow one. The throng of people had spilled on to the street from a nearby gay club clad in the most outrageous fancy-dress costumes and were all drunk to one degree or another. We had to push our way through to the patient. Hunched over him, whispering words of encouragement, was a young man in tight-fitting German Lederhosen with halter. The feather in his green hat bobbed as he looked up at our approach.

'Well! At last! You took long enough.'

Larry never did appreciate this kind of welcome. He pointed at the ambulance.

'You see that white thing we just got out of?'

'Yes, of course.'

'Well, for your information it's an ambulance – not a bloody Harrier Jump Jet! We got here as fast as we could!' With the tone set, and without waiting for a response, he knelt down and glanced at the swollen ankle, then at the patient.

'Hello. What's your name?'

'Philip,' interjected the would-be Bavarian.

Larry looked at him sharply.

'Thank you, but I'm sure he can speak for himself.' Then to the patient, 'So, what have you been up to?'

'He tripped over the kerb,' said the Bavarian, and pointed at the swelling. 'That's where he's getting the pain.'

Larry slowly and deliberately kneaded the bridge of his nose between finger and thumb as he spoke.

'Look! It'll be a lot easier and quicker if you let him answer for himself.'

I went to the ambulance for a splint and returned to find the Bavarian still annoying Larry.

'I think you ought to know that he's got a very low pain threshold. And when I say low – I mean low.'

Larry took the splint and measured it against the injured limb.

'Is that a fact?'

'Yes. You're going to have to be very careful. I think it might be an idea if I hold his leg. He trusts me.'

'No, thank you. We'll cope.'

'I've got my St John's certificate in emergency aid. I could help,' the Bavarian persisted.

'If you want to help,' Larry said, 'go away.'

It had the desired effect.

'Well! Pardon me for breathing!' The Bavarian stood up and, with a dramatic toss of his head, turned on his heel and began to march off. It was then that we made the unfortunate discovery that the Lederhosen he was wearing had no back, unless you count the thong, only a quarter-inch of which was visible. The rest disappeared between a pair of plump, pink buttocks that a Botticelli cherub would have died for. Larry took one look and started to convulse. He'd managed to keep a straight face when confronted by the tutu, but this was the final straw. And I wasn't far behind him, especially when the object of our amusement turned and put his hands on his hips.

'Excuse me! What exactly, may I ask, do you find so funny?'

'Nothing.' Larry's voice went up a couple of octaves in the course of one word. He put his head down and fiddled with the Velcro straps of the splint, his shoulders juddering while he emitted little 'hooo-hooo' noises like an animal in distress. I think 'corpsing' is the word used by actors for uncontrollable giggling at the wrong moment. We corpsed quite often, but Larry had it bad this time. It was infectious too, and I had to bite my lip, even when looking into the scowl forming on the face of a big bloke straight off the set of *Easy Rider*. I looked round at all the other faces. None was friendly, especially that of a large, moustachioed man with a mane of blond hair dressed in a pink gangster suit. I nudged Larry with my foot and spoke out of the corner of my mouth.

'Larry! For heaven's sake, pull yourself together!'

'Hooo-hooo.'

'Larry!'

The patient's tutu rustled as he pushed himself up by the elbows and addressed us for the first time.

'You two aren't showing much respect, are you?'

'Hooo-hooo.'

'Larry!'

Neither I nor the patient noticed him do it, but when I looked down it was to discover that Larry, ever the professional, had somehow managed to get the leg neatly done up in the splint. I quickly set up our carry-chair beside him and prodded Larry again.

'Come on, let's go.'

He raised his head, revealing wet cheeks and quivering lips.

'OK, I'm all right now.' He kept his head down, letting out only the occasional whimper as we manhandled the injured man on to the chair. We were making for the ambulance when the gangster spoke.

'I'm going with him, if that's OK.'

Larry raised his head and, catching sight of the pink suit and dark glasses, quickly dropped it again.

'Hooo-hooo.'

The Bavarian looked at him sternly.

'I'm going too. I wouldn't trust you pair as far as I could throw you.'

'Nooo!' Larry's voice was hardly recognizable. 'Nooo . . . only room . . . for one . . . hooo-hooo.'

With the patient on the stretcher, Larry staggered round to the driver's seat and the ambulance kangarooed off down the road with him barely able to see where he was going. There had been plenty of room to accommodate two passengers but, as Larry pointed out later, wheeling a young man dressed in a tutu through the General escorted by a pink-clad Mafia man was as much as his heart could take. And, to use his own words, 'having that bare-arsed Bavarian tagging along would have finished me off'. I saw his point.

The slides were all packed away when we got back to the Street, allowing Larry to entertain the shift with the story.

'That was as close to wetting myself as I've ever been. The more I tried to stop myself laughing, the worse it got. I tell you, you could have offered me a million quid and I couldn't have stopped.'

'We had to sit in the coffee room for twenty minutes while he got himself under control,' I chipped in, and then added, 'Mind you, it was funny, especially when I noticed that the Bavarian had powdered his arse with blusher.'

'Never! Tell me that's not true!' Larry squeaked.

It wasn't true, but I didn't let on to Larry, as it had the desired effect of setting him off again, to pitying looks from the others.

'He's an embarrassment, isn't he?' Howard said.

Larry made an effort to pull himself together.

'You can talk! Remember that hanging we went out to and you had to get out the house cos you were laughing so much?'

Howard smiled. 'You can't blame me for that. It's something that's bound to happen from time to time when you're working with an idiot.'

'What's there to find funny about a hanging?' Steve enquired, genuinely bemused.

'Well,' Larry said, 'we were called out to someone who'd hanged himself. H went into the house while I turned the ambulance round. I went in a minute or two later and he called me upstairs. There was a bloke standing on the landing with his hand on the banister. I didn't pay him much notice, and as I passed I said, "All right, mate," then I noticed H further down the hall with a woman. He's got his hand over his mouth and his face is all screwed like he's in pain. The woman said in a harsh kind of voice, "That's my husband you're talking to!" I looked round to see what the problem was and only then did I notice the rope from his neck going up to the loft hatch in the ceiling. His feet were on the floor with his knees only a little bent. His hand must have flopped on to the banister by chance when he fell.'

'The only person on the service who says hello to corpses,' Howard interrupted. 'I ask you, what hope is there for the living when he's around?'

Larry grinned. 'You weren't exactly the model professional were you? Running out the house shaking like a leaf on the pretext of getting the paperwork. She must have noticed, poor woman.'

And so, with the genie out of the bottle, the anecdotes flowed until we all ended up back out on the road on various jobs. The case Larry and I were sent to might have been considered funny if it hadn't been quite so ridiculous. It was given to us as 'man with abdominal pain', and the chap certainly looked in pain when he opened the door. He was bent forward clutching his stomach, looking pitiful. I put him at about forty years old, scruffy and, if I'm any judge of these things, not one to jump in the bath very often. Still bent almost double, he led us through to the living room and sat gingerly on the settee from where he grimaced at us in a most unattractive way.

'I think I'm in the shit. I've fucked up big time – God it hurts.'

'Where's the pain and how long have you had it?' I asked.

'It's all over here.' He waved his hand over his abdomen and groin. 'It came on about half an hour ago. I tell you, it's a right bastard, and no mistake.'

I went through the questions expected of me and finished by asking if he had a previous track record when it came to abdominal pain.

'Yeah, I get retention of urine now and again. You know, when you can't piss.'

'Yes, I have heard of it,' I said. 'Is that a problem you've had today?'

'Yeah, the best I've been able to do is a dribble. The thing is, I didn't want to go to hospital and spend half the night hanging around waiting for them to stick a catheter up my dick, so I thought I'd try doing it for myself.'

'What?' Larry and I spoke in unison.

'I know it wasn't a good idea, and I wish I hadn't done it, but when you're desperate – you're desperate.'

'I don't understand,' I said. 'Surely you haven't got the stuff you need to do that kind of thing?'

He rocked back and forth in his seat.

'I used curtain wire.'

'Curtain wire? What the hell's curtain wire?'

'You know – the plastic-coated wire you hang lace curtains up with. It's hollow in the middle so I figured it might do the trick.'

Larry and I looked at each other, then back at him.

'Are you telling us that you've pushed curtain wire into your penis?'

'Yeah.'

Larry scanned the room for the evidence.

'So, where is it?'

'Where's what?'

'The wire!'

'It's inside me. I got it in so far and then it just sucked itself all the way inside – I couldn't stop it.'

Larry and I squirmed.

'How long was it?' I asked, trying to control my revulsion.

'I dunno. Four feet maybe.'

'Four feet!' Larry and I were talking in unison again. 'You've got four feet of wire inside you?'

'Yeah, and it don't half hurt. If you ask me, I think I need to get to hospital.'

And when he got to hospital even the hardened female nurses squealed on hearing what he'd done, while any men within earshot groaned and involuntarily crossed their legs. Any doubts we may have harboured about the truth of his story were dispelled by the X-ray results. The wire showed up as a tangled mass in his bladder, which, for good measure, was also punctured. His condition was serious by any standards, causing him to be whipped away in preparation for surgery. I don't know how it all worked out for him in the end but, if he did survive, I doubt he ever tried that trick again.

We got back to the Street at about half past three to find everyone settled down in their chairs in the hope of relaxing until dawn. They listened to the story of the curtain wire with ill-concealed horror.

'It just goes to show,' Mike said, 'when you think you've personally met every fool there is in the world, there's always another waiting in the wings. Remember that idiot who set fire to his arse, Steve?'

'Of course I do. It was still burning when we got there, or at least his trousers were.'

Larry was intrigued. 'How did he manage that?'

'Well,' Mike said, 'he was gluing down floor tiles in his kitchen with Evo-Stik or something similar. He had a gas-powered fridge and its pilot light ignited the fumes that had slowly built up and within seconds the glue itself was burning. It wasn't a raging fire or anything like that, just a blue flame about an inch high burning its way across the floor. He panics and starts stamping about on it and hitting it with towels, but of course the glue's gone really soft with the heat, and he slips and ends up sitting in the middle of it. From what his wife told us, he got to his feet with his arse burning like a torch. She threw water all over the place and put the fire out while he got out of his clothes. What was left of his trousers was smouldering in the corner when we got there and he was sitting with his arse in a washing-up bowl of cold water trying to cool off.'

This story reminded me of one of my own, and I weighed in before anyone else could beat me to it. Larry and I had been called to quite a posh detached house in Handsworth Wood. The information we had was that a woman had been burned, and the first thing to hit me when the door opened was the ghastly smell of burned hair. The Asian woman who let us in was the patient's mother. She didn't seem particularly concerned or anxious.

'The silly girl's upstairs in her bedroom. Kids! You can't let them out of your sight for a minute.' We followed her up to the bedroom where a girl of about sixteen was lying on the bed under a sheet. A younger girl was standing by the window biting her nails and looked pensive as the woman spoke to her daughter on the bed.

'Show them what you've done then. There's nothing to

be shy about – they've seen it all before.' Without any obvious reluctance, the girl pulled back the sheet to reveal her nakedness. My gaze was straightaway drawn to her groin. Her mother had been wrong; I hadn't seen it all before. It was the first, and hopefully the last, time I'd seen an angry-looking pubis mound. Hairless, red and swollen, it looked very painful. Larry, obviously irritated at my failure to paint a sufficiently graphic picture, interrupted at this point in his own eloquent way.

'It was like looking at a plucked duck that had been boiled for half an hour and left out to cool!'

It seems that the girl had been alone in her room playing with Bengal matches. And they weren't just any old Bengal matches, they were deluxe versions. At least five inches long with two-inch phosphorous tips, they flared intensely in a variety of ever-changing colours for a considerable length of time. She had worked her way through half a box before one eventually snapped on ignition and fell on to her unprotected groin. She leapt from the bed with the burning match sticking obstinately to her flesh and her pubic hair on fire. Alerted by the commotion, her younger sister ran into the room with a mug of water and threw the contents on to the flames. It came far too late to save any of the pubic hair and, predictably, had no effect on the burning phosphorus. They brushed it off with the bed sheets and then had to watch as it began burning its way into the mattress. The younger girl saved the day by fetching a damp facecloth and smothering the flames once and for all. A daft story, which Larry immediately christened 'The case of the burning bush'.

No sooner had I finished than H chipped in.

'How about that moron who tried to gas himself?'

'What, the one on the third floor of Avon Tower?' Mike asked.

'That's the one. He stuck his head in the oven to end it all but, rather than drifting off into oblivion as he expected, he began to feel horribly sick and decided to call the whole thing off until he felt better. After throwing up in the sink, he switched off the gas and phoned his brother to tell him what he'd done. His brother, obviously no brighter than him, told him to stay where he was and that he was coming straight round. Ten minutes later, and presumably feeling a bit better, our man decides to have a cigarette. The explosion blew out the whole window, including the frame and quite a few bricks. The wreckage lay on the grass outside for weeks before the council took it away.'

'And what about him?' Jack asked. 'Did he follow the window out?'

'No such luck. All he had wrong with him was a badly burned ear. Stupid people seem to get away with things that normal people don't. It would have been typical if some perfectly normal person had been walking below and been wiped out by the window landing on his head.'

'There's a difference between stupid people and weird people, isn't there?' Steve said.

Jack looked intrigued. 'How do you mean?'

'Well, the one who blew himself up was stupid, no argument about that. But I went out to a woman on the M6 a few months back who was just plain weird. She'd pulled on to the hard shoulder just past the M5 turn-off and was having a major panic attack when we arrived. I had to calm her down and try to get to the bottom of what triggered it. I thought she might have been involved in some kind of incident on the motorway, but no. And she didn't suffer with any chronic condition that might have set her off either. We were there for a good quarter of an hour and a traffic jam was developing as people slowed down to see why there was an ambulance and police car on the hard shoulder. Eventually she came out with it.' Steve broke off to pat his pockets in search of his ever-elusive pipe. We had to wait until he was belching smoke before he continued. 'The bottom line was that she had a phobia about leaving Birmingham.'

'What?'

'Apparently she'd been trying for years to get out of the place without any success. Every time she made a bolt for it, whether by train, coach or car, the same thing happened. It was the third time she'd attempted going north by car and she still hadn't got any further than the M5 turn-off.' He re-lit his pipe. 'Now, I don't know how you see it, but to my mind there's an element of weirdness going on there.'

Howard gave it some thought before adding a proviso.

'I don't know. There are plenty who say that a day out of Birmingham is a day wasted.'

The only way these sessions were brought to an end was by people falling asleep one by one. Mike's eyes were already closed and mine were starting to get heavy. The last thing I remember was Larry changing tack slightly by including weird people with a penchant for pushing foreign bodies up their bottoms. Even at this early stage in my career, I was pretty sure I'd heard every story there was on the subject, so I closed my eyes and settled back as Larry began his bedside story.

'I had a bloke once who spent the evening stuffing a pound and a half of carrots up his arse and then called us when he got stomach ache.' There was no reaction from the others, so he continued. 'Of course, carrots are child's play compared to getting an apple up there. I took in a bloke who tried it, though. It was half in and half out, completely stuck. They tried all they could think of in Casualty to get it out. Someone even tried using a corkscrew. You'll never guess how they did it in the end.' I don't think anyone but me was awake to offer a guess, and I didn't have the energy. 'Well,' Larry continued, 'they sent round to the doctor's mess for two dessert spoons and managed to ease it out with them. A kind of makeshift forceps delivery I suppose you'd call it. I heard that they didn't sell a single pudding in the doctors' mess for months when word spread that the spoons had been returned afterwards.'

It was the last I heard before drifting off to dream of tutus and gangsters.

# Chapter Twelve

Jack Turner's successful transition from probationer to fully qualified ambulance man was as good an excuse as any for spending an evening in the pub. Strangely, and much as I enjoyed Jack's company, it wasn't an evening I looked forward to with any relish. I wasn't the only one who'd begun to worry about the extent of his drinking and I'd learned not to try to match him drink for drink. Instead, I kept to my own pace and watched from a distance as his personality slowly changed for the worse with every drink he knocked back. When sober, he was a quiet, thoughtful man blessed with natural charm and a selfless, engaging sense of humour. He didn't mind being the brunt of the joke himself – a quality guaranteed to win him a lot of friends at the Street. He enjoyed the conversation and the day-to-day banter of depot life but, if the truth be told, he was just as at home with his head buried in a book. For an ex-night-club bouncer and long-distance lorry driver, his choice of reading surprised me. You seldom found a thriller in his hands; he was invariably drawn to gentle, literary authors like Eric Malpass. I still remember him getting dewy-eyed over Malpass's *Morning's at Seven* and demanding quiet as he read aloud poignant passages to a bewildered messroom.

We found ourselves crewed together more often once he'd passed his twelve-month probationary period. The good rapport we enjoyed meant the hours would slip by effortlessly. It also helped that Jack was ten years older than me and his wealth of worldly wisdom made up for my naivety. For a heavy-set man of brooding appearance, he was surprisingly adept at dealing with situations requiring tact and sensitivity. These were skills I was slowly developing, but there was no hiding my youth. Patients and relatives always turned to Jack as the older member of the crew. He was also handy to have around when we were scraping belligerent drunks off the street after closing time. He didn't take kindly to aggressive people, however big they were, and made it clear from the outset that he wasn't a man to be messed with. It's true that our collective experience still didn't amount to much but, imperceptibly, we were picking up an understanding of what the job was all about. This was brought home to me one night when Jack and I attended a curious case that tested my instinct as much as anything else.

We'd been told that a man had fallen off a wall. The truth was that he hadn't so much fallen off it as dived over it when he and his girlfriend were escaping a taxi driver chasing them for the fare. She was unhurt, but he'd landed on his head. A bouncer from a nearby club had seen what happened and called for us. They were waiting on the pavement in a popular city night spot crowded with bars and clubs. It was a cold night and I had my anorak zipped up, while she shivered in a skimpy top and mini skirt. He was wearing a pair of jeans and sleeveless T-shirt.

'So, what's happened?' I asked.

'It was that bloody taxi driver's fault,' the girl said, hugging herself in a vain attempt to keep warm.

He cut over her. 'No, it wasn't. I went over that wall over there and hit my head.' He pointed at a four-foot wall on the other side of the street. 'I got careless, I suppose. It's a bigger drop than I realized on the other side.'

'After you fell,' I asked, 'did you get up under your own steam and walk over here?'

'Yeah, no problem. I'm all right, no harm done. I don't need to go to hospital or anything like that.'

Despite the bravado, he didn't seem in a hurry to be off and answered my questions patiently, despite his girl-friend whining in his ear.

'If you're not going to hospital, Ben, what are we hanging around here for? Sue and the others are waiting for us in the club and I'm freezing my tits off.'

He responded, mildly, 'Yeah, I know. I just want to speak to these blokes first.'

He was alert and orientated and, although not showing any sign of distress, did admit to having 'a bit of a stiff neck'. He wouldn't let me check it for tenderness and again flatly refused to come with us to hospital. This pleased his girlfriend. And, as I did my best to make him change his mind, she did all she could to persuade him to join their friends in the night club. He prevaricated at every turn and after a few minutes she lost patience and walked off, shouting over her shoulder that she'd get a pint in for him if he decided to turn up. I wasn't quite sure why I didn't leave too; it was a busy night and he'd made it clear that he had no intention of going to hospital. It's not as if I could drag him into the ambulance. It was an odd business. He looked like a tough customer with his skinhead cut, tattooed arms and muscle-enhancing T-shirt; someone who could take a beating and not let it spoil his evening. Yet he didn't make any attempt to follow his girlfriend to the club. It was as if he were standing there waiting for something to happen.

'So what are you going to do?' I asked.

'I'm not sure. What do you think?'

'I think you should come with us to hospital.'

'Nah, I'm OK here.'

'How about if I give your neck a bit of support?' I asked. 'It might make you feel a bit better.'

He gave the suggestion some thought.

'Yeah, why not?'

Jack appeared with the Heinz collar a moment later and handed it to me with a look that suggested I was wasting my time. The Heinz was a rigid contraption that held the head, neck and upper back in a straight line, leaving no scope for movement. I asked him how it felt.

'Yeah, that feels good.'

'You'd look pretty stupid wearing that in the club, wouldn't you?' It was a patronizing remark, but he didn't seem to notice.

'Yeah, I suppose I would.'

'Shall we get you in the ambulance then?' It was going to be the last time I asked and my hope was that now he had the collar on he would see a trip to hospital as being the next logical step. I was getting colder by the minute and it came as a relief and a surprise when he agreed.

He didn't object as we carefully lowered him flat on the stretcher and secured his head to the metal frame with surgical tape. Using the Heinz collar and then immobilizing him further might have been seen as going over the top, especially as he'd refused treatment several times. Part of me felt foolish. My reasoning for taking such care didn't just follow textbook logic either. Sure, he had a stiff neck after a fall, but what really played on my mind, and made me stick to the task, was his reluctance to leave our sides even when his girlfriend walked off in a huff. That he was a tough, macho guy made his behaviour all the more strange. On the way to hospital I decided not to mention my reasoning to the doctors. The simple facts would have to do: fell off a wall, banged his head, got up and walked around, now complains of a stiff neck. Voicing vague misgivings that I couldn't adequately explain would not be helpful, or so I thought at the time. I've come to appreciate that such misgivings should always be mentioned, even if they later prove to be groundless.

We discovered the extent of his injuries when we returned to Casualty later in the night. One of the doctors pulled me to one side and spoke in an almost cheery voice.

'Remember that character you brought in earlier with the neck pain?'

I was guarded, half expecting to hear that he'd made a nuisance of himself.

'Of course. He hasn't been giving you any trouble, has he?'

'It depends how you look at it. He's going to give the orthopaedic people plenty of trouble. He'd fractured his second cervical vertebra or, if you prefer to be more dramatic, he's got a hangman's fracture.'

Hangman's fracture! I'd never heard of it, but it didn't take much imagination to figure out what it meant.

I took a moment to digest the news, then asked, 'Is he going to be OK?'

'Yes, he's neurologically intact. If he hadn't been it would probably have been curtains for him. He isn't going to enjoy the next eight weeks, though.'

I felt a bit weak at the knees. Persuading him to come to hospital and immobilizing him had been based on not much more than a hunch.

The next case we were given gave me cause to wonder if Jack was quite as worldly wise as I had imagined. A young woman had been assaulted and was waiting for us on a canal bridge in Hockley. When we arrived she was sitting on the pavement with her legs drawn up to her chin, looking very sorry for herself. Jack was attending, so I stood back as he approached her and tried to find out what had happened. She was sobbing, and when she saw the uniform she clutched his hand gratefully as if he were her knight in shining armour. He drew back gently and listened as she described how her boyfriend had punched her about the body and then abandoned her in the street. This news kindled both indignation and sympathy in Jack, and when she took hold of his hand again he didn't resist. When her tears stopped flowing, he coaxed her into the ambulance, uttering every reassuring platitude that sprang to mind. It was as good an example of tender loving care as I'd seen in a long time. I took up my place in the driver's seat and watched in the interior mirror for Jack's signal to head off. She was still clutching his hand and trying to rest her head on his shoulder while answering his questions in a forlorn little voice. He was doing his best to fend her off gently when he caught my eye and indicated that we should go.

I was baffled. Surely Jack couldn't have missed what was staring him in the face. The Adam's apple? The narrow hips? The low, husky voice? I allowed myself another glance in the mirror. She hadn't released her grip on his hand and if anything was leaning closer as Jack went about reassuring her with all the concern of a worried father. She was hanging on his every word and, when he took a breath, said something that Jack probably didn't hear too often.

'You're such a lovely man. People like you are precious . . .'

I turned my attention back to the road and smiled broadly. Jack didn't have a clue that *she* was a transvestite. There had been a pub about a hundred yards from where we'd picked him up and the chances were that that's where he'd come from. Tolerance of alternative lifestyles wasn't exactly a hallmark of the late seventies and my guess was that one of the drinkers had taken offence and clobbered him. My initial assumption was that Jack had realized his true gender and was simply being professional. That assumption had been misguided though, and I was in for some fun.

Jack handed over his patient to the triage nurse while I waited in the cab. When he joined me a few minutes later he slumped into his seat with a grunt.

'God, she was hard work. Talk about having the weight of the world on her shoulders. You're lucky you didn't have to listen to her going on.'

'She?' I said lightly. 'What was her name?'

He glanced at me suspiciously. 'Lesley, like you. Why the interest?'

'If her name's Lesley, then it's spelt with an ie not an ey.' Seeing his frown, I decided not to beat about the bush. '*She* was a bloke, you daft sod.'

He smiled, tore off a fresh case sheet and fixed it to the board before replying.

'You don't half talk some bollocks at times.'

'That's an appropriate turn of phrase,' I replied,

'because that's precisely what *she*'s got! I knew you were getting senile but I didn't realize how far gone you were.'

The ensuing row lasted about two minutes and I brought it to an end by slamming a pound note down on the dashboard.

'I'll give you two to one that *she* is a *he*.'

He took the note and held it up to the light.

'This will be the easiest quid I've ever made. I'll be back in a minute.'

He had a face like thunder when he returned to the ambulance and threw fifty pence at me with a few words of warning.

'If you breathe a word about this back at the Street you're a dead man. I'll rip your liver out and—'

'Eat it?' I suggested.

'Yes. And when I've done that I'll burn your house down for good measure. Am I making myself clear? Because I wouldn't want there to be any misunderstandings about this.'

'Yes, Jack. But you don't need to make threats. I'm your mate. The last thing I'd want to do is embarrass you in front of the others.'

He stared at me tight-lipped as I put the ambulance into gear and headed back to station.

When we got back to the messroom I addressed the rest of the shift.

'They missed something out on Jack's training course. They forgot to tell him how to spot the difference between a man and a woman.'

Jack leapt from his chair with a bellow.

'I warned you!'

I'd positioned myself on the far side of the snooker table, knowing that Jack wasn't what you would call fleet of foot. He'd have been hard pressed to catch a three-legged donkey over fifty yards and as we chased round the table I still had enough breath to relate the entire story to the others, embellishing it here and there where I saw fit. With the job done, I made a bolt for the door and out into the garage. Jack didn't follow and a few minutes later I considered it safe to return. When I poked my head round the door he was trying to put over his side of the story but was struggling to be heard over the heckling. In the end he gave up and let it all wash over him. Jack saw the funny side of most things in the end, and it wasn't long before he was joining in the banter, even if it was at his own expense. He could take a joke better than most, which was just as well for me as it meant I would hang on to my liver a bit longer.

I thought it a good idea to make the tea as a peace offering, but by the time I came out of the kitchen with the tray of mugs Howard and Steve had been called out on a job. Jack flopped into a chair with a book while Mike, Larry and I settled down for a few games of Scrabble. We'd been playing – well, arguing to be more accurate – for about half an hour when Jack interrupted the bickering by hurling his book on to the table.

'Thank God that's finished. If I'd been told that I'd ever be sitting in an ambulance station at two in the morning reading a book about bloody rabbits I'd have thrown in the towel there and then.'

'Rabbits?' Larry exclaimed. 'What is it, a cookery book?'

Jack gave him a long stare.

'No, Larry, it's called *Watership Down*. It's an allegory on life: how adversity can lead to triumph. It's a best-seller, if you've ever heard of such a thing.'

Larry placed a word on the board.

'Can't say the title rings any bells. Transvestites are they, these rabbits?'

Jack looked round at the rest of us as if hoping for some moral support. He didn't get any.

'So you didn't like the book?' Mike asked.

Jack puffed out his cheeks.

'That's what worries me. I did like it – I thought it was bloody brilliant.'

Howard had returned from his previous case and wandered back into the messroom while the exchange was going on. He looked slightly flushed as he addressed Larry.

'If you've finished talking about rabbits, I want to talk to you about goldfish.' He held up a water carafe in which a goldfish circled lazily. 'I take it this is your doing?'

Larry looked up and smiled. 'I like the way you blame me for everything.' He turned back to the Scrabble board and pretended to study his options. 'As it happens, you're right this time. I put him in there before the shift started.' He glanced at his watch. 'That's more than four hours ago. You're supposed to change the water at the start of the shift, H. Did it slip your mind?'

The glass bottle Howard held aloft was standard issue for all the Bedford ambulances and was usually housed with a drinking glass in a wooden frame attached to one of the bulkheads. It was rarely used, and the water rarely changed. Howard ignored the comment and pressed on.

'You made me look a right prat . . .'

'You don't usually need any help for—'

'You made me look a right prat,' H repeated, 'and you almost gave an innocent old lady a heart attack. We were taking her home from hospital when she asked for a drink of water. She spotted the bloody goldfish just as I was about to pour it into her glass. She squealed and when she'd recovered gave me a lecture on mistreating wild animals. I had to make up a cock-and-bull story about having just rescued it from a home where it was being abused. And you know what? I don't think she believed me. Heaven only knows what she's going to tell her relatives.'

'How many goldfish can boast to their mates they spent an evening going out on 999s?' Larry interjected while considering his tray of letters. Howard clunked the jug on the Scrabble board, scattering all our work.

'Just like you, Larry, it hasn't got any mates. The two of you should get on well together.'

The emergency phone rang, forcing Jack and me to miss the rest of the conversation and head out into a world where the temperature had dropped below zero. Our destination was a custom-built block of self-contained flats offering sheltered accommodation for the elderly, and a few minutes found us hunched and shivering outside its locked doors. You tend to feel the cold at 2.30 in the morning anyway. But when it's midwinter, the temperature's sub-zero and you add a piercing wind that must have stirred into life somewhere over the Russian steppe and whose icy fingers are rummaging about deep inside your chest, the word 'cold' takes on a whole new meaning. Our reason for being there was to investigate why one of the elderly residents had pulled his emergency cord and hadn't responded to any questions put to him via the intercom.

The home was piloting a security system that we'd heard of, but were yet to experience. The idea was that during the day a warden answered calls for assistance as usual, but at night the calls were routed directly to a central control. Its job was to assess the call by speaking to the resident over the intercom and, if deeming it necessary, call an ambulance. The crew had to press a red button at the front door when they arrived and wait for a sleepy voice to respond. After identifying themselves and giving the flat number, the burglar alarm was remotely de-activated, as was the door lock. Once inside, a master key to the flats was obtained from a small safe on the wall, the lock of which would also have been automatically released.

Jack pressed the button and the device blared out a series of raucous beeps, perfectly pitched to grate on the nerves as we huddled against the wind. Eventually, amidst a sea of static, a metallic voice answered.

'Hello?'

'Hi,' Jack said into the box. 'It's the ambulance service – you should be expecting us. We've been called to flat nine.' There was a pause before the voice crackled back.

'Hello?'

Jack rolled his eyes and tried a bit louder.

'It's the ambulance for flat nine!'

'Hello?'

Jutting his face forward, Jack bellowed into the device.

'It's the ambulance. Let us in!'

As if appraising Jack, the box on the wall crackled for a few moments. Then, presumably not liking what it saw, abruptly fell silent, the connection cut.

'Bloody hell!' Jack shouted in exasperation while I flapped my arms and hopped from foot to foot in an effort to keep warm.

Jack composed himself before pressing the button again. We then waited while the box beeped away for a second time. Two minutes later we were back to square one.

'Hello?' rattled the disembodied voice.

'Hello, it's the ambu—'

Jack was interrupted as the voice, which in my mind was taking on the persona of a Dalek, spoke over him.

'Is that the ambulance? If it is, I am going to open the door.' The Dalek was shouting and leaving gaps between each word, presumably assuming that if he couldn't hear us, we couldn't hear him.

'Yes!' Jack shouted back. 'Who else would it be?'

There was a long pause.

'Well – is it the ambulance?'

'Yes!' Jack was now screaming loud enough to wake everyone within fifty yards. After a few more crackles from the intercom, the lock on the front door buzzed furiously as it was released.

We tumbled into the warmth of the foyer and looked round for the safe containing the master key. I was first to spot the small metal box situated on the central pillar and pulled open the door as instructed. Instantaneously, an ear-splitting screech ripped apart the silence. It was the burglar alarm, but it wasn't like any alarm I'd come across before. It was the mother of all alarms, and in the confined space the noise was unbearable. I can only presume its other function was to act as a fire alarm and, as such, it had been set at the highest level to compensate for any hearing difficulties amongst the elderly residents. Not that I was thinking quite so logically at the time. In fact, I wasn't thinking at all, which I proved by slamming the safe door shut in the instinctive hope of stopping the racket. My first clear thoughts arrived a moment later. Firstly, the noise hadn't stopped and, more importantly, the key was still inside the safe. Deep down I knew what the outcome would be when I tried to re-open the door. Sure enough: it had self-locked. I couldn't hear what Jack was shouting at me, but I didn't have any trouble reading his lips.

'You stupid bleeder!'

The only thing to do was to go back outside to the inter-com and try to get the Dalek to switch off the alarm from his central control and re-open the key safe. Shouting my intentions to Jack, I ran from the building with my hands over my ears. Back outside in the bitter wind I pressed the button, closed my eyes, and leaned my head against the wall while the high-pitched beeps of the intercom mingled with the shriek of the alarm. When I eventually opened my eyes it was to discover Jack standing at my side. With a feeling of resignation, I let my gaze drift across to the front door. My fears were confirmed: the front door had closed itself behind Jack. I looked back at him.

'Who's the stupid bleeder now?'

Fifteen minutes had passed since we'd arrived and all we'd achieved was to set off the alarm and end up back where we started – locked out.

'Hello?' said the Dalek over the intercom.

'Hello,' I shouted back. 'The alarm's gone off! Can you switch it off and let us back in?'

'Hello?'

'Switch off the bloody alarm!' Jack bellowed over my shoulder.

'Listen,' the Dalek was shouting as well now, while taking care to enunciate each word slowly as if speaking to a pair of congenital idiots. 'The alarm has gone off . . . we have contacted the area warden . . . she will attend and de-activate it.'

'Open the bloody door!' Jack shouted at the intercom.

As if offended, it hissed for a few seconds and then went silent. He looked at me and voiced my thoughts.

'You know, they shouldn't let us work together.'

Twenty minutes later a car pulled into the car park and an impressively large middle-aged woman heaved herself out of the driver's seat. She was wearing a heavy winter coat pulled over a pair of pyjamas and in her hand was a large bunch of keys. Making no attempt to communicate over the noise, she swept past us and opened the front door. Once inside, she marched over to the control box and, selecting a key, switched off the alarm. The sudden silence was bliss, a bit like the dentist's drill being taken away from a tooth. It was only then that it struck me how totally ineffective the alarm had been. It hadn't roused a single person in the block and no one from the surrounding houses had come out to investigate. And where were the police?

The warden turned to us with something approaching a scowl on her face.

'Which flat is it? And don't dare tell me it's number nine.'

'You got it. Number nine,' I replied.

'Oh no! I don't believe it – not Albert again. So help me I'll swing for that man one day!'

She set off at a pace down the corridor with us following as fast as we could, laden down as we were with our resuscitation equipment, oxygen, first-aid bag, blanket and carry-chair. When we arrived at the flat she pushed open the door and walked straight in. I stared and shook my head.

'It was open all the time! We could have by-passed the key safe and come straight up half an hour ago.'

'You certainly could have,' answered the warden. 'He never locks his door.'

We found Albert snugly tucked up in bed with the covers pulled well up past his chin. All we could see of him was a bony, hooked nose, a pair of droopy eyes and a few wisps of white hair. The bedside light was on and music was playing softly on the radio.

'What's wrong now, Albert?' The warden's voice was tired, but all the same it had an edge to it.

'Nothing,' Albert mumbled from under the sheets.

'What do you mean, "nothing"? You pulled the emergency cord didn't you?'

'No.'

'Albert! I'm really not in the mood for playing games. Why did you pull the cord?'

'I didn't pull it.'

'Oh yes you did! Why?' The edge in her voice had taken on a hint of menace, causing Albert to shrink back a little further under the sheets before replying.

'Well, it . . . it's the radio . . . I can't get to sleep with it on and I wanted someone to switch it off for me.' As an after-thought, he added meekly, 'I didn't think they'd send you.'

Albert was almost hidden under the blankets by now. The warden stared at the top of his head and seemed to be summoning up the energy to continue. She started quietly, but got louder as she spoke.

'Albert, you're not seriously telling me that you've called

me out in the middle of the night to switch off your radio . . . are you?'

Her hands were on her hips as she leaned over the bed. Albert had now completely disappeared under the sheets and chose not to answer.

'Is that what you are telling me, Albert? Albert!' The warden persisted.

'I didn't think it would be you who came.'

'I bet you didn't! Do you know that all the alarms have gone off and an ambulance has been sent? They're supposed to be helping people who need them, not switching off radios for silly old men who should know better! Do you hear me?'

Giving up on getting any hint of contrition from beneath the blankets, she turned to us.

'I'm sorry. What can I say?'

'You don't need to say anything,' I said as we gathered up our bits and pieces. 'We'll leave you to it.'

She lowered her voice and took on a gentler tone as she walked us to the door.

'I don't like to scold him, but what else can I do? If I were to let him get away with it, he'd be pulling tricks like this every night of the week. He cries wolf too often as it is.'

Jack smiled at her. 'Honestly, don't worry about it. I'm just grateful he's OK. Especially after the time it took us to get to him.'

The warden looked back at the besieged figure in the bed.

'Poor old Albert. He was a schoolteacher for forty years, you know. He hasn't got any relatives left alive; he's all on his own these days. It's such a shame things have to come to this.'

# Chapter Thirteen

Howard's goldfish happily explored his little world for three weeks until it became noticeable that all was not well. H voiced his concern to Larry.

'Every now and then he does a couple of laps upside down. If you ask me, something's up with him.'

Larry peered into the tank. 'He might just be showing off.'

Howard glanced at him scornfully. He'd taken it upon himself to re-house the fish and keep it well fed. Being the good-natured chap he was, he took the job seriously.

'It could be his swim bladder . . . Maybe if we took him to the vet . . .' The words were no sooner out of his mouth than the fish turned turtle and drifted to the surface, still and flaccid. 'Bloody hell, the poor little bleeder's just pegged it!' Howard was genuinely dismayed. 'I don't know, this bloody place must have a curse on it. We can't even keep a pot plant alive for more than a month, never mind a goldfish.'

'It was a witnessed cardiac arrest!' Larry said, with exaggerated excitement, 'We might be able to do something for him.'

H gave him another look. 'Very funny! And before you bother saying it, no, I'm not going to do mouth-to-gill resuscitation. He's a goner; let's leave his dignity intact at least.'

And so it was that our newest companion, his dignity still intact, left Henrietta Street for the last time via the gents' toilets.

Larry was being ironic when he expressed hope that something might be done to save the fish as it was a witnessed cardiac arrest. The vast majority of patients who go into cardiac arrest are pretty well doomed, for no other reason than that the time lapse between the heart stopping and a meaningful attempt to get it restarted is desperately short. In the great scheme of things, a witnessed arrest, or arriving within a minute or two, represents our best chance of successfully resuscitating someone. It doesn't happen often, and when it does the results can be gratifying, as they had been the previous Sunday morning. Our patient wasn't a goldfish, but a businessman who thought that his day off would be best spent by going over some paperwork in the office.

Steve turned the ambulance into the small car park to find a solitary Jaguar parked close by the main entrance of the single-storey building. He pulled up alongside and we made our way inside without bothering with the bell. To the left of the reception desk was an open office door, through which we could see a man sitting behind a desk. There are times when you don't need an ounce of training to realize that the person you are looking at is desperately ill. He was cowering in his chair like a wounded animal at bay. Pain and fear clouded eyes set in a face bathed with sweat and the colour of porridge, and he seemed to have shrunk into himself as if attempting to retreat from the world. It wasn't the first time I'd seen someone's life hanging by such a fine thread, but that made it no less disconcerting. He was dying – I had no doubt about that. It was an effort to keep my face impassive as a wave of alarm coursed through me. I had to remain steady, and even resisted glancing at Steve. There was no need to look for guidance: we were both well aware that we had to get him out of that office and into hospital without losing a moment. I also knew it had to be done calmly; nothing should be allowed to add to the anxiety he was already under.

Cardiac monitors were still some way in the future for ambulance crews, not that we needed one as far as this diagnosis was concerned. I asked the minimum of questions while fitting the oxygen mask before moving him on to our carry-chair. He had crushing central chest pain and felt horribly nauseous, but couldn't vomit. He was in the midst of a massive heart attack. He knew it, and we knew it; there was no need to burden him with distractions. We could have given in to the temptation to run with him to the ambulance, but we didn't. Steve could have driven with sirens blaring and thrown us all over the place in his haste, but he didn't. Everything was done swiftly and efficiently. I made sure he didn't notice me take the bag and mask used to assist a patient's breathing from its case and place it out of sight. I knelt in the gangway to be at his level and talked to him. I have no idea what I said, but it wasn't cheery-chappy ambulance-man talk; there's a time and a place for that, and this wasn't it.

One benefit of working in the inner city is that we're seldom more than ten minutes from the nearest hospital. In this instance it couldn't have been more than six. Six long minutes spent watching the life ebb from him. He didn't say anything. His breathing became more irregular and his face slowly took on an impassive look that belied the situation. Then he spoke.

'I'm dying.'

Dreaded words. I'd been warned in training that when a patient expresses a premonition of his own demise it should be taken very seriously. The medical term is 'impending doom'. This was the first time I'd encountered it, and I blurted out the first words that came to mind.

'No, you're not. I won't let it happen!' I had no control of events, yet my voice carried a conviction that surprised me. I went further and attempted to lighten a moment as dark as any I've known. 'Nobody's ever died on my ambulance, and you're not going to be the first.' His eyes held mine as the flicker of a smile passed over his face. I can still see it; it was as extraordinary as it was fleeting. My fingers were closed on the pulse at his wrist as I watched the smile fade and his breathing slow. I was reaching for the bag and mask as the ambulance came to a halt at the Casualty entrance.

The back doors were flung open by the waiting resuscitation team and, as Steve and I unloaded the stretcher, I did my best to give a brief history to the doctor in charge. A nurse found the patient's carotid pulse but then, as we crossed the Casualty threshold, announced that she'd lost it. We didn't stop, and a second later were dragging him across on to the hospital trolley while the nurse tore open his shirt, sending a shower of buttons across the floor. I pulled the stretcher into a corner of the room and watched. Each person knew exactly what was expected of them and worked in near silence. While the ECG electrodes were being positioned across his body, one of the nurses started cardiac compressions. The anaesthetist fed an intubation tube into his trachea and began rhythmically inflating his lungs. A needle was slipped into a vein in his arm, ready to be used as access for delivering drugs and fluids. The ECG reading was analysed and two paddles were placed on the patient's chest with a warning for everyone to stand back. Thunk! The man, who minutes earlier had told me he was dying, jerked. An arm slipped from the table and dangled unnoticed as a doctor studied the results on the ECG machine. His voice was measured, but it didn't disguise his delight.

'We've got a rhythm.' He eyed the monitor cautiously for thirty seconds. 'Yep, it's looking good.'

Drugs were being eased into the patient's veins while the anaesthetist kept his lungs enriched with oxygen.

Strangely, I didn't feel any elation. It was more a sense of relief, as if I had a vested interest in the outcome.

I followed his progress anonymously for the next few weeks. He went to intensive care, from where he was transferred to cardiac care, and then eventually on to a general ward before being sent home. It was an outcome I wouldn't have predicted when I first laid eyes on him. Steve was sanguine about the whole thing.

'He's one hell of a lucky bloke. It's little short of a miracle he didn't go on you in the back.'

'It wasn't a miracle,' I said. 'I told him he couldn't. I said it wasn't allowed.'

Steve smiled. 'Oh really? So that's one of your rules, is it?'

'It is from now on,' I said. 'I told him that nobody had ever died on my ambulance and he wasn't going to be the first.'

Steve began cleaning his pipe with a spent match.

'Good for you! Did you also tell him that you've only been on the job five minutes?'

I grinned. 'No, I didn't think of mentioning that.'

I would have given anything to have known it at the time, but my new rule would never be broken, staying intact for over three decades.

Steve blew through his pipe and, seemingly satisfied with the result, was about to slip it into his pocket when a woman of about thirty-five tapped on his window. He wound it down and looked at her enquiringly. She smiled at him.

'He'd got a perforated ulcer after all. You said that's probably what it was, didn't you?'

Steve smiled back. 'That's right! How's he doing now?'

'Just fine. He'll be back on his feet any day.' She turned to go and then had another thought. 'I don't think I had chance at the time, but I want to say thanks very much. You were so kind to Colin and I know he appreciated it.'

'I'm only glad we could help. It's great to know that everything worked out for the good.'

She gave him a lingering smile and was on her way. Steve slowly wound up the window.

'Well, that was nice of her,' I said. 'I thought she was going to kiss you. Who was she?'

He examined his pipe thoughtfully.

'I haven't got a bloody clue. It happens from time to time. People never forget you when you turn up and drag their relative out of the house, but it's not often I remember them.'

It was true, but I knew I wouldn't forget the man we had just brought in, and thought it would be nice if he tapped on my window one day.

I was destined to attend a similar case of impending doom years later, a case made all the more poignant as it involved Steve. He had been my role model and, as far as I was concerned, had set a benchmark for everyone else. Much of his talent came from within and was personified by an air of benevolent kindness which engendered a feeling of reassurance in every patient who came under his care. It was a persona that never slipped. Even on station, surrounded by the general hurly-burly and banter of depot life, he managed to remain a pillar of calm, gently puffing on his pipe and at peace with the world. It was a sad day for Henrietta Street when he retired, and I missed his presence for a long while afterwards. I still saw him from time to time when he popped in for a coffee, but these visits became fewer and fewer. I hadn't seen him for a couple of years when my crew mate and I were called to his house in answer to a 999.

His wife showed us upstairs to the bedroom. He was propped up in the bed, his normally slicked back, Brylcreemed hair in a state of disarray.

'Steve!' I said with an air of forced joviality. 'We were in the middle of watching a film. If I'd known it was you we were coming out to I'd have waited until it was finished.'

He gave the faintest of smiles.

'Hello, Les. I'm afraid I'm not too good. In fact, I feel terrible.'

The lack of reaction to my comment immediately rang warning bells in my head. At the very least I'd expected him to say something like, 'If they'd said it was you they were going to send, I'd have called a taxi instead.' I moved over to the bed to get a proper look at him. He said he felt terrible: well, he looked terrible. Pale and drawn doesn't convey the jaded exhaustion written over his features. I reached for his wrist and asked him to describe how he felt as I counted off his pulse.

'I don't know. I just feel awful. No strength – I can hardly even manage to keep my eyes open.'

'Any pain?'

'No. No pain.'

'Nausea?' I asked.

'No. I feel hot, my legs feel so hot.' His voice trailed off.

He wasn't sweating and his temperature was normal. His breathing wasn't laboured and his blood pressure, though a bit on the low side, didn't give cause for concern. We rigged him up to the three-lead ECG machine, which showed a normal rhythm.

'Can you be more specific, Steve?' I asked, in the hope of finding a starting point.

'No, mate. Just tired and hot.'

Tired and hot? We weren't getting very far, but I did have two points of reference. Firstly, he looked bloody awful and, secondly, I knew him as well as anyone and I knew that he wasn't the kind of person to seek help until he saw no other course of action. Calling for an ambulance would have been anathema to him. That he allowed himself to be lifted on to our carry-chair without complaint and carried downstairs only increased my unease. The Steve I knew would have done his utmost to avoid such ignominy. I was worried and annoyed: worried for my friend, and annoyed that I couldn't begin to understand what might be wrong.

On the journey to hospital I probed and questioned, but the only symptom I could add to my vague collection was the observation that he displayed a general air of rest-lessness. I passed on what precious little I'd learned to the triage nurse while she studied the ECG strip. It all sounded a bit lame as I repeated it, but she could see for herself how ill he looked and agreed that all wasn't well. She then directed us into one of the cubicles where we were to transfer him on to a hospital trolley. I hesitated. I wanted him to go to the resuscitation room for immediate attention, but couldn't justify the request without basing it on firm reasoning. I leaned a bit closer to the nurse so Steve couldn't overhear, just as I'd watched him do so many times in the past when he'd been worried about a patient.

'Look, I'm not asking because he's a friend or anything like that, but couldn't we put him in the resuscitation room? It's just that I'm concerned about him; he's not the kind of person to feel sorry for himself or exaggerate how he feels.'

She looked at Steve, then back at me.

'I can see he's not well, but I need to keep that room free. Put him in the cubicle for now and I'll send a doctor in as soon as one comes free.'

Steve stopped me in my tracks as we were preparing to move him on to the hospital trolley.

'I'm going, Les. I think this is it.'

I looked down at him. His eyes were closed and he didn't say any more. He looked serene, completely at odds with the way I felt.

'Steve, don't talk like that,' I said in alarm. 'You're not going anywhere.'

He didn't look up as I turned on my heel and retraced my steps to the triage desk. The nurse was finishing with another ambulance crew when I butted in.

'My patient's just told me that he thinks he's dying.' When I added the trigger phrase 'he's got impending doom', she looked up sharply and, to her credit, didn't hesitate.

'OK, take him into resusc.'

Her compliance was a relief, as I'm not sure what I'd have done if she'd refused. A minute later Steve was on their trolley and we were backing out of the room with our stretcher. A nurse began attaching him to a twelve-lead ECG while a doctor slipped a needle into his arm. I closed the door and went looking for a coffee. When I popped my head in ten minutes later, he was sitting up surrounded by staff, still looking drawn and pale. I didn't want to distract anyone by asking the trite question 'Is he going to be OK?' so I returned to the ambulance and sat in deep contemplation.

The lad I was working with that day had started on the service some time after Steve retired. He could see I was preoccupied and asked tentatively, 'Was he a good friend of yours?'

'Yes, he worked at the Street for years. He was quite a character. You must have heard of him, Steve Baxter?' He looked unsure. 'One of the nicest blokes you could meet. Surely you've heard his name mentioned?'

'Sorry, I can't say I have.'

I thought of the jobs Steve and I had done together, and

how much I'd learned from him. Of the times he'd rescued me from making a fool of myself, and of the times I'd watched in admiration as he'd treated people in desperate straits while still finding time to reassure relatives distraught with worry. Of the times we'd laughed, chatted and played snooker together. And now, so soon after stepping down from a job to which he'd given a good part of his life, his name didn't even strike a chord with the generation following so close behind. It's the way of things, I suppose, but no less sad for that.

As soon as we'd dropped off our next patient I made my way to the resusc room with little thought other than to discover how Steve was faring. He was wearing a hospital gown and sitting up looking much like his old self; even his hair had miraculously returned to its normal elegant state.

'I see they've combed your hair for you,' I said as I took up a seat by his bed.

'No, that was Mary, my wife. Heart attack or not, she insists that I look my best.'

'Heart attack? You've had a heart attack?' I had been about to ask what the diagnosis was, and a heart attack hadn't featured on the shortlist of possibilities I'd drawn up in my head. 'There was nothing on the ECG to suggest that it was your heart. You weren't in any pain . . . I don't understand.'

'It happened just after you left. It was weird. The doctor was busy telling me that the ECG was clear, when he suddenly announced that I was having a heart attack –

he could see it happening on the screen. Not that I had any doubts. While he watched it, I felt it.'

'So the way you were beforehand was a kind of build-up?'

'I suppose so, but it's not something I've heard of before.'

I sat back in my seat and tried to take it all in.

'So what happens now? You look so well.'

'I'm waiting to be taken up to coronary care. They've pumped me full of all kinds of stuff. I suppose I was lucky to be here when it happened. Thanks for everything, by the way.'

'There's nothing to thank me for – I did bugger all,' I said. 'I only brought you in. I didn't even have a clue what was wrong with you.'

Steve thought about it. 'I suppose you're right. You never were good for much more than carting people about.'

I grinned. He was definitely back to his old self. He went on to make a complete recovery. I occasionally bumped into him round the hospital when he came for out-patient appointments. We chewed the fat when we had chance, but as time passed I saw less and less of him.

Let's jump forward in time once again, about sixteen years. I was taking an elderly lady to hospital for some routine tests. She was accompanied by her son and as the three of us fell into conversation on the journey she mentioned that her late husband had once been an ambulance driver. We hear this kind of thing now and again, and more often than not it turns out that the person in question did the occasional stint for the St John at weekends. Nonetheless, I enquired further.

'Did he do emergency work?'

'Oh yes, but there weren't any fancy ambulances like this in his day. He worked at Henrietta Street in town. Do you know it?'

She had my full attention now.

'Yes, that's where I'm based. What was his name?'

'Stephen, but I doubt if you were there at the time. He retired in the early eighties.'

It wasn't an uncommon name, and I glanced at her surname on the case sheet. Mary Baxter. Stephen Baxter? Then the penny dropped.

'Steve! Of course I know him! They put me on his shift when I came out of training school in seventy-seven.'

She looked pleased. 'Well, fancy that.'

Then the fact that he'd died hit home and I was left groping for words.

'I'm so sorry to hear that he's passed away. I had no idea. When did it happen?'

'Eighteen months ago. They said it was his heart.'

He'd been gone eighteen months and I hadn't known. How could that be? I felt angry with myself for not keeping in touch with him, and angry that the ambulance service hadn't made an announcement at the time. Surely they kept some kind of record concerning past employees? Or perhaps they didn't. I felt guilty and passed on my regrets as best I could.

'I'm really sorry I wasn't at the funeral. I didn't know.'

'Don't worry,' Steve's son said. 'Nobody from the ambulance service came.' He didn't sound bitter, but the news made it all the worse.

'That makes me feel terrible,' I said. 'It can only be because nobody knew. Everybody liked your dad. He was a gentleman and great at his job. He was really good to me when I first started.'

'Well, it's nice to hear you say that,' Mrs Baxter said with a smile. 'Tell me, was it you who came out to him when he had his first heart attack?'

Her question came as a surprise. I'd only been vaguely aware of her at the time, and found it remarkable that she had such good recall almost two decades later.

'Yes, yes it was me. Fancy you remembering that after all these years.'

'It was when you said you worked with Stephen that it came back to me. You looked so worried at the time, but what I remember best was your lovely long blond hair. Where did it go?'

All those years ago Steve had said that relatives rarely forget you, and here was his wife proving his point. It can be a funny old world.

The sad way I learned of Steve's passing gave me cause to reflect on a lot of things, not least how each generation of ambulance personnel eventually fades away without leaving anything tangible to be remembered by. Their names quickly become a memory to some and completely unknown to others. But they do leave something:

they leave their wisdom. It passes through the line to each new generation grappling with a job that can be as baffling as it is wonderful. Medical knowledge and procedures are learned in the classroom; determining how to cope with the vagaries of life isn't. You can't teach someone how to be composed when those about them are losing their heads. You can't teach someone how to manage the hysteria of a bereaved mother or calm a terrified patient. These skills are passed on and can be accrued only by watching and learning. I'm not claiming there was anything remarkable about Steve. He was just one of many. To me, though, he was a guiding light and I'm grateful to have known him.

# Chapter Fourteen

Jack, a skilled hairdresser, didn't show much enthusiasm when Larry suggested he should treat the rest of us to free haircuts. His initial refusal was emphatic, not to say spirited, and it took a surprising length of time before his resistance crumbled under Larry's constant badgering. From then on, he morosely chopped away at our hair every time the night shift came round. There was a price to pay, though. He ignored any views we might have on length or style and demanded silence. If someone had the temerity to ask for it to be left on the long side, he'd cut it short. If you asked for it short, he'd leave it long. And there was another cost. Although these sessions took place during the night shift when it wasn't so busy, there was always the possibility of answering a 999 call with half a haircut. Sometimes we had to wait until the following month to get it finished. But it was free, and that was the main thing.

It was a haircut night when Mike and I returned from a

job at about 1 a.m. Sid, our local beat copper, was sitting at the table with a cup of tea looking melancholic as usual. He was friendly enough, but never had a great deal to say for himself and would usually be asleep in a corner within five minutes of arriving. We found it rather odd, but the ethos of the day was to live and let live, and we left him to it. In another corner, Jack was listlessly clipping away at Howard's head, which protruded from a sheet taken from one of the ambulances. As usual, Jack was grumbling about being the only one on the shift who had to pay to get his hair cut, but we'd heard it all before. I threw my coat on to an empty chair as the phone rang. Steve took down the case and spoke to H.

'That's us, mate. Someone's got themselves beaten up at the Locarno.'

I took Howard's place under the sheet as they trooped out to the garage and ten minutes later all there was to be heard in the messroom was the snipping of scissors and the gentle clicking of snooker balls as Larry pursued his hopeless quest one day to beat Mike. I'd quite forgotten about Sid asleep in the corner until his radio squawked into life. We all jumped, Sid included. He sat up abruptly and then got to his feet, straining to make sense of the garbled message.

'Sounds like one of your blokes has been assaulted. I've got to go.'

Mike put down his cue. 'Where?'

Sid was on his way out of the door. 'A night club in Hurst Street.'

We all looked at each other.

'That's got to be the job Steve and Howard went out on,' Larry said, and snatched up the phone to the control room. A minute later he was in possession of what little information Control had: one of the crew members had been attacked and the other was driving him to hospital.

My haircut half done, and with Jack showing little inclination to continue, I took off the sheet and joined the others. Mike was on his feet, pacing the room with a face like thunder. After a couple of circuits he announced that he and Larry were going to the hospital to find out which one had been hurt, and how badly.

'What about Control?' I asked.

'Bugger Control.' Then he relented. 'Don't worry, I'll tell them on the radio.' And with that they were gone, leaving Jack and me to await developments. Not that we had much time to dwell on things: the phone rang within a couple of minutes, sending us out to transport an elderly man with retention of urine to hospital. Annoyingly, our destination hospital was several miles from the one where Steve and Howard had ended up. We got back to the Street an hour later to find Mike, Larry and Howard sitting round the table finishing off a pot of tea.

'So what's happened?' I asked. 'Where's Steve?'

'Steve,' Howard answered, 'is in hospital, and that's where he'll be staying for the next few hours.'

I sat down beside him. 'Is he badly hurt?'

'His nose is broken and he's going to have a couple of beautiful black eyes by morning.'

'How did it happen?' I persisted.

Howard drained his cup.

'All we were told when we got the job was that someone had been assaulted outside the Locarno. When we got
there the fight was more or less over, just a couple of
skirmishes going on further down the street. It seemed
safe enough and as there was a lad sprawled in the gutter
with a girl bending over him and waving at us, Steve
decided to get out to see what he could do for him. He
opened his door and had just about got one foot out of the
cab when some yob ran across and punched him in
the face. There's no way he could have seen it coming and
he fell back on to me, squirting blood everywhere. Some
other kid started thumping the yob who'd hit him and I
drove round the corner and parked up to see how Steve
was. He hadn't been knocked out or anything, so I carried
on to the hospital.'

I could scarcely believe what I was hearing. That we
were at risk in the city at night was plain enough, but I
always imagined that if trouble was coming our way we
would at least be in a position to do something about it.
To be the subject of an outrageous and unprovoked attack
was something I'd never even contemplated. Mike was
still fuming at the injustice of it all, especially as Steve
was a particular and long-standing friend of his.

'What gets me,' he said, 'is the cowardliness of it. That
yob wouldn't have dared pull anything like that face to
face. I just wish it had been me he'd had a go at. He'd
have spent a good deal longer in hospital than Steve will.'

We didn't doubt him. He was a powerfully built man who'd learned a lot of tricks in the Marines and it would have been a foolish person who deliberately tangled with him, despite his age.

This had been brought home to me a few months earlier when I'd been working with Mike on a late shift. I'd stopped at a newsagent's for the evening paper and returned to the ambulance to find a youth urinating against the back wheel. I was outraged and shouted at him, asking what the hell he thought he was doing, even though it was perfectly clear that we both knew exactly what he was doing.

'Having a piss. You got a problem with that?'

Mike leaned his head out of the cab window and, seeing what was unfolding, leapt from the ambulance with a bellow.

'You little runt – I should rub your face in that!'

The youth zipped himself up and regarded Mike with disdain.

'So why don't you try it, you fat git?'

I cringed. Nobody spoke to Mike like that, least of all a pimply youth he could have crushed with one hand. But what could he do? We were in full view of the public and it surely wasn't worth risking his job to get even with an uncouth yob. The uncouth yob must have come to much the same conclusion, and confidently held his ground as Mike advanced on him, eyes burning. I barely saw Mike's hand move; the youth certainly didn't. Apart from the pain, I would imagine the next thing he was aware of was being on his knees hoping he'd die soon.

At last I had discovered why Mike often carried his torch with him even when it wouldn't be needed. It had a slightly elongated handle, and it was this handle that made contact with the youth's testicles. It wasn't much of a blow; in fact, it was delivered with the barest flick of the wrist. But it was delivered with the skill and accuracy of an expert. It's a common misconception, especially amongst women, that a blow between the legs will instantly incapacitate a man. Nine times out of ten it won't. It will hurt, as a blow anywhere on the body might, but not enough to render the victim helpless. However, and this is the point, if the assailant finds the precise spot, and it's a tiny spot, the pain inflicted is out of all proportion to the force used. And it's not a pain easy to imagine. It's a river of fire that starts at the point of contact and streaks into the centre of the body like a comet before scything upwards past the abdomen and into the solar plexus. And as if that's not bad enough, the agony is accompanied by a feeling of nausea so intense that the victim's breathing goes haywire, leaving him retching while searching for a breath he thinks will never come. So it must have been for the yob on all fours, head down and looking as if he were trying to eat the pavement. I doubt if he ever had the urge to relieve himself against an ambulance again.

Howard put the kettle on and we were soon sitting round discussing the assault over endless cups of tea. As the conversation meandered one way and another, it struck me that none of the others had a similar story to tell, apocryphal or not. Usually there's no stopping the flow of anecdotes once a subject has been broached, but in this case there seemed to be a dearth of them. The truth is that assaults on ambulance staff were rare. They still are, considering the thousands of cases dealt with each day, but back then you were even less likely to be attacked. I have wondered why this should be and, leaving the urinating yob to one side, it seems to me that at the time the public had an ingrained respect for the ambulance service and those who worked in it. Most people still have today, but there's no escaping the growing section of the community that holds little respect for anything, least of all themselves. Those who chose to test the boundaries of tolerance in years gone by did so in the knowledge that retribution, and not just from the courts, was a very real threat – something that's an alien notion nowadays.

Sid looked in later that night with the news that the assailant had been arrested and was now spending an uncomfortable night in the local nick.

'A bouncer from the club was holding him by the scruff of the neck when we got there,' Sid explained. 'He'd broken up the fight that started after Steve got thumped and made sure he collared him for us.' Sid sat down and eyed the teapot. 'The cheeky bastard wanted to make a complaint against the bouncer because he'd given him a couple of smacks. Our sergeant told him to shut up or we'd finish the job.'

We thanked him and poured him a cup of tea before he resumed his seat in the corner and closed his eyes. Steve was off work for just over a week, and I believe received a payment from the Criminal Injuries Board for what was adjudged to be permanent impairment to the functioning of his nose.

We might not have been assaulted very often, but there were plenty of times when we felt we might be. I once took a middle-aged man to hospital with his son travelling as an escort. Halfway there the father went into respiratory arrest and I ended up having to breathe for him using a bag and mask. It can't have been nice for his son to watch what was going on, but I don't think even the emotion of the moment justified him shouting at me as I worked, 'If he dies, so do you!'

I like to think that it didn't influence the eventual outcome; then again, maybe it did. For one reason or another, the patient survived and the threat was never put to the test.

It's not a perfect world, no matter how much we wish it to be. Everything, from verbal abuse to intimidating stares, was and still is part and parcel of the job. When trouble is brewing, it's up to us to be alert and see it coming before things have chance to turn nasty. It's also an intuitive thing. Gauging other people's moods and their potential for violence is a fine art. People under the influence of alcohol or drugs are more difficult to read, as are the emotionally distraught or mentally unbalanced.

Like a snake sniffing the air with its tongue, we learn to pick up on the atmosphere and respond the best way we can.

Diabetics with low sugar levels were a constant threat. They're usually stabilized on scene without too much trouble these days, but we didn't have the means to accomplish that in the late seventies. If the patient had slipped into unconsciousness, then we had the relatively simple task of managing their airway and whipping them off to hospital. It was a little more problematic when they were hovering in a kind of deranged limbo prior to unconsciousness. At best they become downright obstinate and irrational; at worst they see everything around them as a threat and react accordingly. Coaxing a sixteen-stone man downstairs when he thinks you're a creature from Mars intent on his destruction comes with its own problems. But, when the patient thinks *he*'s the creature from Mars and is intent on *your* destruction, then things become altogether more tiresome. Luckily, diabetics are rarely able to coordinate a focused attack. It's more a case of them lashing out randomly at anything that happens to be within range. All we had to do was see it coming and get out of the way. At least that was the theory.

The first of many memories I have of being on the receiving end of a diabetic's wrath was set in a Safeway supermarket. The man and his wife were just about to start shopping when he signalled that all was not well by trying to walk through a stack of parked trolleys. The resulting clatter brought out the staff, who persuaded him to sit in a chair they found for him. They then called for an ambulance while his wife tried to force-feed him a Mars bar in an effort to get some sugar into him. Of course, it didn't work; it never does when things have gone too far, and when we arrived all she'd achieved was smearing chocolate all over his face. I can see him now sitting there like an ageing Dudley Moore in his gabardine mac, scarf and flat cap, staring through the chocolate with a dreamily benign expression on his face. He was in his late sixties, about five feet six and, in the great scheme of things, didn't appear to offer much of a threat. I approached him, said hello, and was promptly kicked between the legs. It was a random kick that, luckily for me, didn't hit the magic spot I mentioned earlier. Battle then commenced. Despite our opponent being no more than seven stone, it degenerated into quite a melee as we fought to get him on to the ambulance without doing him any harm in the process. Heaven only knows how it must have looked to the people coming in to do their weekly shop.

Encountering people with mental-health problems was worrisome at times. Most of them, it must be said, are harmless, which is just as well, as there are plenty of them about. If you ever wondered what happened to the guy you saw walking down the road shouting at pigeons and having arguments with bus shelters, then the chances are he eventually ended up in the back of an ambulance. They were easily dealt with. The real threat came when we wandered innocently into a situation and found ourselves face to face with a dangerously unhinged individual. If it happened in the street, then we at least had room to manoeuvre; if it happened indoors, then the possibility of making a quick getaway was somewhat reduced. Such was the case when Howard and I found ourselves in the back parlour of a small terraced house in Handsworth. The patient's mother had made the call, claiming her son was unwell. She was certainly right about that, but it would have been nice if she'd mentioned that he was a violent schizophrenic who hadn't taken his medication for over a week.

She was about sixty, with a world-weariness about her that found its way into her voice.

'I'm glad you've come. It's James, my son – he's not himself. I think he needs to go to hospital to have his medication reassessed.'

Not much the wiser, we followed her through to the back room, where James was sitting on the sofa. I guessed him to be in his early thirties and he was dressed in the nondescript way of someone with little regard for his appearance. He looked up, startled, as his mother introduced us.

'There's two ambulance men come to see you, James.'

His initial frown transformed into a smile.

'Come in and sit down.' He looked at his mother. 'The ambulance service has always been good to us, hasn't it, Mum?'

'Yes, dear. They want to have a little chat with you about the noises coming from the ceiling.'

For me, this news was a bolt from the blue, and I looked to see how Howard would react. He didn't. He rarely reacted to anything, and kept his friendly gaze fixed on the young man, whose leg had begun to beat rapid time on the floor.

'It's not noises! It's people talking to me, and what they say is private! Why can't you get that into your thick head?'

She responded tentatively, playing down his outburst.

'I know it's private, dear, but these are ambulance men. I thought you might want to talk to them about the voices.'

He got to his feet and paced the room, casting her angry glares as he shouted, 'You stupid old bag! It's private! How many times have I told you that it's fucking private?'

I stood up, alarmed by this second outburst. Howard stayed in his seat, as calm as if he'd called round for afternoon tea. He waited for James to finish before speaking.

'We don't mind what we talk about, James. I usually rattle on about Aston Villa when I get half a chance.' It had the desired effect.

'Huh! They're for the drop unless they sign someone decent to strengthen the midfield.'

I sat back down while they talked football. They chatted for about five minutes, in which time James's leg stopped vibrating and the smile returned as he spoke to his mother.

'How about a cup of tea, Mum?'

His mother, perhaps lulled into a false sense of security, felt confident enough to mention his medication.

'James, don't you think it might be a good idea if you went with these nice men to hospital and got your medication sorted out?'

He was out of the chair in a flash, all Howard's good work undone.

'That's it! I've had enough!' He looked at us. 'You two bastards . . . fuck off!' Then, to his mother. 'And you, you silly old bat, you stay where you are!'

'James, love, please . . .'

With a sweep of his arm he sent all the ornaments on the mantelpiece crashing to the floor.

'Don't *love* me! Don't ever *love* me!' He moved towards her with his fists clenched. Howard appeared between them, holding up his arms.

'Wow, steady on. Let's all settle down, shall we?'

James pushed him in the chest, only to find that Howard wasn't the kind of person to be pushed aside very easily. He wasn't very tall and the weight he was carrying gave him a low centre of gravity. When James swung at him for a second time, Howard reacted by grabbing him and pinning his arms to his sides. Before I knew what I was doing, I'd joined in and caught hold of James from behind in a bear hug. At that moment Howard walked forward like a baby rhino, forcing the three of us to totter backwards and fall on to the sofa, one after the other. I was underneath and struggling to breathe, while James squirmed above me trying to fight off Howard. I could hardly believe what was happening, but knew that there was no going back. In an inspired move, I managed to bring my legs up and round his chest in a scissor lock. He writhed in an effort to dislodge me, but I clung on like a limpet until he seemed to have had enough and gave up.

Howard pulled a hankie from his pocket and wiped the sweat from his face as he eased his bulk further up James's legs. We were all breathing hard and, when I felt able, I cast H a questioning look.

'What now?'

He gave his face another wipe. 'Just hang on. He'll go again in a minute.'

I was wondering how he could be so sure, when James suddenly exploded with renewed fury. His strength was little short of amazing, and I found myself thrown around like a rodeo rider while Howard bounced up and down on James's legs like an animated medicine ball. It was a good thirty seconds before he fell quiet. Howard dabbed his face again and spoke to James's mother.

'I'm sorry about this, but you're going to have to call the police for us.'

She was horrified, and appealed to her son.

'James, baby, let go of them. We don't want the police here, do we?'

James didn't answer; he was waiting for the lactic acid to drain from his muscles before erupting again.

'Please,' Howard said. 'Just call them. There's nothing else for it.'

James was a spent force by the time the police arrived. He was handcuffed and taken to be assessed by a police psychiatrist. In case anyone should wonder, under the Mental Health Act ambulance crews have no more power than the man in the street. It takes two doctors with the aid of Social Services to have a person sectioned before removal to a place of care. Without any authority or jurisdiction, we had restrained James in an effort to protect his mother, as any private citizen might have. If his mother hadn't been there you wouldn't have seen us for dust; a tactical retreat in the hope of living to fight another day is always the preferred option.

It won't come as a surprise to hear that it's probably drunks who offer the greatest threat to our personal safety. There's no denying that they can be violent, though usually in a more predictable manner than drug-users or the mentally unstable. But not always. One drunk in particular stands out in my memory. Howard and I picked him off the street after he'd fallen from a bench and gone to sleep. He'd hurt his knee and we dutifully set off for the hospital at a modest pace, with me in the back and Howard driving. He did his best to answer the questions I put his way, although it was clear he just wanted to rest his tired eyes. We were less than half a mile from the hospital on a stretch of dual carriageway when he opened his eyes and addressed me directly.

'I've changed my mind about the hospital. I want to get off.'

It was his decision, and I looked through the window to see where we were.

'We're nearly at the hospital. You might as well wait until we get there.'

'No. I want off now.'

Howard heard the conversation from the driver's seat and shouted through, 'I can't stop now, anyway. The traffic's moving too fast. Tell him he's got to wait.'

I looked at the drunk. 'You heard what he said. You'll have to hang on for a couple of minutes.'

There was a sudden blur of movement. For a split second I thought he was going for me, but when he swept past I realized he was making for the doors. There was no time to think. I lunged at his back and by chance caught hold of his waistband just as he grasped the handle. The back doors can only be opened by releasing the left one first and, as an extra safety precaution, the handle has to be raised rather than lowered as you might expect. He got it right at the first attempt. The door swung open with him determined to go with it. I tried to pull him backwards but was horrified to discover that his hand was curled round the door frame and he was actually pulling me forwards. It's one thing heroically trying to stop someone leaping to their probable death, but quite another when you find yourself about to join them in the enterprise. Not caring if I broke all his fingers in the process, I yanked with all the strength at my command. It worked. We both fell backwards, him on top, with me desperately trying to get him in the scissor lock that had been so successful with the schizophrenic some months earlier.

During the struggle the door swung open to its full extent and locked into the restraining clips on the side of the ambulance. This gave the two women following behind in their car an unimpeded view of the unfolding struggle. What they saw must have seemed a little odd as we all sped along at forty miles an hour. They would have seen a defenceless patient thrashing about on his back, desperately trying to escape a deranged ambulance man intent on crushing him like a boa constrictor. They would have seen the ambulance man hook his arm round the leg of the stretcher and use it as an anchor as he dragged his helpless victim further into his lair. The last thing they would have seen as the ambulance turned into the hospital drive was said ambulance man giving them a cheery wave with his free hand. I probably shouldn't have waved, but I couldn't resist it once I had the moron safely under control. After all, it was the first, and probably the last, time I'd see two women sitting side by side in a car rendered speechless. No doubt they made up for it afterwards. They might still be dining out on the story to this day.

Howard parked up outside the Casualty doors. He'd been aware of the rumpus but, as it had all been over so quickly, he didn't realize how close we'd come to ending up on the road. The drunk and I were getting unsteadily to our feet as he dropped the step and looked at my rumpled state with concern.

'What the hell's this cretin been doing to you?'

'You'd better ask him for yourself,' the drunk responded. 'He's fuckin' nuts if you ask me. I'm going to report him the first chance I get.'

Howard slowly turned his gaze on him.

'What? You idiot! I wasn't speaking to you. Get out!'

The drunk obliged and began weaving his way down the drive without a backward glance. I watched him go, wondering whether to laugh or cry. Had luck not been on our side he might have done for us both. At least there was one positive: if anyone in the pub asked me if I'd saved any lives recently, for once I'd be able to answer in the affirmative.

Every so often the national press will carry a story about someone killing themselves by jumping out of a moving ambulance. I'm sure the reaction of most readers is to wonder how such a thing could be allowed to happen. Well, if they read this, they now know. The truth is that some people are just so weird it's impossible to second-guess them. Of course, alcohol can play a large part, but that can't be the whole story, otherwise there would be a few hundred people a day plunging to their deaths. It happened again many years later, though despite giving it his best shot he didn't manage to get the doors open, and we ended up rolling about on the stretcher like a couple of schoolboys until my driver pulled us apart.

Looking back on Steve's broken nose, I think it's fair to say that all his experience and guile counted for nothing in the face of an attack that came out of the blue. Only being in possession of a sixth sense would have saved him. Something similar happened to me eventually. The patient was an oddball, I'd realized that much, but at no point did it cross my mind that he might be capable of violence.

The call had been passed as 'man bleeding in the street'. He was sitting on the pavement with his feet in the gutter when we arrived. A refuse truck was parked nearby with its engine idling. The driver and his mate were out of their cab, looking at our man ruefully. Across the front of his shirt he had a bright splash of blood that seemed to have emanated from somewhere on his face. I was crewed with a lad called Neil and one of the workmen looked up as we approached.

'Hello, mate. It was me who called you.'

'So, what's happened?' I asked.

'I don't really know. We were coming down the road and saw him sitting there with blood on him. I stopped in case he needed help or something. We've been here at least ten minutes and he's hardly said a word to us. He's a strange one, if you ask me.'

I knelt next to the man and got a better look at him. I judged him to be about twenty-three and he seemed well dressed in a casual way, clean and healthy looking, although admittedly a bit on the skinny side. When I asked his name and what had happened, he chose not to answer, although it was clear that he could hear me. The blood was still dripping on to his chest and, as I angled myself to get a better look, I asked him to hold back his head. He obliged, revealing a cut under his chin no longer than half an inch. As with a cut you might get shaving, it had refused to stop bleeding, making the whole thing seem ten times worse than it really was. I folded up a piece of lint and taped it over the wound.

'How did you manage to cut yourself there?' I asked the question in a breezy kind of way, hoping he'd be more forthcoming.

He looked over at the driver. 'He did it. He hit me with that bloody great lorry when I was crossing the road.'

The driver's jaw dropped. 'That's total bollocks!' He waved an arm towards the refuse truck and looked at me. 'If I'd hit him with that you'd have to scrape him up with a shovel!' Then he turned his attention to the patient. 'I stopped to help you, you prat! More fool me.'

The young man spoke to no one in particular. 'I want him prosecuted.'

The two men glared at him for a moment, then headed for their truck. The driver leaned his head out the window.

'Tell him to watch out, because if I see him again I'll make bloody well sure that I run him over.'

With that they were gone, engulfing us in a cloud of diesel and evil-smelling rubbish fumes.

The patient sat opposite me on the ambulance, still refusing to cooperate in any way. It was odd. He looked respectable enough and there wasn't any smell of alcohol about him. He might have psychiatric problems, or maybe he was high on something. I had another go.

'Look, mate, let's try again shall we? What's your name?' He ignored the question and looked out the window. 'OK,' I said. 'Unknown male it is then.' If he wasn't going to play ball, then that was fine by me and I turned my attention to jotting down a few notes on my report form. It was then it happened. I was aware of sudden movement accompanied by an enraged shout.

'*Bastard!*'

Instinctively, I ducked, recoiled or cringed – I don't know which. Whatever I did, it saved my nose and the blow landed on the side of my forehead instead. In almost the same instant he was on me with enough momentum to topple us over the armrest of my seat and on to the floor. My position was hopeless. Crushed between the bulkhead and the seat with him on top of me, I couldn't get purchase on anything to force him off, and was kept busy anyway trying to deflect his flailing arms. It could have lasted only three or four seconds. Neil, alerted by my patient's initial shout and the subsequent scuffle, wasted no time in hitting the brakes. The ambulance had barely come to a halt when he launched himself through the communicating door and hauled my assailant off by his shoulders. He had him face down on the stretcher with his arm twisted up his back by the time I got to my feet. My head was throbbing and my back ached ominously as I opened the back doors to breathe in some cooling air and gather my thoughts.

It's often said, by me included, that the police are never there when you need them. Well, I can now put the record straight. Parked five feet behind us was a police car with its blue light revolving. They had by chance been following us along the two-lane highway when Neil made the emergency stop and switched on his own blue lights to warn other road-users that we were stationary. Both officers were out of their car, curious to see what might be going on.

'Christ. What's happened to you?' the first one said. I couldn't understand how he would know anything had happened to me, until I raised my hand and felt the swelling on my forehead. It must have been angry-looking, especially set against a face drained of colour. I don't think I said anything and he looked past me into the ambulance. Neil had adapted his restraint technique and was now sitting on the patient, looking quite relaxed about the whole thing.

Two minutes later the offender was in handcuffs and on his way to Steelhouse Lane police station. He appeared in court the following week and was convicted of assault, his defence being that he was under the influence of drugs at the time. Part of his punishment was to pay me £100 compensation. Everybody at the Street was amused at the idea, and from collective experience predicted I would receive the first £10 in fifty-pence instalments and then nothing. They were wrong. I got a cheque for the full amount within days. Either his parents, mortified at what he'd done, coughed up, or he was overcome by genuine remorse when he looked back at his actions in the cold light of day.

# Chapter Fifteen

From a distance, the tramp seemed little more than a jumble of rags in a corner of Birmingham's New Street Station. Closer inspection revealed him to be as cold as the marble floor on which he rested. A blotchy mauve smudge had formed under the skin, marking the pooling of body fluids where his cheek pressed against the unyielding surface. His half-open eyes stared unseeingly across the concourse towards the departure board, where people crowded unaware, or perhaps uninterested, that an anonymous life had come to an end. I leaned back and considered the dishevelled body. There was no point trying to resuscitate someone long gone and I said as much to Howard, who nodded in agreement. Then, as I turned away, my eyes fell on a pair of highly polished black shoes worn by one of the bystanders and a vague feeling of disquiet crept over me.

I'd first noticed them from the corner of my eye as I knelt amongst the bottles and discarded fast-food wrappers to get a closer look at the tramp. It wasn't so much the shoes, I realized, as their owner who was making me uncomfortable. I could sense his gaze and somewhere in the back of my mind I had the feeling that I knew this silent observer. He'd been standing by the body with two other men when we arrived. All three were similarly dressed in dark business suits and overcoats, reminiscent of professional mourners. I'd paid them scant regard at first, but now I allowed my gaze to drift upwards to the man himself. His rather dated dark grey suit was worn with waistcoat, pocket watch and what might have been a starched white shirt and black tie. Greying hair was immaculately combed back from a deeply lined forchead, which dominated a face of stern authority. But what gave the game away, and made my heart suddenly jump into my mouth, was that stubby grey moustache. Any doubts of his identity were dispelled. He was the city Coroner.

The last person on earth I would want to be watched by was watching me. He was my headmaster, my bank manager, my first girlfriend's father; in fact, he was every authority figure I'd ever known all rolled into one. I'd already announced my decision about the tramp, but what if the Coroner didn't agree? What if he expected me to try to revive the body? His expressionless face did nothing to dispel the feeling of self-doubt beginning to seep through my veins. A voice in my head said, 'Change your decision, go through the motions and make it look good. There's nothing to lose.' Another voice said, 'You can't bring a man back from the dead. Don't make yourself look an ass in front of the Coroner by pretending you can.' The latter won the day; the die was cast. The Coroner regarded me, well aware of the turmoil he was putting me through. After a calculated pause, and with perhaps the slightest of smiles, he spoke.

'That's OK, young man, you're right. The poor fellow is indeed quite dead.'

Even though I knew the truth of the statement, I could have hugged him.

It gave me cause for reflection, and not for the first time. We're forever in the public eye but seldom know who might be standing nearby, scrutinizing our every move. All patients are treated honestly and with equal care and attention but, when it comes down to diagnosis and sub-sequent treatment, opinions can vary and actions can be misconstrued. Sometimes, when faced with a barrage of advice and suggestions from complete strangers, we have to ignore it all and stick to our guns, knowing that a certain amount of hostility, not to mention complaints, might come our way.

There are times when it's perhaps best not to know who is watching. A few weeks earlier Howard and I had been called to a synagogue where a man had collapsed with chest pains. Waiting for us at the entrance was a smartly dressed man in his late twenties. He held out a hand in greeting and introduced himself as a doctor. Shaking hands with someone when you arrive at a job is unusual in itself, but when that someone is the very person you'd expect to be mopping the patient's fevered brow, it's perplexing to say the least. He gave a running commentary on what he knew of the patient's condition as he guided us into the building. An elderly man with a history of cardiac problems had apparently been taken ill with severe central chest pain during the service.

'They seem to think that he's had another heart attack,' said the doctor, in conclusion.

This was getting stranger.

'They seem to think? Who are they? Haven't you examined him yourself?' I abruptly stopped talking as we entered the body of the synagogue. In stark contrast to its rather bleak exterior, the interior was as imposing as it was beautiful. Unlike a church, the seats were arranged parallel with, and facing, the central aisle. Every seat was taken. The service had been stopped, leaving the congregation with little else to do but watch silently as we made our entrance.

About thirty yards away at the far end of the aisle stood the rabbi in all his finery. The hush was complete. Everybody's attention was on us and I felt as uncomfortable as I have ever done. The doctor led the way down the middle of the aisle and I spotted a couple of people standing by a man slumped in his seat just to the right of the rabbi. As we approached, I repeated my unanswered question from the corner of my mouth.

'Haven't you examined him?'

'Me? No. I wouldn't be allowed near him. He's got his cardiologist with him, a personal friend I think. He just about trusted me to come and meet you.' He continued to put me at my ease by going on to describe the congregation.

'Half the people here are doctors, consultants or one type of specialist or another.'

I felt my heart sink a little, but he wasn't finished.

'The other half is made up of lawyers, solicitors and the like.'

My heart sank a bit more; I didn't want to be here.

We reached the patient and one look was enough to see that his distress was genuine. The cardiologist spoke earnestly into my ear as I took stock of the patient. He was a distinguished-looking man of about sixty, his tie had been loosened and the perspiration from his grey face had soaked his collar. His pain was such that he sought to relieve it by hugging himself. With what I could see, and from what I was being told, there was little doubt he was having a heart attack. I must admit his condition worried me to the point where I felt he could go into cardiac arrest at any moment. 'Please, not here, keep going' was all I could think as I placed an oxygen mask over his face. We weren't equipped with defibrillators or the drugs that are available to modern-day crews; the best we could offer were oxygen, speed and reassurance. But even speed was a problem.

He was a large man by any standards and, adding to the difficulty, he was sitting in the second row about five seats from the end. He couldn't do much for himself, and it must have appeared an ungainly struggle as we slid him

along to the edge with me leaning across the pews in front
and Howard working from behind. When we eventually
manoeuvred him on to the stretcher I was in a sweat, and
not just from the exertion. Every eye in the building was
boring into the back of my head, making it feel like an
eternity before we had him safely out of the synagogue
and into the ambulance.

The hospital was only a short drive away and I was
beginning to feel a bit better about things, when the
cardiologist spoke. He named a private hospital and said,
'I've phoned them and they'll be waiting for you.'

My heart, which had just about regained its normal
position, sank back again. There was no question of going
to this private hospital, which, apart from anything else,
was about three miles further away.

'Look, I'm sorry,' I said. 'But we have to go to the
closest Casualty and there's one just a couple of minutes
away.'

His eyebrows came together. 'You don't seem to understand. They have all his medical files there. They know
him, and they're waiting for him.'

The patient's son, a big man in his mid-thirties, was
standing by the ambulance steps.

'He goes to his own hospital!'

It wasn't a request. It was an order delivered by a man
used to having the final word.

'I'm sorry, we can't go there,' I said.

'He's my father, and he goes where I say.'

I didn't like this one little bit. It was the first time I'd found myself in direct confrontation with a relative who wasn't drunk. I knew I was in the right, but it was still difficult. I had to be decisive. Speaking deliberately, and trying to exude a confidence I didn't feel, I said, 'We're taking your father to the nearest hospital because it's in his best interest.' Then, with a touch of bravado, I added, 'There's no time to discuss it; we're going now.'

The son gave me a hard stare and, perhaps admitting that the time for arguing was later, said, 'OK, let's go.'

The stand-off was over, for the moment.

Howard and I went over the merits of the case after safely dropping our patient off at hospital and concluded that the stand I'd taken had been the correct one. The man's life had clearly been in danger and passing one hospital to get to another would have been madness. He was now in safe hands and could be assessed, stabilized and then, if deemed prudent, transferred to the private hospital. But still we felt uneasy. Like it or not, when people of influence complain and demand their pound of flesh, more often than not they get it.

Such thoughts were still on my mind when, half an hour later, another patient brought us back to the same hospital. The waiting area was crowded with people from the synagogue and when it was time to leave we tried to make an unobtrusive exit. We made it unnoticed through the doors, only to walk straight into the son on his way back in after nipping out for a cigarette. He spoke as we tried to slip past.

'Excuse me!'

'Damn it, here we go.' H spoke under his breath as he turned to face what we both knew was going to be trouble. Howard decided to meet it head on. 'Look, if you're not happy with the way we   '

The man held up a hand. 'No, no. I just wanted to say thank you very much for looking after my father. You were absolutely right about coming here. He's doing fine, and the treatment he's getting is wonderful, truly top class. Thanks again.'

H blinked. 'Oh, good. I'm glad he's OK.'

The son bestowed a parting smile and turned back into the hospital. It was odd. One moment we were rehearsing our response to a complaint and the next we were being thanked. It only went to underline what I already knew: I still had a lot to learn about this job.

When it comes to being watched there can be no more pitiless spotlight than television. Medical documentaries were in their infancy in the late seventies and none, as far as I was aware, had broken the new ground of highlighting the adventurous life of an ambulance crew. When we heard that a film crew was coming to the Street with that very purpose, it was generally agreed that only an idiot would put himself forward to play the lead role. And we were proved right when Larry volunteered. It turned out to be an illuminating experience and demonstrated the wisdom of having a rather large pinch of salt to hand when watching this kind of guff. The programme was filmed at the Street a month or so before screening and was billed as a 'fly-on-the-wall' documentary portraying a day in the life of a 'typical' ambulance crew. It had been shot over an eight-hour shift and Larry was the undoubted star – a status he'd assumed with worrying ease. There was a problem, though. Despite his entire working day being compressed into twenty-five minutes, precious little of interest had happened. Hours of inactivity, interrupted by the occasional routine job, had left the producers pulling their hair out and relying heavily on the voice-over to create an atmosphere of subdued tension.

When we all settled down in front of the telly, it soon became clear that the Larry we were watching on the screen bore little resemblance to the Larry we all knew. As the programme progressed, he shifted uncomfortably in his seat. Under our accusing stares, he kept his gaze firmly fixed on the screen.

'Larry and his partner,' the voice-over breathed, 'have found time to snatch an unexpected cup of tea between emergencies.' Cut away to Larry pouring two mugs of tea. 'Larry knows to grab these rare opportunities when they present themselves; the next chance might be hours away . . .'

'Rare opportunities?' Steve shouted at the screen. 'The lazy bastard gets through at least a gallon of the stuff a day!'

Larry flicked him an irritated glance.

'If you just shut up and watch, you might pick up some tips about real ambulance work.'

Steve was twenty years senior, and the book he threw

at Larry's head missed by only a fraction. Back on the silver screen, Larry was doing his best to maintain an air of tension as he sipped his tea. Suddenly the emergency phone rang. The effect was little short of amazing. He shot from his seat like a greyhound from the trap. The camera, fighting to keep up, managed to catch his purposeful stride as he crossed the room; it even caught the keen look of anticipation as he picked up the receiver. It didn't miss the concern written over his face as he responded to the operator's words in clipped mono-syllables. Replacing the receiver, he turned to his partner.

'We've got a 999 on the other side of the city. A young girl's taken an overdose. It's a bit of a trek, so we'll have to get a move on!'

Here was a man whose only reason for being was to serve others; here was one of life's unsung heroes.

The presence of a camera begs the question: how would Larry behave if the film crew weren't there? Rather differ-ently, I fancy. The first few rings of the phone would go unanswered until someone lost patience and shouted at Larry, 'That's for you, you lazy git!'

Larry would look up from his newspaper in frustration.

'It can't be me – I've only been back five minutes from the last job!'

Once persuaded that he was indeed next out, he would resentfully heave himself from his chair, cross the room and, yanking the receiver from its cradle, bark into it, 'Yes?'

Grunts would follow as he wrote down the case, the

irritation in his voice increasing as the last bit of information was imparted. 'What? That's miles away! You can't
be serious!' After being assured that they were serious,
the phone would be slammed back down as he turned
to the room.

'Guess where they're sending us?'

Nobody would bother to guess, in the sure knowledge
that they'd be told whether they liked it or not.

The programme continued to amuse us greatly. The
highlight came when Larry was shown transporting said
teenage girl to hospital. She'd swallowed a mixture of
vitamin pills and iron supplements. Not exactly a life-
threatening concoction but, not being experts in
toxicology, we're obliged to take any overdose to
hospital. Larry, though, for the benefit of the camera, was
taking it very seriously. The patient had to remain anonymous, so as an alternative to the camera lingering on her,
we were treated to Larry's face in uncomfortable and
intimate close-up. Worry lines, which I'd never seen
before, appeared as if by magic as he leaned forward
offering fatherly advice to the teenager. She clasped his
hand in gratitude as he bestowed on her the fruits of
his accumulated wisdom on life and why it's so wonderful. The sad truth is that most city crews will, on average,
take two or three overdose cases to hospital every week.
And, virtually without exception, it's an utterly tedious
and thankless task. At best the patient will try to unburden
a mountain of emotional turmoil on your shoulders or,
and only marginally worse, will subject you to a torrent of

personal abuse for getting involved. I know it sounds a bit hard-hearted, but the people who make genuine attempts on their own life usually succeed. They are the ones who need help and, ironically, the ones who don't get it.

If Larry's artificial concern was toe-curlingly embarrassing for us to watch, then how on earth was he feeling? Steve decided to find out by quoting back a few of Larry's words in a suitably whining tone.

'You have to trust me ... We can talk through your problems if it'll make you feel better . . .' then, reverting to his own voice, 'I wouldn't "talk through" my Thursday-night shopping list with you.'

It might have been my imagination, but Larry seemed to go a delicate shade of red as he struggled to respond.

'Just because you don't know how to bond with your patients, don't—' He broke off at the sound of sirens coming from the television. The on-screen activity had gone up a gear. The ambulance sirens were now blaring, accompanied by a shot of the grimly determined driver fighting his way through the city traffic. Larry gaped at the screen for a moment, then seized the chance to divert attention away from himself by spluttering indignantly: 'We never used the sirens!' He gave us a beseeching look. 'We'd never use the sirens for someone who'd taken too many vitamin pills!'

The production team had obviously thought things needed 'spicing up' and had added sirens on to the soundtrack when the editing had been done. Now, with his own disingenuous performance conveniently pushed to one side, Larry loudly denounced the film crew for 'faking' it.

When my turn came to appear on TV a few years later, I was still naive enough to miss the point of the whole thing. They were spending the weekend at our station while other cameras were situated at fire and police stations. The idea was to combine all the film to portray a typical weekend for the emergency services. Much of their transmission went out live in fifteen-minute segments, intermingled with pre-recorded material. Being filmed at work was not a prospect any of us relished, and the objective of every crew was to keep as far away from the cameras as possible. Paul, my crew mate at the time, and I managed to evade them until mid-morning when the phone rang on station. We were the next crew out and I picked up the receiver with a resigned sigh, uncomfortably aware of the sound boom hovering over my head like a dead rat and the shoulder-held camera to my left panning in. I could feel myself reddening and prayed the case would prove to be innocuous and of no interest to the producer. My prayer was answered. A doctor had visited a three-week-old baby at home and decided that the infant was in danger of becoming dehydrated and needed to go into hospital to be monitored. My grip on the receiver relaxed. I couldn't have dreamt up a more boring job. Putting down the phone, I turned to the film crew with a shrug and an apologetic smile.

'Sorry, it's not a 999 – only a baby that needs to go in for some routine treatment.'

The producer's eyes widened.

'A baby! It's a 999 now!'

We were filmed 'rushing' the baby to hospital while the team carefully avoided showing that the blue lights were switched off and the child spent the journey fast asleep in her carrycot. Instead, lingering close-ups of the anxious mother were interspersed with equally anxious looks from me. I never did figure out how they managed that, because all I was concerned about was whether I'd remembered to comb my hair or not. It was a different matter for anyone watching though; it was a life-or-death event and open to no other interpretation. I don't deny that the baby needed urgent treatment, but it certainly wasn't an emergency in my understanding of the word. To add insult to injury, the viewers were left with the earnest promise that regular updates of the baby's progress would be broadcast at intervals throughout the programme. In this the production team were true to their word, and even finished the evening with the grateful mother giving an emotional thanks to everyone who had helped 'save' her child, including the ambulance crew. She didn't know what she would have done without us.

'Gone by taxi, perhaps?' was the caustic remark made by someone behind me as we watched it later on TV.

Of course, I'd no idea at the time that the case would later be inflated way beyond its importance. In fact, after dropping mother and child at the Children's Hospital, I found myself apologizing to the producer for the rather dull day he'd had so far. He, in possession of the bigger picture, was quick to assure me that things were turning out just fine. While we talked, another case came over the radio. It originated from the police and the information given was that an elderly lady had been scalded. I asked if the crew was going to tag along. The producer thought about it.

'Old woman scalded? Er . . . no. I think we'll give it a miss. We need to change some equipment back on station anyway. We'll pick up another crew there.' With that they all bundled into their support car and headed back to the Street. I watched them go as Paul looked up the address in the A–Z. Their lack of interest was surprising, but I can't deny that it was a relief to see the back of them.

We arrived at the tower block and headed up to the third floor. The door to the flat was open and, getting no response to our shouted hellos, we made our way down the hall to the lounge. A dowdy, middle-aged woman with greying hair pulled into a severe ponytail was backed into the far corner of the room. She didn't look at us, but kept her gaze locked on an elderly woman slumped in a wheelchair a few feet away. The woman's chin was resting on her chest, leaving the top of her head in clear view. Her thinning hair was wet and matted, but it didn't hide the multitude of angry red blisters covering her scalp and neck. Her arms were also lobster red and ravaged by burgeoning blisters. I flinched at the sight. Despite being forewarned that someone had been scalded, I wasn't prepared for such appalling injuries. It was made worse by the knowledge that for someone of her age, her injuries were life-threatening. I looked round for some explanation of how she'd come to be scalded, but all I could see was a normal living room. Had there been an accident in the kitchen? The bathroom? While I mechanically broke the seals on the sterile burns sheets, I spoke to the grey-haired lady in as calm a voice as I could muster.

'How did this happen?'

She didn't answer. Instead, the patient raised her head to reveal a face every bit as disfigured as her arms and neck. She pointed confidently at the other woman and spoke in a steady voice.

'It was her – she did it.'

It's a rather unnerving fact, but people suffering even as much as 90 per cent burns can remain lucid and communicative for the short while before clinical shock sets in. She carried on talking as Paul and I began easing off her upper clothing in preparation for wrapping her in the sterile sheets.

'I've given her my whole life and she repays me by doing this.'

'I'm sorry, Mum . . . I didn't mean to.'

'What did she do?' I asked as I pulled away her cardigan.

The old woman looked up at me. 'She threw boiling water over me. I couldn't stop her . . . I'm helpless in this damn chair, and she knows it.'

Her daughter's voice came back weak and pleading. 'I didn't know what I was doing. I've looked after you these past twenty years since Dad died, haven't I? I've done my best. But still nothing I ever do is good enough. You complain about everything. I just couldn't listen to you going on any more.'

The two women's voices were rising in competition in a way that suggested it was a well-practised ritual. Through accusations and counter-accusations, a picture emerged. The daughter had put the kettle on for a cup of tea and while it boiled her mother harangued her from the other room. She listened to the criticisms and complaints until something inside her took over. She picked up the boiling kettle, walked over to her mother, and poured its contents over her head.

It was only later that I had a chance to dwell on the sad culmination of a long and troubled mother–daughter relationship. Our priority now was to get the woman to Birmingham's Accident Hospital, which was home to one of the country's leading burns units. Despite having instigated the call to Ambulance Control, the police had yet to make an appearance, which meant that we had little choice but to take the daughter with us. I wasn't troubled by the prospect. Whatever demons had been unleashed earlier were now back in their bottle, and it was better she remained under our watchful eyes.

When we were ready to leave she suddenly turned into one of the bedrooms. Frustrated at the delay, I called after her.

'What are you doing? We have to go!'

'She'll need her coat and scarf. It might be chilly when we come back.'

I was lost for words. She had no understanding of the seriousness, or the consequences, of her actions. It wasn't a case of denial; she was in shock, the like of which I'd never seen before.

'That's fine,' I said. 'Fetch her coat, but be quick – we've got to get your mum to hospital.'

The police arrived as we were putting the old lady on to the ambulance and after a quick word with us they arrested the daughter. She was bewildered, protesting as they steered her towards their car.

'But she can't go to hospital on her own. She needs me to be with her.'

The officer made no comment and, in true police style, protected her head with the palm of his hand as he coaxed her into the back seat.

I was never to learn the ultimate fate of either woman, in large part because I made no effort to do so. The whole episode was deeply unsettling and I had no desire to follow the macabre trail any further than necessary. People outside the service often ask how we deal with the 'bad sights' we come across. They expect a practised reply, and seldom have the patience to listen when I try to explain that it's rarely the bad sights that have a lasting effect. It's the emotional legacy gained from dipping into other people's tragedies that's hard to shake off.

I wasn't thinking along such lines when we got back to the Street. All I wanted was a cup of tea and the chance to relax behind a newspaper. It wasn't to be. The film crew were still hanging about and the producer wandered over and asked about the case he'd declined to cover. He was an amiable chap, in an English kind of way, and listened intently with beetled brows as I recounted the story. When I finished he leaned back and shook his head.

'My goodness, that's just awful. Really awful. The things that go on behind closed doors are enough to take your breath away.'

Oddly, to my mind, he showed no regret that he and his crew had missed out on an incident that might have had his viewers sitting up in their seats. I put the point to him and waited as he sucked in air through the gap between his front teeth.

'Well, the truth is . . . even if we'd been there we wouldn't have used it in the show.'

'I know you couldn't have filmed her or her injuries,' I interjected, 'but surely the incident itself was worth recording as an example of what, as you say, goes on behind closed doors?'

'I'm afraid not.' He illustrated his point by counting off on his fingers the different aspects of the case. 'Let's see, we have family conflict, which develops into drama, which then turns violent and ultimately tragic. Other than sex, it's got everything that soap operas get away with every night of the week. But we're filming real life here and we have to protect our audience by being very careful about what we show and don't show.'

'But your audience will go away with the impression that they've just witnessed a typical day for the emergency services in Birmingham, when that plainly isn't true,' I said.

He smiled. 'I can't argue with that. But you're forgetting that we're going out before the nine o'clock watershed. That means it's babies and kittens for us, I'm afraid.'

# Chapter Sixteen

Otto leaned across the table and told me in heavily accented English why he'd called for an ambulance.

'Vot I vont – is for you to shoot me!'

I groaned and made no attempt to hide my irritation.

'For God's sake! This is the second time you've called us out today . . .'

Otto's eyes narrowed. 'Swine! Take out your gun unt shoot me!'

'We don't carry guns, you daft bugger!' I shouted back.

'Liar! I am thinking zat you do have zem. Zey carry gunss in zi Fatherland!'

'No, they bloody well don't! And don't start on about the Fatherland. You've never been near Germany in your life, and you can stop talking in that stupid accent!' I finished with a long, menacing stare that I hoped would shut him up.

It didn't. Jumping to his feet, he clicked his heels

violently together and barked out, 'You have your orders! Now – shoot me!'

My patience was all but spent.

'You're a bloody idiot! We're leaving now. Don't dare call us again!'

With that, Larry and I turned for the door, but Otto was too old a hand at this game to let us get away so easily.

'I have taken an overdose of zee Paracetamol.'

His statement had the desired effect. We turned back into the room. Gritting your teeth isn't something you're taught in training school; it's something you learn to do all by yourself within a month of joining the service.

'Show me the bottles.'

'Ze pillsss ver in packets, not bottles.'

'OK. Show me the bloody packets then!'

'Zey are long gone. I threw zem all avay.'

Larry, who so far had resisted the temptation to join in the conversation, leaned forward and pushed his nose within two inches of Otto's.

'You win this time, Otto. We'll take you to hospital. But be warned, when the day comes that they do just give us guns, I will come round here and take great pleasure in shooting you on the spot!'

Otto, or to use his real name, Eddie Dawes, was beyond redemption. It took only a few cans of strong lager to turn him from an introverted oddball into a barking eccentric who liked nothing better than to take on the persona of a Third Reich officer. After heavy drinking sessions, he'd take his obsession on to the street and entertain the neighbours by goose-stepping back and forth, bellowing out *'Deutschland über Alles'* at the top of his voice until the police turned up. I don't quite know why, but when the mood took him he even lured fire engines to his council Reichstag. For him, though, the emergency service of choice – and I don't mean to sound smug about it – was the ambulance service. We were his passport to Valhalla, or, as most people would call it, the local Casualty department. A place he liked to visit at least five times a week.

Eddie was a 'regular'; one of a small but determined band of people who make it their business persistently to harass the emergency services. Like all the regulars we had to contend with, Eddie was well acquainted with the system and could manipulate it effortlessly. Claiming to have taken an overdose is always a winner, as there's no way we can disprove it.

Some of these characters are alcoholics, and some are the hapless victims of the 'care in the community' scheme, suffering from an array of personality disorders ranging from psychosis to schizophrenia. Some, though, are simply lonely, inadequate people adrift in a world that doesn't seem to notice them, or, if it does, isn't inclined to admit it. Perhaps they're so anonymous, even to themselves, that the only way to confirm their existence is by seeking attention from those who are duty-bound to give it. Ambulance crews, nurses and doctors, for example, not to mention the clergy. For our part, we have no choice but to take them obediently to hospital, knowing full well they'll be booted straight back on to the street as soon as decorum permits. And our reward? A glare from the triage nurse that would stop a charging rhino in its tracks.

I was unaware that such a band of brothers existed when I started on the shift. Not that that happy state lasted long. Dave Harper was the first I remember clearly. He was a scruffy, smelly individual with a personality perhaps even more odious than his appearance. I was in the messroom when I first heard his name. Mike had come back from a job and, after throwing his coat on a chair, addressed the room in general.

'What do you want first – the good news, or the bad news?'

'Go on then, if you must,' Steve said. 'Start with the bad.'

'Dave Harper's back in town.'

The name meant nothing to me, but the hostility it inspired in the others made me prick up my ears.

'Are you sure? April's hardly started,' Larry spluttered. 'He never turns up in Birmingham before late spring!'

'Oh, I'm sure all right,' Mike said wearily. 'I've just dropped the little bastard off at the General.'

Dave Harper spent the summer months on the streets of Birmingham, heading south only when the first hint of autumn chilled the air. With the unerring instinct of a migrating wildebeest, spring would see him head north again, arriving shortly after the first cuckoo. The news of his early arrival got Larry thinking.

'Maybe it means we're in for a good summer.'

'Could be,' Steve said. 'It certainly means it's going to be a long one. So what's the good news, Mike?'

'I think he had a bath when he was down in Cornwall.'

Dave Harper never strayed far from the city centre and entertained himself by getting involved in low-key mischief whenever he saw the chance. When bored, which seemed to be quite often, he would create a scene in a shop, café or some other public place. There would always be a big kerfuffle that would inevitably involve the police, but he'd seldom be arrested, as the last person any clued-up policeman wanted in the back of his car was Dave Harper. When he fancied a trip in an ambulance he had two ways of achieving it: getting beaten up, or lying down in the street and pretending to be dead. And, I must say, he was very good at playing dead. So good, in fact, that members of the public would sometimes do all they could to revive him while waiting for us to arrive. If this meant performing mouth-to-mouth – then so be it. We would pull up in due course and rush forward to take over, only to be stopped in our tracks when it was clear who the patient was. Aware of our presence, Dave would move into phase two of the performance by shrugging off the helpers and then turning on them: 'Get your hands off me, you bastards!' And then to us, as if we were old mates, 'Hello, lads. I was having a kip when these stupid fuckers all jumped on me!'

You can imagine the reaction of the would-be

life-savers as they came to terms with being conned into exchanging bodily fluids with a tramp.

Taking a beating never seemed to bother Dave, which was fortunate because he took an awful lot of them. It was rare to see him without his trademark black eye or thick lip, and it wasn't difficult to understand why some people were overcome by the urge to whack him. His habit was to shout abuse at strangers. A bald head, a fat belly, a big nose – it didn't take much to set him off. I suppose most people saw him as a 'street nutter' and walked on by. But the law of averages demanded that every now and again someone would turn round and flatten him.

The worst of his vitriol was reserved for the ethnic minorities. Whenever the opportunity presented itself, he would let forth a stream of racial taunts. These opportunities presented themselves quite often in a place like Birmingham. The memory of such an incident, which still has the power to send a shudder through me, was born in the city's main social security office.

As was his wont, Dave had picked up his money before making himself comfortable in a corner and quietly 'dying'. We were led through by an elderly commissionaire keen to tell us how he'd successfully resuscitated the 'patient' by vigorously rubbing his arms. Mike somehow kept a straight face.

'Good for you! Where did you do your first-aid training?'

'Well, I did a St John's course a few years—'

Mike broke in sharply when he recognized Dave lying serenely on the floor.

'Shit! It's you again! Get up, Harper, you stupid man!' This novel approach to patient care left the commission-aire and quite a few others in the room looking at him in wonder. To Dave, though, it was the friendly voice of an old acquaintance and he sat up with a little smile. The smile turned to a frown as he took in the bemused stares from those around him.

'What are all you bastards looking at?'

Mike walked over and pulled him to his feet.

'I don't want to hear another word out of you, Harper.'

But Dave had spotted two West Indian men sitting opposite and let loose the vilest stream of racial slurs I've ever had the misfortune to hear. I don't know if he was labouring under the illusion that we offered him some kind of protection, but he continued until Mike clamped his hand hard over his mouth and forced his arm up his back.

Meanwhile, the two West Indians, both tall, powerfully built men in their late twenties, were on their feet and advancing in a disturbing manner. To make matters worse, I was between them and their quarry with no obvious means of escape. The fury in their eyes was unmistakable, leaving me in no doubt that something really ugly was going to happen. I panicked and shouted out the first things that came into my head, jabbing my index finger against my temple.

'I'm sorry! He's a nutter! He's mad! He's escaped from an institution! We've been hunting for him all day. The police are waiting for him outside. They're going to take him back to the loony-bin and throw away the key!'

To my amazement, it worked. They halted, and stood clenching and unclenching their fists while considering their next move. The tension in the air slowly subsided, and when they settled for verbally venting their rage on me, as if I'd somehow been aiding and abetting, I was delighted, savouring each syllable in the grateful knowledge that the moment was over.

While I was receiving my verbal ear-bashing, Mike was dancing Dave from the room. I say dancing, because Mike's favourite way of persuading someone to go where they didn't want to go was to grab their waistband from behind and yank every spare inch of trouser material hard up between their buttocks. He would carry on pulling until the victim was forced on to tiptoes and then, using his spare hand, he would propel the hapless man swiftly forward by the scruff of the neck. The effect was to throw the victim off balance and leave him looking as if he were running in zero gravity – a kind of precursor to Michael Jackson's moon walk. It's a remarkably effective technique, and Dave Harper found himself on the receiving end more times than he probably cares to remember. For the life of me, I can't think why it's not taught in training school.

Murder was in my heart when I eventually made it back on to the street looking for Dave. I don't really know what I'd have done or said to him, but it was probably just as well that Mike had already sent him packing. I can't say that my temper had mellowed a great deal when we came across him a couple of days later playing dead in Lewis's food hall. Luckily for him, I couldn't vent my true feelings, as he was surrounded by a crowd of concerned shoppers. People just don't understand it when you bawl out a patient who, as far as they are concerned, was trembling on the edge of oblivion only moments earlier. He actually had me wishing for an early winter, when the Cornwall Ambulance Service would once again have the pleasure of his company.

Dave wasn't a one-off. He had contemporaries equally adept at raising the blood pressure of the calmest ambulance crews. One of them, and someone also destined to haunt us for years, was Tony Franklin, a reptilian character who I'm sure would have been capable of making Mother Teresa's skin crawl given half a chance. A one-trick pony, perhaps, but he had that trick honed to something little short of an art form.

His speciality was the pseudo fit – a tried and trusted ruse used by a legion of regulars over the years. As the title suggests, it's when someone pretends to be having an epileptic fit in the hope of attracting a crowd, and ultimately an ambulance. The performance needn't even be particularly proficient, as it doesn't take much to fool your average layman. Of the people playing this game, Tony was the best I ever came across. He could fool just about anybody, even out-of-town ambulance crews. Over a period of years he turned up all over the city with monotonous regularity and in the end we all became heartily sick of the sight of him. One evening he fooled a gaggle of nurses in a city night club.

The majority of dancers were oblivious to our presence as the doorman led us through the melee to a group of girls bending over a man's body on the dance floor. It was impossible to make myself heard over the thumping music, so I tapped one of the girls on the shoulder to gain her attention. She looked up in relief and started talking excitedly, gesticulating towards the man at her feet. I couldn't hear a word and pointed at my ears while shaking my head. She cupped her hands and shouted into my ear.

'I'm a nurse. This lad's had a fit and then went into respiratory arrest. We managed to get him back!'

I found it improbable but, on the other hand, drug abuse can sometimes affect the respiratory system, so with this in mind I knelt by the patient and reached for his pulse. It was then that I recognized Tony. We'd been spared the part of the act where he foamed at the mouth and thrashed about on the floor, but we were in time for the final moments of the second act, which involved him holding his breath for an inordinate length of time while gently wetting himself. I think wetting his pants was his masterstroke. Any doubtful member of the public seeing this believed it to be proof of just how serious his condition was. I mean, what normal person would do a thing like that?

So there he lay, eyes tightly shut, striving to mimic death while the mucus smeared across his face writhed rhythmically under the ever-changing colours of the disco lights. He'd probably judged that it was about time for the ambulance to arrive and was gearing himself up for a grand exit on our stretcher. I didn't want him to get his way, so with a sigh of resignation I leaned over and gave him a rough shake.

'Come on, Tony, wake up. The show's over!'

This had no effect. He had his audience to think of, after all. Steve knelt down opposite me and together we tried to sit him up, but his body became rigid. The harder we tried, the greater the resistance we met, until it was like trying to bend a plank of wood. Tony knew that we knew that it was all a sham, but he wasn't going to admit to it with so many people watching. Steve then attempted to open one of his eyes with his thumb, but Tony clamped them shut so tightly that his face took on a ghastly grimace. There was nothing else for it; we were going to have to give him exactly what he wanted and load him on to our stretcher.

There are plenty of ways to 'wake' somebody who doesn't want to be woken, but in such a public place our actions could well be misconstrued and were better left until we got on the ambulance. As it happened, our actions had already been misconstrued. Behind me the group of nurses was becoming agitated, and one began angrily tugging at my sleeve.

'You don't seem bothered!' she yelled over the noise. 'Don't you realize he almost died? We brought him back!'

'He's play-acting,' I shouted back.

'Play-acting? He went into respiratory arrest!' In case I didn't understand what she meant by that, she spelled it out. 'He stopped breathing! We've been taking turns giving him mouth-to-mouth.'

I didn't know whether to laugh or cry. The thought of these pretty young girls queuing up to press their lips against Tony's drooling mouth didn't bear thinking about. And as for him, he must have thought that it was his birthday and Christmas rolled into one. Shaking my head, I tried to explain.

'Look, I know him – he's a regular. He does this all the time. Believe me, there's nothing wrong with him.'

'I'm going to report you!' she yelled.

'Fine, you do that,' I shouted back.

Her reaction was understandable. She wasn't to know that Tony had been on our ambulance at least twenty times in the past under very similar circumstances.

Things had worked out better than Tony could have hoped for. When he eventually heard the ambulance doors shut behind him, he decided to quit while he was ahead and before we got to work on him.

'What's happened?' he asked, as his eyes flickered open.

I didn't bother counting to ten.

'Oh come on, Tony, give it a rest. You've won, so don't push your luck. Now sit up properly.'

He complied listlessly and sat rubbing his eyes.

'Well?' I asked. 'What rubbish have you got to tell me this time?'

'You shouldn't speak to me like that.' His face screwed up unpleasantly and a few tears joined the mucus still clinging to the corners of his mouth. Weeping was another effective strategy. As I say, he really was very good. 'I don't know what you want me to say,' he continued. 'I can't think, my mind's a blank. Which hospital are you taking me to?'

'Dudley Road.'

The tears stopped and a look of concern passed over his face.

'Sister Howells isn't on duty tonight, is she?'

'Sister Howells? I thought your mind was a blank.'

'Some things are coming back,' he said feebly.

Much to my regret, Sister Howells had retired a month earlier. She'd been a formidable woman who ruled Casualty with a fist of iron. And, more to the point, she didn't have a moment's patience for the likes of Tony. It was with some reluctance that I passed on the news of her retirement and then had to watch as his face took on a look of relief, which gently grew into a nasty little smile.

While most regulars stick to tried and tested routines, some develop a more varied and dangerous repertoire. One of the more cavalier amongst them was Matt Fellows, a heftily built man in his forties. His speciality was to lie down in the gutter and pretend to be the victim of a hit-and-run accident. There was, of course, never any evidence of physical injury, but he'd honed the technique of appearing to be deeply unconscious to the point where even experienced crews were left in a quandary. Our best efforts to 'wake him up' would usually fail (and there aren't many people who can resist our best efforts), leaving us to consider the possibility that maybe, just maybe, this time it might be genuine. This would mean having to spend time trussing him up like a chicken in case of any hidden injuries to his back or neck before taking him to hospital. An hour later he'd be sitting on the wall outside Casualty with a coffee in one hand and a fag in the other, chatting to some other reprobate.

Once, in what was an act of pure frustration, the attending crew decided it was necessary to expose his arms and legs to check for injuries. Taking a pair of scissors, they cut both his trouser legs from hem to crotch. Finding nothing wrong, they cut up the arms of his jacket; again they found nothing untoward and felt he was at last safe to be moved. He was later seen walking home from the hospital with his shredded clothes flapping in the breeze.

Any hope that this may have acted as a deterrent proved groundless. He continued his bizarre pastime until the inevitable happened. One evening Matt lay down in the road, made himself comfortable and waited for a passer-by to call an ambulance. No one knows how long he lay there, but it probably wasn't long before the articulated lorry came along. In the darkness the driver failed to notice him and Matt finally met his Waterloo in the manner of his own choosing. The driver was convicted of causing death by careless driving, or something similar. The dreadful injustice is that the court probably knew nothing of Matt's peculiar habits. We only found out about the prosecution weeks later, otherwise a delegation from the Street would have been sent to plead the poor man's case.

And then there was Roger Aston, who, unlike Matt, was not content with feigning injury. He went out and actively pursued the real thing. I first came across him when he'd fallen down a flight of stairs and broken his wrist. I took him to hospital and thought no more of it. Two weeks later I found myself splinting his broken leg after he'd been 'clipped' by a car. I remember feeling sorry for him because the plaster was still on his arm and he was obviously going to find life difficult over the next few weeks. It dawned on me as time passed just how often we saw him in and around hospitals, sporting a plaster cast on one limb or another. His name gradually became known amongst the ambulance crews, and even though it never occurred to us that his 'accidents' were anything but accidents, we started to regard him as a pest.

In the early days he was forgiven, as he had a sunny disposition and most of what happened to him seemed to be nothing more than bad luck. As time passed, though, suspicions grew that these mishaps were not accidents, but that he was intentionally putting himself in harm's way with a calculated recklessness. As he became older, he occasionally diversified from broken bones into other areas, such as mysteriously picking up various medical conditions like asthma, multiple sclerosis and epilepsy.

His mock asthma attacks were reasonably effective on the public, but he never really became master of the pseudo fit, usually keeping it in reserve if nothing else worked. Always he returned to his first love, which after all was what he did best, and that was breaking bones. This went on for years and gradually, due to the persistent damage he inflicted on himself, he became partially disabled. He could still walk without needing any assistance, but some department of the hospital one day presented him with a wheelchair. Crafty as ever, Roger realized its potential and quickly began exploiting the benefits it had to offer. It was good for gaining attention, very good for getting sympathy, and excellent for falling out of, hopefully breaking something in the process.

If he had stuck to his wheelchair he would still be plaguing ambulance crews to this day, but old habits die hard and he couldn't resist one more brush with a car. I didn't attend his swan song, but the general feeling was that he simply couldn't move quickly enough and what should have been a glancing blow proved to be anything but. Like an ageing matador in the bullring, his trained reflexes let him down. It was perhaps only by a split second, but it was a rather important split second and, with his mortal coil shrugged off, he went swiftly to that great hospital in the sky.

It's strange, and inexplicable, but there never seems to be more than half a dozen of these characters around at any one time. It's as if it's an exclusive club that admits a new face only when one of the existing members cashes in his chips. And there's always someone waiting to join. The result is that the fraternity is a perpetual and highly irritating presence on the streets of Birmingham. We sometimes feel sorry for them, and on rare occasions almost sympathetic to their plight. These emotions are only ever fleeting, however, as our tolerance and forbearance is tested to the limit time after time. Members of the public, not realizing quite what we're dealing with – like the nurses in the night club – can find our attitude towards these reprobates brusque, if not downright rude.

I will leave the last word with Paul Rickards, an old man who made my skin crawl. In appearance there was nothing extraordinary about him. He was about seventy-five, below average height, reasonably well kempt and, if caught at the right angle, possessor of a not unpleasant face. It was when he opened his mouth that you quickly discovered he had a mind like a cesspit, a mouth like a sewer and a moral code King Herod would have found disturbing. He'd been in and out of prison throughout his life and found the advancing years no reason to curtail his dishonest lifestyle, being evicted from one sheltered housing complex for pilfering from residents' rooms while they played bingo. He'd been booted out of another for what would nowadays be called 'inappropriate touch-ing' – or, as he would put it, 'grabbing a handful of tit'. When you consider that the 'handful of tit' might belong to a ninety-year-old woman, then it will give you some measure of the man.

He went everywhere in a wheelchair. I don't quite know why, because he was as fit as a flea and fooled nobody. Despite being read the riot act time and time again, he had no compunction in denying an ambulance to someone who might be in genuine need just to meet his own selfish ends. He was forever calling us out for the most spurious reasons. And why? To get a free cup of tea from the Women's Royal Voluntary Service (WRVS) at the hospital. The good ladies who gave up their time to provide snacks and drinks saw him as a charming and vulnerable elderly gentleman, little realizing they were the only women in Birmingham he was careful not to insult. Our frustration can be imagined when we watched him munch biscuits and sip tea under their fond care. It might be wondered why we didn't simply refuse to take him. Well, it was tried, but it proved difficult to explain to the members of the public who were clustered around why we were refusing to convey a helpless old man in a wheelchair complaining of chest pain.

If I'd been paranoid, and I have a sneaking feeling that's the way I was becoming, it would have been easy to imagine that everything he did was designed to make life difficult for us. For example, when he fancied spending a couple of hours with the WRVS ladies he'd whistle up an ambulance without a qualm. But, and here's the rub, simply abusing the service wasn't enough for him: he always chose to 'collapse' in the most awkward place he could think of. Upstairs on a bus was one of his favourites. One such occasion lingers in my memory, as I nearly landed myself in hot water with a hospital administrator.

The bus had been emptied of its passengers, allowing me a clear view down the aisle as I stepped on board. And there it was – Paul's distinctive wheelchair, plastered in Aston Villa stickers, neatly stowed in the luggage recess. I let out a groan of recognition and looked at the driver. His reaction suggested that he'd run into Paul before.

'The silly old sod's upstairs with one of our inspectors. Good luck.'

We made our way wearily upstairs to find him slumped across one of the bench seats with the inspector standing over him taking notes in his little black book. He snapped it shut when he saw us and pulled me aside.

'I'm glad you're here. The poor old boy's got chest pain. If you ask me, he's having a heart attack.'

I hadn't intended to ask him, and rather than replying I turned my attention to 'the poor old boy'. His face was twisted into something between a gurn and a grimace that was as horrible as it was unconvincing. Valiantly, he managed a few words.

'The man might be right. I might be having a heart attack.'

This left us with little choice but to carry him back down the spiral stairs while he shouted warnings and instructions with every step.

My partner had barely closed the ambulance doors when Paul took the initiative.

'So where have you been? I could have died ten times

over in the time it took you to get here! That bloke from the bus company was a right pain in the arse.'

I ignored him.

'If you don't mind me saying so, you don't sound much like a man in distress. How's the chest pain now?'

'It's gone off, no thanks to you.'

'It's funny how that always seems to happen once you're on the way to hospital,' I said as I started work on the report form. 'Now, what's your name? No, don't tell me – I think I know it. Paul Rickards, isn't it?'

He scowled at me. 'You think you're so clever, don't you? You sarcastic bleeder. It's about time you showed some respect for your elders and betters.'

'Betters!' I spluttered. 'You're a disgrace. Someone out there could be having a real heart attack and end up dying because we're wasting our time with you! Have you ever thought about that?'

'Why should I? It's not my fault if the government don't put enough ambulances on the road, is it?'

The conversation continued along similar lines until we reached our destination.

I should have known better, but there are times when you can't help yourself, and hostilities were still in full flow as I wheeled him through the hospital doors.

'I'm warning you,' I said, without caring who over-heard, 'show a bit of respect to the nurses and keep your trap shut, or I'll take pleasure in personally kicking you back out on to the street. Am I making myself clear?'

His reply was typical. 'Get stuffed!'

It was then that I noticed the administrator standing close to the triage desk. He was holding a clipboard and watching me curiously. He scribbled some notes as we approached and then looked with concern at Paul.

'Is everything OK, sir? Is there some kind of problem?'

Paul jerked a thumb towards me. 'You should teach these kids to show a bit of respect. I don't expect to be spoken to like that at my age.'

The administrator nodded in agreement. 'Quite. May I suggest that you—'

Paul's attention was diverted by the sight of an amply proportioned nurse leaving one of the cubicles and heading off down the corridor. His face creased into a trademark leer as he stared after her and let out a low whistle.

'Would you just look at the arse on that!'

The administrator's Adam's apple bobbed as he followed Paul's gaze.

'Really, sir, I don't think you should—'

Paul ignored him and continued in a voice loud enough to be heard twenty feet away.

'Man, that's what I call a fucking arse!' He was almost slavering. 'Look at those buttocks! You could feed a family of four on just one of 'em. I tell you what, mate,' he looked up at the vacant, silly face staring down at him and winked, 'you're a lucky bastard working in a place like this.'

Visibly shocked, and obviously not a man used to confrontation, the administrator turned on his heel and was gone. I was delighted, and had to overcome an urge to hug Paul. The chances of the chinless wonder writing a report describing my outburst were a good deal more remote than they had been a minute earlier.

# Chapter Seventeen

'Return to station . . . and have a cup of tea.'

Howard's eyebrows narrowed as he stared suspiciously at the radio.

'Were they talking to us?'

I stopped chewing on my sandwich and considered it.

'They must have been. It was our call sign – who else could they be talking to?'

Howard was still wary.

'Have a cup of tea? What's that all about?'

'It could be they're sending us back because the police want to interview us. They're bound to want a statement after that last job. But I don't get the cup of tea bit.'

Howard thought about it.

'No, the police don't move that fast. You know what I think? I think they might be giving us a stress break.'

'A what?'

'A stress break. Someone told me that firemen get them when they come back off a nasty job. Their control simply marks them down as being unavailable for an hour.'

'Really? Sounds like a good idea to me.'

Howard continued in a less optimistic tone. 'Of course, it might just be that they've got a long-distance job lined up for us.'

'Well,' I said, 'let's hope that it's one of these stress breaks and, if it is, I'm not going to look a gift horse in the mouth.' I put the ambulance into gear and pulled out into the traffic as Howard rummaged through his bag for the newspaper.

As I headed back to station to enjoy what would indeed prove to be our first ever stress break, I mulled over the case we'd just attended. It certainly had been a nasty one by any standard. A young man had hidden himself in the bushes by a railway track and jumped out in front of the first train to come along. He was killed instantly, and messily. But it wasn't the gruesome aspect of the job that preoccupied me; what I found intriguing was Ambulance Control's apparent concern for our sensibilities. Was it a new policy dreamt up in a management meeting after someone had read an article in an American medical journal? And if they thought we needed time to recuperate, just how did they think we would spend it? If they imagined we'd throw our arms round each other and 'talk through' our feelings, they couldn't be more wrong. The truth was that we would probably put our feet up and be dozing within five minutes of getting back. Were we strange? Were we callous and indifferent? In search of some kind of answer, I reconsidered the suicide in an attempt to analyse why we had apparently remained unaffected by it.

We had been about a hundred yards from the closest access point to the railway line when Howard leaned over the brick wall and looked at the scene in the cutting below. A yellow-coated railway worker was standing near the body. H shouted down at him.

'Is he dead?'

'What the fuck do you think? He's been hit by a train doing sixty miles an hour!' There was a definite note of irritation in his voice.

If H was affronted, he didn't let it show as he shouted back, 'I was only wondering.'

The truth was that if the victim was dead then our involvement was more or less over before it started. If, on the other hand, the victim was still clinging to life, we had to ready ourselves for an intricate and harrowing rescue.

With his first question answered, H asked another. 'Is the power off?' This was something we had to make sure of. Apart from being fried, our insurance would be rendered void.

'Of course the power's off! Do you think I'd be fucking standing here if it wasn't?'

'OK, keep your hair on,' H responded. 'We'll be right down.' The niceties over, we made our way down to the track and silently trudged towards the body. As we got near, I had to step over a partially unfurled turban lying between the rails. A glance at the victim left me in no doubt that it belonged to him. The long, shiny black hair the turban normally secured had cascaded loose over his shoulders. A perfunctory glance was enough to confirm that he was dead; his chin was resting on his backbone. Our work was done. It was now up to the Railway Police to arrange for the removal of the body. Once back in the cab I reached into my hold-all for a sandwich and idly watched Howard fill in the patient report form.

He wrote down a résumé of his findings in his usual meticulous way and finished by describing the victim as 'an unknown white male in his mid-twenties'. I was mystified.

'Why have you written that?' I asked through a mouthful of cheese sandwich.

'Written what?'

'You've called him white. He was a Sikh.'

'No he wasn't.'

'Of course he was. Surely the turban gave it away?'

'What turban?'

'What turban? The one lying beside him. The one we had to step over to get to him.'

'I didn't see a turban. He was white.'

We were going in circles and, exasperated, I said, 'I'm telling you, he was Asian. Why would I lie? If you don't believe me, go and take another look.'

He returned a few minutes later and, after screwing up the report form he'd so carefully written, mumbled, 'I can't understand it. I was sure he was white.'

At the time I put it down to Howard being uncharacteristically unobservant. Now, as I reconsidered, I came up with another possibility. Could it be that he had only seen what he needed to see and no more? The patient was as dead as anyone could be and, having established that, might Howard simply have switched off? If so, was it done as a form of self-protection, a way of avoiding close involvement and remaining detached? It seemed a neat enough theory, but when I looked at my own reaction, I started to feel uncomfortable. What had made me fancy a sandwich within minutes of viewing the mangled remains of a human being on a railway track? What kind of person would discover an appetite after taking in such a scene? Surely only an emotional cripple – someone who had long since lost any kind of empathy with his fellow man. It made me think all right.

Back on station I tried to justify my behaviour. Maybe I was clutching at straws, but could it be that from the moment I laid eyes on the victim, the emotional part of my brain had simply switched off? I'd taken in the facts, but not for an instant had I allowed myself to consider the enormity of what I was looking at – the result being that, as soon as I turned away, the whole episode was effectively wiped from my conscious thought. It was relegated to some dark area of my mind from where it could be retrieved easily, but only on my terms. Afterwards, when I might describe the case to colleagues, or give a statement to the police, it would be as if I were talking of something I'd seen from a million miles away, so distant that I might just wonder if it really had happened at all. Maybe, in eating my sandwiches, I was subconsciously exorcizing the ghost of this particular job by immediately returning to the mundane. Who knows?

There are so many ambulance officers about these days that you hardly dare open a cupboard without running the risk of one falling out. This is in stark contrast to life in the late seventies. There was, of course, the station manager, but he didn't really count. All the others remained hidden away, appearing only if there were praise or reprimands to be dished out. So it came as a surprise when one wandered into the messroom shortly after Howard and I got back from the train job. I went on the defensive when he came over and spoke to us.

'All right, lads? Don't suppose there's a chance of a cup of tea, is there?'

Howard, ever the diplomat, smiled cautiously.

'Of course, have a seat and I'll sort one out.'

A few minutes later the three of us were sitting self-consciously sipping our tea. H broke the silence.

'So what brings you to the lion's den?'

'Oh, I was in the area . . . you know how it is.' Then, as an afterthought, 'Had a busy day?'

'Not really,' Howard replied.

The officer took a sip of tea.

'I hear you had a nasty railway job.'

News simply doesn't travel that fast. Howard and I glanced at each other with the same thought in mind: he'd been sent as a shoulder to cry on. Howard wasn't going to make it easy for him.

'Depends on how you look at it.'

'Well, you know what I mean. These things tend to stay with you afterwards.'

'Really?'

'I would have thought so, don't you?'

Howard considered the question and then looked him in the eye.

'No, I don't. Anyway, we were just going to get the Scrabble out. Do you fancy a game?'

The officer shifted uncomfortably.

'Er, no, I don't think so. So what happened to your patient?'

'Got bladdered by a train.'

'Nasty!'

'I suppose so.'

The officer eased back in his chair.

'It's lucky these jobs don't come along too often, isn't it? We'd all go nuts if they did.'

'Would we? I think you're going to have to speak for yourself on that one.' Howard placed his cup on the table. 'Have you ever been out to a suicide on the railway?'

'No, I was spared that when I was on the road.'

'Really? Well, if you ever do find yourself at one you'll have to pop in for a chat afterwards and we'll compare notes.'

Perhaps stung by the sarcasm, the officer sat in silence for a few moments before announcing his departure.

'Oh well, must be on my way.'

Howard had other ideas.

'Talking of nasty jobs, remember that bloke who fell

into the chemical vat, Les? The one who had most of his skin burned off and was running around screaming when we got there?'

I nodded. It wasn't a memory I particularly wanted to resurrect.

'I'm sure there are worse cases than that, though. Now let me think . . .' Howard's voice had taken on a tone so unfamiliar to me that I looked at him in puzzlement as he continued. 'Oh yes, I can think of one. She'd been unfaithful to her husband and when he found out he stabbed her to death. And then, like you do, he cut her head off and, just in case she hadn't got the message, rammed it up between her legs. I can't think why the relatives called for an ambulance. It's not as if we were going to sew it back on, was it? Yes, that was a nasty job – definitely worse than the train one, wouldn't you say?'

Howard's outburst was all the more shocking when measured against his normally serene demeanour. If I felt uncomfortable, then what of the officer? His face was impassive as he conjured up a final platitude.

'Dreadful. It's maybe good to get these things off your chest.'

Howard eyed him coldly, as if examining his shallowness.

'Do you want to hear about another really nasty job before you go?'

'If it's something you want to talk about, then yes.'

'It happened last year to Will Dobson and his partner. They were sent to help an elderly lady who'd fallen at home. She wasn't hurt and they put her back into bed. When they came on duty two days later there was one of you lot waiting for them. He told them that they were suspended and to go home until further notice. When they asked for an explanation, all the officer had to say was that it was something about theft. That's a nice thing to be met with when you turn up for work, isn't it?' This was a true story that I could vouch for. 'It seems,' Howard continued, 'that the old lady's pension money had gone missing and the family had lodged an accusation of theft on the grounds that nobody but them had been in the house.'

The officer looked uncomfortable, unsure where this was going.

'We don't have any choice but to suspend people if they're accused of theft . . .'

'That's true enough,' H interrupted. 'It's the way they were treated from then on that was nasty. They eventually got a letter outlining the charge and were told to stay away from any ambulance buildings or offices until the matter was settled. Their statement was taken and they heard nothing else from the service, no visits offering *support* or anything else. They were guilty until proven innocent, and they were treated like pariahs.'

The officer had lost some of his bonhomie.

'I really don't know what you expect me to say. The service policy is quite clear in this kind of case. Things have to run their course.'

Howard's look turned from cold to icy.

'The service has suddenly decided to try to ease the stress we might be under. Can you imagine the stress of being accused of something you haven't done and having no way of disproving it? The stress of sitting in a police station answering questions. Of watching people cross the street when they see you coming. When your family and friends want to know why you're not at work and you don't want to tell them you've been accused of being a thief. That's stress. And where was the service when these blokes needed some genuine support? Nowhere! Do you know what happened to Will Dobson in the end?'

The officer shook his head. 'No, I'm on a different division.'

'He had a heart attack three weeks into his suspension. He was about fifty-seven with years of experience under his belt and that was him finished – he never came back. And guess what? At almost the same time the family found the missing pension money stuffed in a corner of the old woman's wardrobe. And what did the service do? They sent both men a letter and told them they could return to work at the start of their next scheduled shift. No visit, no sorry, just a letter.' Howard stood up. 'When it comes to nasty jobs, that's the worst one I've heard about. Now, if you'll excuse me, I've got to get some fresh sheets for the ambulance.' With that, he left the messroom.

We watched him go and then the officer turned to me.

'I don't know what's wrong with your mate, but he needs to talk to someone.'

'He just has, hasn't he?'

He eyed me as he retrieved his cap from the table.

'Don't tell me you're another smartarse?'

'Another smartarse? Howard's not a smartarse – he was just getting something off his chest. That was the idea, wasn't it?'

He was about to say something, but thought the better of it and instead headed for the door.

'Thanks for the tea. See you about.'

'Yeah, see you about.'

And so ended my first and, come to think of it, my last ever counselling session.

Howard came back into the messroom with a smile on his face.

'Well, that's got rid of him. I don't suppose he'll be coming back here in a hurry.'

His anger was gone.

'You certainly let off some steam,' I said. 'Was that true about the woman having her head cut off? I've not heard you mention it before.'

'No, you won't have done. I save that story for dinner parties, or at least I would if I ever got invited to one.' He smiled again, back to his normal self. 'I'm afraid it is true though. It happened three or four years ago and, if I'm honest about it, it did give me one or two sleepless nights at the time.'

'So,' I said, 'did it help to go off on a rant?'

'Yeah, I think it did. But only because it gave me chance to put the record straight about Will Dobson. He was a friend of mine; he looked after me when I started and was a thoroughly decent bloke. To think his career ended like that still makes me angry. Anyway, stress breaks and concerned officers sniffing around is just a fad. It'll soon be a thing of the past.'

He wasn't wrong in his prediction. There is a phone number you can ring these days. I don't know if anyone uses it, but I don't suppose they'd tell me if they did.

Any gloom quickly surrendered to the irrepressible atmosphere of Henrietta Street. Nothing was allowed to interfere, but I was beginning to wonder if beneath the high jinks and banter of daily life there might lurk a streak of cynicism I'd missed until now. More than two years down the line, I'd developed a deeper understanding of why newcomers to the job were, at best, tolerated. They had to serve an apprenticeship not just measured in terms of time, but in the gathering of experiences that would lift them to another plane and a true level of empathy with their more seasoned workmates.

Looked at in these terms, and even though I still had plenty to learn, I'd picked up enough emotional bumps and bruises to feel myself now to be part of the shift. I wasn't so naïve as to imagine myself impervious to whatever the job might throw at me, but I hoped I had all the mechanisms in place to help me cope and had become reasonably adept at distancing myself from events. Then along came a hot Sunday afternoon and with it a case so sad that it has become something of a metaphor for all the distressing cases I've been involved in since.

Steve and I were returning to the Street for an overdue meal break when we were called up and given the location of an ambulance which had broken down on the way to hospital. We were to collect the patient and continue the journey. The controller broke off in mid-flow for several seconds. When he came back on air there was no mistaking the urgency in his voice. The patient we were to collect was a five-year-old girl in cardiac arrest. Resuscitation efforts were in progress. My heart sank on hearing the message. Nobody wants a case like this, and Steve summed up our feelings in a single word.

'Shit!'

On went the blue lights and sirens, one of the rare occasions I was glad of them.

Her parents had taken her to a summer fete being held in a local park. One of the attractions was a brass band playing from a bandstand erected for the occasion. I don't know if it was exposed wiring, or if part of the metal structure had unaccountably become 'live', but when the little girl ran across and sat on one of the bandstand steps, she was instantly electrocuted. Her heart and breathing stopped. Panic ensued. Tannoy appeals brought an off-duty doctor and nurse from the crowd who set about performing mouth-to-mouth and cardiac massage. They kept working until the ambulance arrived and then travelled with her to hospital without faltering in their efforts to save her life. About a mile from their destination, the ambulance broke down.

The other vehicle's back doors flew open as we pulled up alongside and a flurry of bodies tumbled out. First the doctor with the limp body of the girl clutched to his chest. Behind him, the nurse and the ambulance attendant, both pale and tight-lipped. Behind them came the child's parents. They were ashen-faced and trying to move quickly, but their efforts were so awkward and leaden-footed that they needed support. Steve and I helped them on to our ambulance and sat them opposite the stretcher where their daughter lay. She was on her back, the doctor was breathing into her mouth and the nurse had resumed cardiac massage. I gave the doctor the bag and mask I'd connected to the oxygen in advance, allowing him to supply her with a source of richly oxygenated air by rhythmically squeezing on the bag. Portable defibrillators were still in the future and there was nothing else to be done. It was a two-person operation leaving me little more than a spectator.

There was nothing I could do for the parents either. Even if I could have found the words, they wouldn't have heard them. What energy they had left was concentrated on the little form of their child. She was a pretty girl, the very picture of innocence. Her hair had been arranged into pigtails and she had on a pale green summer frock. I couldn't drag my eyes from her. What had she been like before the accident? Full of life and fun no doubt, chasing around the park. The sun was shining, her parents were close by and nothing could harm her. But she was harmed, struck dead in an instant by a sinister and invisible force. It took but a moment to rob that little body of life and destroy the hopes and dreams of all those around her.

The full impact of the tragedy and all its ramifications slowly ebbed into my being, leaving me feeling wretched and defenceless. Not being directly involved in the efforts to save her life gave me time to dwell on the nightmare as it unfolded in front of my eyes, and turned the journey into the worst I've ever experienced. By the time we reached the hospital I was acutely depressed. She hadn't responded. Her parents hadn't spoken or moved.

We rushed her to the resuscitation room where the hospital staff gave their all for almost two hours. Eventually they stopped trying; they had gone well past the time when logic had told them to stop. Life in a hospital Casualty is peppered with drama, crises and tragedies, large and small. When finished with one patient the staff simply turn to the next. This time it was different. Everyone, even the porter who held open the door, was deeply affected. I think we all felt a personal sense of failure that was hard to overcome. When a child is in danger or distress, instinct impels us to go to its aid, gather it up and offer protection. When all efforts fail, then it's hard not to feel responsible in some way, and hard not to blame yourself. You go over and over the events in your head to try to pinpoint how you failed. There is, of course, never an answer. So you run through it all again, just one more time.

Since then I've been to children killed on the roads.

More times than I care to think of, I've run to the ambulance with a baby, found lifeless in its cot, in my arms. I can recall them all vividly, but my defences always managed to hold up. Years later, though, and with a heavy heart, I still think from time to time of that little girl from the park.

# Chapter Eighteen

Jack and I spent the rest of the day speculating on what might have killed the man in the pub car park. No matter how much we mulled it over, we still couldn't make sense of it. Even the job description we were given had been ambiguous: 'Man trying to commit suicide'. No mention of how he was trying to do it, just that he was trying. In the event, we discovered that death had come to him many hours earlier, in the middle of the night. We found him sitting behind the wheel of a white Mercedes tucked neatly in a corner of the White Hart car park in Handsworth. He wasn't slumped in the seat; he was upright, his head tipped back slightly as if asleep. I put him to be in his mid-thirties. He was tall, athletically built, well groomed and, from what I could see through the large brown stain on the front of his shirt, of smart appearance. A cursory examination was enough to establish that he'd been dead for some time. Rigor mortis had firmly set in.

So what had killed him? My immediate thought was

that he'd had some kind of internal haemorrhage. The stain on his shirt had emanated from his mouth and was probably dried blood; it seemed sensible to imagine that a sudden catastrophic bleed had done for him.

'The thing is,' Jack said, 'there's no blood anywhere else. You'd think he'd have had a few seconds of thrashing about when it all happened.'

He was right. The interior of the car was immaculate, not a spot of blood to be seen.

'And his hands,' Jack continued. 'No blood on them either. Surely he'd have put them up to his face. Mind you, it could be that he didn't have time to react.'

It was curious. I was no expert on these things, but I found it hard to imagine he didn't have at least a few moments of awareness before expiring. We were still debating it when a police motorcyclist pulled into the car park. He tucked his helmet under an arm and wandered over.

'Hello, lads – what have we got?'

'A sudden death. He's been here a good few hours by the look of it.'

He peered into the car.

'He seems a bit young just to peg it. Is that blood all down his front?'

'Looks like it,' I said.

'Any injuries? Stab wounds or anything?'

'None that I can see, but we haven't moved him to check round the back.' Then I added a line I'd picked up from TV. 'There isn't any evidence of a struggle taking place.'

'So you think it's natural causes, then?'

This put me on the spot but, as my opinion didn't carry any weight in the great scheme of things, I stuck my neck out.

'It's a strange one, but I don't see that it's suspicious.'

I had a couple of days off after that and at lunchtime next day I prepared myself baked beans on toast before settling down in front of the television to watch the news. The first item on the local bulletin talked of a shooting in Handsworth the previous morning. My ears pricked up. Shootings were rare; in fact, other than as a means of suicide, they were virtually unheard of. My first reaction was relief that someone else had been sent to it rather than me. Then, as I wondered why I hadn't heard about it at the time, the TV picture switched from the studio to a reporter at the scene. Behind her was red-and-white police tape cordoning off the area and behind that was the car park of the White Hart. In the far corner was a car draped in a tarpaulin. I came close to coughing a mouthful of baked beans across the living-room carpet.

From what I picked up from the commentary, it seems the victim had been shot through the head from close range. Shot *through* the head eventually proved to be journalese speak. Shot *in* the head would have been closer to the mark. But such niceties didn't concern me at the time. I was in shock. How could I have attended a murder by gunshot and not have noticed? In a panic, and in need of reassurance as much as anything else, I tried to get in touch with Jack but every time I rang the call went unanswered.

When I clocked on for the afternoon shift two days later, I had it all figured out for myself. The killer must have been sitting in the passenger seat with the gun close to his victim's head when he discharged it. They were probably talking or arguing when oblivion came without warning to the unfortunate man. If it was a small-calibre bullet fired from a low-velocity pistol, it was conceivable that it entered the victim's skull and then went for a trip round his brain rather than exiting cleanly from the other side. Unconscious at the very least, and with death only moments away, the blood I thought came from his mouth must have come from his nose. It was gratifying to find out later that I was more or less correct in my amateur analysis. Not that it prevented Jack and me becoming the butt of jokes at the Street and far-flung depots I'd never even heard of.

Jack was in the corner with the *Telegraph* folded back at the crossword page when I came into the messroom, while the others were sitting round the table idly chatting. I joined them as the conversation turned to the murder.

'Who went out to it, anyway?' Steve asked.

'It wasn't me and Larry,' H said. 'It might have been a crew from West Brom, I suppose.'

Jack, crossword finished, put the paper on a nearby chair and stood up.

'It was me and Les.'

'Really?' H said. 'How come you didn't say anything about it at the time?'

Jack wandered over and took a seat, oblivious to my slight shake of the head and panic-stricken stare.

'We didn't realize he'd been shot at the time. There was no way of telling.'

I had to resist holding my head in my hands and rocking back and forth. My plan had been to play down the whole thing, not mention that we were ignorant of the manner of death, but simply say there was nothing we could do and leave it at that. What they didn't know wouldn't hurt them. With the rabbit out of the bag, Larry turned his attention to me.

'Is that right? You went out to someone with his head blown off and you didn't notice?'

I sighed. 'His head wasn't blown off. The bullet must have entered above his hairline and not come out. There was nothing to see unless I picked over his scalp like a chimp looking for ticks.' I knew I was wasting my breath, but I went on to describe the case in detail anyway. Larry leaned back and slapped his hands down on his thighs when I'd finished.

'That's priceless! A bloke's shot in the head and you think it's a burst ulcer.'

'Who mentioned ulcers?' I protested. 'I said it might have been a ruptured aorta.'

They were enjoying themselves and it wasn't long before Mike weighed in.

'It was only a few months ago when that woman hanged herself and you pair diagnosed death by natural causes. Or am I getting you mixed up with another crew?' Knowing there was more to come, I folded my arms and leaned back. 'Then there was that woman who set fire to her husband, and from what I heard you gave her a month's worth of care and sympathy.'

A year earlier, Gerard Lynch of gas-mask fame had attended an accident in the city centre. A car had left the road and ploughed into a shop front. The driver had run off and it was only by good fortune that nobody else was hurt. Gerard chewed the fat with the police and firemen for a bit, then pushed off. The car was removed by low-loader to a police compound. It was quite some time later that a dead body was found in the boot. Again, it was murder. You couldn't possibly have blamed Gerard for not finding the corpse, but when word got round that he'd been to a road traffic accident and left a body behind, the ribbing was merciless. He couldn't even visit the toilet without being told to check the cistern for bodies before he flushed it. But, as they say, if you can't take it, then don't give it out. If I remember rightly, I had joined in with as much enthusiasm as anyone else when it came to berating Gerard. Now it was payback time – and I had to put a brave face on it for weeks afterwards. When I gave my police statement, the officer told me that the motorbike cop had also been made to look foolish by not flagging up a suspicious incident immediately. He probably blamed me, and every time I spotted a police motorcyclist out on the road I felt it only prudent to sink down in my seat and look the other way.

When they'd finished with me, talk turned to murders of the past. I didn't feel in the mood, and when the emergency phone rang it was a relief to get out on our first job of the afternoon. As we headed for Ladywood, Jack was unrepentant about letting slip the truth about the murder.

'If it gives them a bit of amusement, where's the harm?'

'That might be one way of looking at it if there was no way of stopping them finding out,' I said. 'The trouble is that we're now going to be known as the crew who didn't notice our patient's head was blown off. Mark my words, Larry will see to that.' Then, for good measure, I added, 'Handing that lot the ammunition to shoot you with is just plain barmy.'

Jack smiled. 'That's a very apt comparison.'

'When I first started,' I continued, 'Bob Philips had a very expensive first-aid bag that he'd bought and kitted at his own cost. You could have done a heart transplant with what he'd got in it. Anyway, he took it on holiday to France with him and lost it . . .'

'What? Why on earth would he take it on holiday?'

'Don't ask,' I said. 'It's just the way he was. The mistake the silly sod made was to mention his loss at the Street when he got back, as if he was looking for sympathy. That summer he started getting postcards from the missing bag. He didn't particularly see the funny side, especially when he read what the bag had to say to him. And it continues to this day. Our lot don't half get around: Mexico, Canada, Thailand – you name a place and the chances are the bag's sent him a postcard from there. He got a particularly disgusting one from the red light district in Amsterdam that the boss confiscated. You must have seen some of them pinned on the notice board.'

'Yes, I wondered what they were about. Have you sent any?'

'Of course. If you can't beat 'em, you've got to join 'em. Anyway, do you see the point I'm trying to make?'

I brought the ambulance to a halt outside the address and pulled on the handbrake.

'Here we are then.'

Jack opened his door, then had a thought. 'You haven't even told me what the case is.'

'Oh, it's just a maternity . . . woman in labour.'

With my track record, I should have known better than be so blasé. The door was opened by a man in his mid-twenties. He was pleasant, and his smile was warm enough, but there was something vacant about it. He showed us into the front room where a blonde woman of a similar age lay on the sofa. Her smile was expansive in an almost childlike way. Jack smiled back, then with all the smiles over, he ran through one or two stock questions to try to establish how close she was to delivery. Her answers were unfocused and left us in some doubt.

'Let's make sure I've got this right,' Jack said. 'Your waters have broken and you were getting contractions earlier, but now they've stopped?'

'That's right. They were coming quite fast and I started pushing.'

'You were pushing?'

'Yes, I can feel the baby. It's almost out, I think.'

Jack's face was a picture, as I suppose was mine.

'Almost out? The baby's almost out?' There was a definite sense of urgency in his voice. 'I'm going to have to take a look. Is that OK with you?'

She hitched up her maternity dress and smiled again.

'Of course.'

The top of the baby's head was clearly visible. I turned on my heel and made for the ambulance to radio for a midwife and collect the maternity pack containing all the bits and pieces we might need for a delivery.

Nothing had changed when I came back into the room. Jack was kneeling in front of the woman trying to coax her into making an effort to push. She was doing her best, but without the natural impulse of a contraction she wasn't getting very far. The circumstances were outside my experience and training. I didn't know what to do or say. I also didn't know how big a threat the baby's predicament was to its well-being. Plainly, there was nothing we could do to stimulate the delivery, which left us with two choices. We could wait it out for the midwife, or gather up the woman and hightail it to hospital. I discounted the latter. If she'd been in distress to the point where we were genuinely fearful for her safety and the baby's, then the risky journey to hospital might be justifiable but, as it was, there was nothing about her to give us any concern. The baby was another matter. Never, before or since, have I wished so fervently for the quick arrival of the midwife.

Doing nothing as a course of action was new to me and

I didn't like it. Then the stalemate was broken when the woman gave a little exclamation of surprise.

'Oh! Something's happening.'

A moment later the baby's crinkly little head nudged fully into the world. We waited for the next contraction. Despite our increasingly frantic pleas for her to make a greater effort, it didn't happen for five minutes. Five minutes is a long time when you're counting every second and I'd broken into a sweat by the time the baby's shoulders slipped out. The battle was over. I gave a silent prayer of thanks as we carefully eased the little body fully into the world. My immediate impression was that he was a healthy weight and, considering the shock of the pro-longed delivery, not a bad colour. It was as I leaned over him with the mucous extractor ready in case his airway needed clearing that I realized he had yet to take his first breath. His airway was clear, but he wasn't breathing. The nervous tension I'd been so happy to see the back of moments earlier returned with a vengeance. I placed two fingers on his chest and felt a faint, rapid beat. I grabbed a piece of towelling and gave his chest a vigorous rub in the hope of stimulating him into taking that first vital breath. Nothing. I picked him up by the feet and sharply tapped his bottom as I'd seen done in the movies; again, no result. My thoughts were now in a wild jumble and my pulse was racing. I had to breathe for him, and the only way to do that was by mouth-to-mouth inflations.

I tilted back the little head and was suddenly horror-struck at the prospect of blowing into lungs so tiny and fragile that I might explode them and not even know I'd done it. I had no choice – three quick breaths. The sour taste of the baby's face remains with me to this day. It didn't work. I tried again with a little more pressure. Sweat was pouring off me and I felt faint. I wasn't trained, or even prepared, for this kind of thing happening. I was out of my depth and sinking fast. I could hear Jack talking to the mother, but the voice I heard most clearly was the one in my head. 'Brain damage . . . brain damage,' it kept saying. 'Lack of oxygen at birth means brain damage.' I was vaguely aware of the midwives arriving. Two of them – they never send two – why two this time? I had my face pressed to the baby's, still gently blowing as he was taken from me. He was in the midwife's arms, the umbilical cord had been cut and she was moving towards the door, leaving her colleague to care for the mother. As we ran out to the ambulance I noticed she'd placed a tiny oxygen mask on the baby's face. What was the point of that? He wasn't breathing – I knew he wasn't breathing; wafting oxygen over him was futile.

Less than five minutes later our little bundle was taken by a flurry of gowned nurses. Our part in the drama was at an abrupt end and the battle for the baby's life was carried on elsewhere. We stood by the ambulance with a cup of tea and tried to talk through the case, but there was precious little to be said. I felt agitated and angry. I wanted to jump into the ambulance and go looking for a so-called instructor and demand to know why I hadn't been better prepared. I also felt guilty. Guilty that for a short while Jack and I held the fate of a tiny life in our hands and had not measured up. But it was too soon to collect my thoughts in a rational way, so much was a blur. I had no memory of the mother's reaction, nor of the young man who met us at the door. In fact, I didn't recall seeing him again after entering the room.

Such was my despondency that I didn't even dare imagine that the baby would pull through. But, and I'm really pleased to say this, pull through he did. Two weeks later we received a letter of thanks from someone at the hospital with the wonderful news that he was alive and holding his own.

The rest of the shift was on station when we got back. They only needed to glance at our faces to see that something was wrong. They listened to the story in silence and to my surprise had very little to say when I finished. The only one to speak was Larry, and all he had to say was, 'That's a tough one, all right.' I think it drew them all up in their tracks to hear of a nightmare job beyond even their experience, especially when it came from the two least experienced members of the shift. Phyllis, our cook, who was never known to venture into the messroom, came round with a cup of tea each for Jack and me. She didn't say anything, and was back in her lair before we had chance to thank her. It was kind of her; a small token that said all that needed to be said. The banter remained dormant and was not resumed until the next day – quite a mark of respect.

Life goes on, but I won't pretend it was easy to see out

the rest of the day with the baby's unknown fate never far from our minds. To make matters worse, it was our luck to run into a young man later in the evening whom I can only describe as a total idiot. Our work can be frustrating at the best of times, but when you have the burdens of the day weighing heavy on your shoulders it can be tough keeping your temper with some people. In that respect, this guy tested us to the limit. He'd tripped and fallen on a bus and from the start I found it hard to believe a word he said. I couldn't put my finger on the reason straightaway, but the more I listened to him, the more suspicious I became. Nothing about him rang true. Suspecting that I was being lied to was bad enough, but what really galled me was that I had no choice but to accept what he said and keep my thoughts to myself. It's not the done thing to look a patient in the face and call him a liar.

We'd been forced to get into the bus via the small emergency exit at the rear, as Malcolm – at least that's what he said his name was – had contrived to fall into the footwell of the front entrance and ended up jamming himself between the inward-opening doors and the vertical handrail. He was curled up in the foetal position with his head resting against the doors and both feet almost out of view under his thighs. He was about twenty-two, conscious, alert, a good colour, and seemingly in good spirits. When I knelt down and spoke to him I was met with a smile and an apology.

'Sorry about this, mate, but I'm stuck and can't seem to get up.'

I was sympathetic at first.

'That's OK. We'll get you out of there in a minute, but let's make sure you haven't broken anything first, shall we?' As I spoke I took his pulse and found it to be ticking along nicely at a steady eighty. The next thing to do was to check for any injuries and, starting at his head, I worked down his body in the usual manner and found that he had no pains, bruises or any other symptoms. That is until I reached his waist.

'Any discomfort here?' I asked, pressing gently on his pelvis.

'I don't know. I can't feel anything at all.'

I pressed down a bit harder and got the same response.

'I can't feel my legs either,' Malcolm offered, without being asked. 'Can't move them, for that matter.'

I was startled. 'What are you saying? Do you mean they've gone numb?'

'They've gone dead.'

'Can you wiggle your toes for me?'

'Nope.'

'Can you feel this?' I gave the inside of his thigh a pinch.

'Nope.'

'Have you got any sensation below your waist – pins and needles, anything?'

'Nope.'

'Look, what you're describing could be serious. Are you quite sure you can't move or feel anything below your waist?'

'Definite!'

His replies were delivered in a breezy, carefree manner, not the kind of attitude you would expect from someone who might have a broken back. Questions circulated in my mind. Why had he waited until I reached his legs before telling me he couldn't move them? Surely anyone with such a potentially serious injury would have been shouting it from the rooftops. They would be horrified, terrified even. There should have been frantic questions in a search for reassurance as the realization struck home just how catastrophic the injury might be. There was none of this from Malcolm, no hint of shock or fear – the opposite, in fact: he seemed completely unconcerned by his predicament. I couldn't escape the feeling that he was relishing the situation. The thought that he was describing false symptoms and deliberately lying was bizarre, but nothing rang true.

My suspicions didn't matter, though. If he described the symptoms of a broken back, then he would be treated for a broken back. For obvious reasons, spinal injuries have to be approached with the utmost care, and immobilizing and then extracting Malcolm was going to be tricky. He was eighteen inches below us, jammed into the small space between the step and the doors, making it nigh on impossible to get at him from inside the bus. The only answer was to work from the outside, which meant somehow getting the inward-opening doors out of the way first. This task was beyond us, and the only solution that sprang to mind was to call the fire brigade.

I straightened up and moved back the couple of feet to where Jack was standing. He'd been listening to the conversation and chipped in with his thoughts.

'Do you smell the same rat as I do?'

'Yes,' I said. 'It's a bloody big one, isn't it?'

Jack leaned in a bit closer. 'If I had my way, we'd just drag the bastard out and send him packing with a boot up his arse.'

What would normally have amused me now irritated me.

'Oh, that's a good idea, Jack. Why didn't I think of that? Let me see. Maybe because it wouldn't read too good on the patient report form when, under symptoms, I'd written "Broken back" and, under treatment, written "Sent packing with one of Jack Turner's size twelves up his arse". Now call me a worrier if you want, but I can't help but feel someone checking the case sheets might just pick up on that.'

Jack looked offended. 'All right, keep your hair on. But the bloke's a con merchant . . . he's playing us for a couple of fools.'

'I know he is,' I said. 'But we're still going to have to get the fire brigade out. If you call Control and get it arranged, I'll have a word with the driver.'

The bus driver was still in his seat and taking remarkably little interest in the proceedings. With his elbows on the steering wheel and his chin resting on his knuckles, he stared impassively through the windscreen. I leaned over and spoke to him.

'How did he end up down there?'

The driver eased back in his seat.

'Good question. Fucked if I know.'

Not exactly the response I was looking for, but I pressed on.

'You must have seen him fall.'

'Yeah, I saw him fall, but don't ask me why he fell. I was pulling into the stop and he was standing in the aisle beside me. Just as we stopped he flew forwards and hit the windscreen and then fell down into the footwell.' He pointed at a long, snaking crack running down the big pane of glass to the left of his own windscreen. 'He could see that I was stopping and, believe me, I didn't brake hard. If he was eighty years old and had been standing on one leg at the time, I could understand it. As it was, there was no reason for him to fall.'

The driver hadn't made a direct accusation, but his thoughts were clear enough and only served to reinforce my own opinion.

Events proceeded as follows. Jack radioed through to our Control and, after asking for the fire brigade, requested another ambulance to be sent. We would need the extra hands; it would take more than two of us to manage the injury described with the necessary care. With the wheels set in motion, there wasn't much else we could do but wait for the reinforcements. While we waited, an inspector from the bus company arrived in a Mini van. He assessed the situation and called out a maintenance team without telling us. The next guests at the party were the police. They'd been told that someone had been run over, but when they discovered what had really happened they still had a procedure to follow and took notes because it was an 'accident in a public place'. They interviewed the patient where he lay and found him only too happy to cooperate. Steve and Mike turned up shortly after the police, and close on their heels came the fire brigade with blue lights flashing and sirens wailing. The fire officer hurried over and listened intently as we explained that the doors had to come off. He considered the problem before snapping out instructions to his men, who scuttled off to fetch the required equipment. They returned laden with heavy cutting gear and started to set it up at the front of the bus.

Just as they were about to start work, a huge break-down truck from the bus company pulled up. The vehicle had barely stopped before one of the two-man crew jumped out and made a beeline for the firemen. He knew exactly what they were about to do and wore a horror-struck expression.

'Stop! Don't do that!' he yelled at them. 'Leave them doors alone!'

He was just in time. The firemen hesitated and looked to their officer for guidance. He thought for a moment, then, without trying to hide his reluctance, told his men to down tools, their fun spoiled at the last moment. The mechanic squeezed past them to inspect the doors and let out a sigh of relief when he found they were still intact. Here was a man who had clearly witnessed the destructive powers of a motivated fire crew before.

With the arrival of the mechanics, we were all now in place – fifteen of us, plus five vehicles. Malcolm's rescue could commence.

The mechanics started removing the doors using spanners and screwdrivers. Any passengers agile enough to climb down from the emergency exit were invited to use it, leaving a few elderly ladies sitting patiently in their seats. Noticing their plight, the fire officer had one of his men stand inside the bus by the door and another positioned outside at ground level. The ladies were then organized into a line and, one by one, carefully lifted by the first fireman and passed into the arms of the other below. It wasn't the kind of rescue that would make the evening papers, but judging from the schoolgirl giggles and squeals coming from the old ladies, for them it was a dream come true.

Meanwhile, work progressed on the doors and in due course they were neatly stacked on the pavement. We now had plenty of room to work and didn't have much difficulty immobilizing Malcolm and placing him on the stretcher. He was then loaded on to the ambulance and we drove off, leaving the mechanics putting their bus back together. During the journey to hospital I quizzed Malcolm again about his symptoms. He cheerfully informed me that there was no change in his condition and he still couldn't feel a thing below the waist. I would have liked to test the reflexes on the soles of his feet, but he was wearing a pair of sturdy boots that laced high up on the ankle and, strapped up as he was, it wasn't practicable. I had to bide my time until we had handed him over to the hospital staff.

A little later I was standing in the corner of a hospital cubicle watching the doctor and a couple of nurses gingerly remove the restraints from Malcolm's body. They too had been surprised by the patient's sunny disposition, but proceeded with utmost caution. At last the boots, then the socks, came off and the doctor ran his biro up the exposed sole of Malcolm's left foot.

'Did you feel that?' he asked.

'Feel what?'

'OK, can you feel this?' The doctor used more pressure and Malcolm's eyes widened a little.

'No, I didn't feel anything.'

With a flourish the doctor applied the biro for a third time, gritting his teeth as he did so. Malcolm yelped and his leg jerked away from the pain.

'Did you feel that?' Somehow the doctor kept any hint of irony from his voice.

'Yes, yes, I felt something that time.' Beads of sweat had broken out on his forehead. The doctor attacked the other foot with similar results. He had, of course, detected the expected reflexes at the first attempt but was determined to get Malcolm to demonstrate to everyone, but particularly to himself, that the game was up. He then got Malcolm to draw up both knees, which he managed with much face-pulling and grunting. Finally, purely as a precaution, the doctor ordered X-rays to be done and left the cubicle.

So what had it all been about? Malcolm had forced a busload of passengers out into the cold, taken two ambulances, a fire engine and a bus out of circulation, wasted police time and then wasted the time and resources of the local hospital. Why? Did he have it in his mind that he might get some compensation from the bus company? How on earth had he expected to fool the doctors? Perhaps he just fancied being the centre of attention for a while. Only Malcolm could answer these questions and there was precious little chance of that happening. When we returned to the hospital with another patient an hour later, he was standing outside Casualty smoking. He recognized us and, flicking the cigarette away, came over.

'I'm glad I caught you. I just want to say thanks, lads. You did a great job. I was really worried back there for a bit.'

I shook my head in wonderment as he continued. 'It must have been some kind of temporary paralysis, trapped nerve or something. I've read about stuff like that in magazines. It's gone now, though – look.' By way of demonstration he hopped from one foot to the other in a little jig. Jack stared at him coldly.

'Are you looking for a good smack, mate?'

'No.'

'Then you'd better fuck off quick, because you're about to get one.'

# Chapter Nineteen

You might spend months dealing with nothing but routine cases while other crews seem to be permanently in the thick of things. It's almost embarrassing when friends ask if you've had any interesting cases lately and you are reduced to scratching your head before answering in the negative. Don't get me wrong; the cases I lightly describe as routine are in fact the backbone of all the good work done by the ambulance service. Chest infections, breathing problems, retention, back pain, abdominal pain . . . the list goes on for ever. And, of course, what we class as routine is anything but that for the patients and families involved. I enjoyed these quiet periods and every case helped add to my bank of knowledge. It was especially informative when working with someone like Larry. He had an instinct for the job that the modern-day obsession with tick boxes could never expose. Just watching him work his way through an array of what some might consider humdrum cases was educational.

For example, one day we were given the task of transporting to hospital a woman whose doctor suspected she might have an intestinal obstruction. She was to undergo tests which might or might not lead to an operation. There was obviously nothing in the way of treatment that we could offer, which meant that the case fell into the category of a routine job. And that's exactly how it would have read to anyone who cared to glance at the case sheet afterwards.

The patient lived alone and opened the door to us looking thoroughly ill at ease. She was elderly and, despite her efforts to sound cheerful, it wasn't difficult to see through her tight, pensive smile.

'Hello boys, I didn't expect you to be here so early. Come in.' She led us into the back parlour and lowered herself into a chair opposite the television. Larry took up a position near the window.

'So how are you feeling this morning, Mrs Homer?'

'Call me Doris, love. I'm not so bad, but I really don't feel up to going to hospital. I was wondering if I could ring the doctor and rearrange it for next week?' She seemed ready to shed a tear and Larry looked at her with concern.

'Hey, come on, Doris. Nobody wants to go to hospital. There isn't anyone who hates the places more than me, but your doctor wants you to pop in for a check-up. You'll be home again before you know it.'

She nodded. 'I know I have to go. It's just that—'

She was interrupted by the sound of a key in the door

and a moment later a lady of similar age bustled into the room and made her way through to the kitchen without slowing down. She nodded at us as she passed.

'Morning.'

Larry stared after her. 'Who was that?'

'That's Jessie,' Doris said. 'She lives down the road.'

We could hear the fridge being opened and then rustling sounds. Larry leaned his head round the door and peered into the kitchen. When he'd seen enough he spoke to Doris.

'Are you on first-name terms with all the burglars round here?'

Doris looked confused. 'How do you mean?'

'That woman, Jessie, she's stealing stuff out of your fridge.'

Despite herself, Doris gave a little laugh and seemed tempted to join in the joke.

'No, I don't know all the burglars' names, only some of them.'

'I know you're living in a bloody rough area,' Larry continued, 'but even so, strolling in and robbing someone's food before they're even out of the house takes the biscuit.'

Jessie came back into the room with her shopping bag bulging.

'I'm not taking any biscuits, you cheeky bugger, just the butter, milk and cheese.' She had another thought. 'Oh, and I helped myself to that loaf while I was about it, Doris.'

Larry looked at Doris. 'Do you want me to call the police and get her arrested?'

She shook her head and laughed again. 'No, prison was where she learned all her bad habits in the first place.'

Jessie looked up at Larry. 'You daft lump! Come on, get out of my way. I've got to get upstairs and sort out her overnight things.'

Larry watched her edge up the steep flight of stairs and shook his head.

'She's even going to nick your clothes while she's here. I don't know what the world's coming to.'

Still chuckling, Doris got to her feet.

'Do you know, Jessie and I sat next to each other in the infant class seventy-odd years ago? We've been best friends ever since. She's going to come round to feed the cat and keep an eye on things while I'm away. It's better she takes the butter and stuff rather than it going off.'

Doris's fears were pushed into the background as the banter continued on the way out to the ambulance. When they were settled in their seats, I raised the step. Larry had picked up the patient report form and was ready with his pen.

'Right then, Doris, the first thing I need to know is how old you are – and don't knock off a few years. Jessie will tell me if you do.'

'I'm eighty-two.'

Larry looked up in surprise.

'Blimey! That's amazing. I'd never have guessed.' He looked at me. 'Hey, Les, did you hear that? I'd have thought she was a darn sight older, wouldn't you?'

She squinted at him. 'You're a cheeky monkey! I'm not too old to put you over my knee, you know.'

I shut the doors and went round to the driver's seat, smiling to myself. I could hear little of what was being said over the engine noise on the way into hospital. What I could hear clearly enough was the ladies' high-pitched laughter competing with Larry's chuckles. A glance in the interior mirror revealed Larry sitting between the two of them, chatting away, his arms folded and his long legs stretched out on the stretcher opposite. The patient report form had been abandoned and he looked thoroughly at home; all that was needed was a crate of ale and Blackpool as our destination.

With Doris safely in the care of the hospital staff, Larry and I, as protocol demanded, went in search of a cup of tea. We were chatting with the receptionist when Jessie came scuttling out of a cubicle and made a beeline for Larry.

'I'm glad I caught you. I wanted to say thank you very much and tell you what a wonderful young man you are.'

Larry looked genuinely startled, as probably did I.

'Well, I've always known what a wonderful person I am, but it's the first time I've heard someone else say it.'

She smiled. 'No, honestly, you did absolute wonders for Doris. She took it very badly when the doctor told her she had to come into hospital today. I've never seen her so upset. She didn't sleep a wink last night and was on the phone to me at six o'clock this morning in tears. She was dreading the ambulance coming. Now she's sitting in there with a smile on her face. I wouldn't have thought it possible, and it's all down to you. I just wanted you to know that you've made a frightened old lady's day.'

Larry watched her head back to the cubicle and then turned to me with a slightly bewildered, not to say pleased, look and, for once, had very little to say.

Larry's skill as a communicator lay in his innate ability to assess people and pick up on atmospheres in the blink of an eye. The line he took with Doris might have been out of the question with someone else, in which case he would have adapted his approach accordingly. We develop these skills with time but, as with most things, some people are better at it than others. Larry was good. If gravitas was required, then he became a funeral director. If, as in the case of the elderly ladies, light-hearted nonsense was needed, he could switch it on in an instant. In all the times I worked with him, I never knew him to make a misjudgement. There was, however, one thing he wouldn't make any compromises over, and that was discourtesy. Those members of the public who thought they could be rude to us with impunity and imagined that our uniform prevented us from responding in kind were quickly put right. But again, Larry's reaction would be tailored to the occasion. If it was a drunk berating him, Larry would become a drunk and give as good as he got. If it was a yob, Larry would become a yob. If subtlety was required, Larry would be subtle.

Boorish behaviour isn't just confined to drunks and

yobs. Plenty of people are capable of it, as was demonstrated when we were called to an exclusive district of Birmingham to take a chronically ill lady to hospital. Again, the appointment had been arranged by her GP the day before and we arrived just after 8 a.m. Her husband let us in and from the start made no effort to hide the fact that he was an impatient, bad-tempered man – the kind of man who would have managed to look irritated even if you had just told him he'd won the Pools. He was in his mid-fifties, with pinched, angular features, greying hair and an expensive suit. He seemed more interested in arranging his cufflinks than looking at us.

'We were told to expect you at seven thirty; it's now eight fifteen. Waiting for you to make an appearance means that I'm now running three-quarters of an hour late.'

A civil greeting might have drawn an apology from us even if it wasn't our fault, but on this occasion neither of us cared to offer one. He gave us a glance as if to check we were suitably chastened. 'Anyway, she's through here. Follow me.' He marched off into his opulent house with us in his wake, grudgingly admiring the decor.

His wife was in a downstairs bedroom propped up with cushions.

'They're here at last, Marjory. Are you ready? We can't waste any more time.'

'Of course I'm ready!' she snapped back. 'Just see to yourself.'

She was polite enough to us, albeit in an unsmiling and

distant kind of way. Her husband checked his tie in a mirror, then pottered around putting bits and pieces in his pockets as we assessed the needs of the patient. We spoke only when necessary. There was an air of frostiness between the couple that was enough to chill the room and we didn't want to get involved.

'OK then, Marjory,' he said as he pulled on his gold watch, 'I'll be off now. I'll phone the hospital this afternoon to see that you're settled in.'

'You mean you'll get Helena to phone.'

His expression of permanent exasperation deepened, and for a moment he looked like the managing director of an insurance company that he probably was.

'I will telephone myself. I always telephone. Of course, if you' rather I didn't, you only have to say.'

She stared at the wall. 'Suit yourself.'

He patted down his pockets and spoke to us.

'Her overnight bag is in the hall – and make sure you don't forget to take her medications with you. They're on the table.' And then he was gone. Thirty seconds later he was back, jangling his keys against his thigh. 'That contraption of yours is blocking the garage doors. Could you please move it?'

Describing the ambulance as a contraption was a calculated put-down, as if he wanted to belittle any status we might have. It was too much for Larry.

'Contraption? I'm not a Contraption Man.'

'What do you mean?'

'If my vehicle had "Emergency Contraption" written

on the side, then that would make me a Contraption Man. But it doesn't say that, it says "Ambulance". It wouldn't sound right if you heard on the news that two "*Contraption* Men" rescued someone from under a bus, would it? The public would lose confidence in us if we were called—'

'Will you just move it!' The man's face had gone taut. Larry looked at him with an expression of innocence. 'Move what?'

'Will you move – your ambulance, immediately.'

Larry might have been inclined to move it if the word 'please' had been thrown in and 'immediately' had been left out. As it was, he turned back to the woman.

'No. Our patient's needs take priority over traffic flow. We'll be out when we're ready.'

The man turned on his heel and made for the door.

'Right! You haven't heard the last of this.'

It was gratifying to notice the slightest of smiles flit across his wife's face, and as the door slammed behind her husband she made a tempting offer.

'Have you boys got time for a nice cup of tea?'

I don't know if Larry heard any more about it. Even if he did, it wouldn't have bothered him. 'Treat as you would be treated' was his motto and he wasn't going to compromise. I don't suppose he would last long in the modern ambulance service, where appeasement is the order of the day and complaints are investigated by highly paid managers with a rigour that can take your breath away. It's a shame, because people like Larry were, and still are, a godsend from the patient's point of view. I've always said that if I found myself upside down in a crashed car with two broken legs and looked up to see Larry's silly grin hovering over me, I would breathe a silent prayer of thanks. Nothing fazed him.

This was demonstrated when we went to the aid of an eighteen-year-old girl who had been hit by a car and tossed into the gutter. Her right thigh bone was broken mid-shaft, splayed out at almost ninety degrees and left resting on top of her good leg. It was a sight that would make most people, and I include myself, catch their breath and squirm. Not Larry. He knelt down beside her and, after establishing that she was conscious and orientated, did a full body check. Satisfied that the injured leg was the chief priority, he started chatting to her in a conversational way and rounded things off by saying, 'There's a good chance you've broken your leg,' as if it were hardly worth mentioning. It was the understatement of the year, but he was determined she should be as relaxed as possible. She must have been aware of the fracture, but I doubt she realized for a moment just how grotesque it was.

Despite her tight jeans, we were able to establish that the bone hadn't punctured the skin and were ready to straighten the leg out, or at least Larry was. My job was to get a firm grip of her upper thigh and pelvis and, as Larry put it, hang on for dear life as he brought the broken leg round to join the good one. He had a few more words with the girl and persuaded her to relax all her muscles, as it would make it easier for us to move her leg into a better position for the journey to hospital, making it seem that she was doing us a favour by agreeing. I have to say that she was a most compliant patient and kept her eyes fixed on the sky throughout. Larry grasped the injured limb and, with a nod to me, started to pull without at first altering the angle. The girl grimaced but didn't make a sound. I was astonished at the amount of strength it took to counter the effort Larry was putting in as he swung the leg round without allowing the broken ends of the bones to touch. When he had it in what he considered to be the optimal position, he slowly released the traction. She grimaced again and her ordeal was over. Her legs were side by side. It was then a matter of putting on a bit more traction and splinting her up.

I don't know which was the more praiseworthy, the girl's fortitude or Larry's skill, but when I looked at the injured leg it seemed to me that the doctors wouldn't have much to do. There's usually a fair amount of swelling involved when the femur is fractured. Perhaps her tight jeans masked the worst of it, but there wasn't much evidence of the damage when we handed her over to the triage nurse. She listened to Larry's description of her condition and how we had found her and then straightened the leg. A young Casualty doctor happened past and, having missed the beginning of the story, stopped to listen to the rest. Larry leaned over the girl and pointed at the middle of her thigh.

'It's just there: mid-shaft fracture, clean as a whistle.'

The doctor craned his neck and regarded the leg sceptically.

'I think it might be an idea to let the X-ray decide that, don't you?'

To my surprise, Larry said nothing, so I opened my mouth to remonstrate, only to be stopped by a sharp kick on the ankle from Larry. The doctor, having made his point, disappeared into a nearby cubicle while we and our patient disappeared into another.

Back in the ambulance, Larry smiled when I asked why he didn't explain to the doctor about the fracture.

'For a start, he didn't ask, and that was rude. When he gets to see the X-ray the fracture will jump out at him. He might just look back on his remark and feel a little embarrassed. These young doctors have to learn not to dismiss us as jumped-up porters and listen to what we have to say. There's no way an experienced doctor would have been so arrogant.' He mellowed a little. 'I suppose it's not really his fault – he has to learn somehow.'

'So you see it as helping him out with his education?' I suggested.

'Yeah, I suppose you could put it that way.'

And he was right. It's quite noticeable that the higher up the medical tree a doctor has climbed, the more likely he is to give us his full attention.

Larry's practical bent wasn't confined to treating patients. He could be relied on to find a way round any obstacle, no matter how problematic it might be, as he did in the case of the newsagent and the dogs. We had reports of a shopkeeper having collapsed and arrived to find four or five elderly ladies outside, anxiously peering in through the window. One was wearing a bright floral headscarf and expressed her relief at our arrival.

'Oh, thank goodness you're here. Poor Mr Johnston's on the floor. I don't know if he's breathing or not.'

Larry and I gazed through the window and could just about see the patient's head and shoulders protruding from behind the counter. We stared at him intently and came to the conclusion that he was breathing, but was unconscious. There was no way of forcing an entry and I asked the ladies, in hope rather than expectation, if they knew of a key-holder we could contact. After some lip-pursing and frowning, the lady in the headscarf answered in the negative.

'No, love, he lives on his own above the shop. I don't know of anyone else who might have a key. But that doesn't matter anyway – the door's not locked.'

'The door's open?' Larry said in surprise. 'So why are we all standing out here?' He turned the handle and instantly got the answer to his question. A sudden scuffling sound from within was quickly followed by a furious cacophony of deep-throated barking. Woof! Woof! Woof! Larry slammed the door closed and used it for support while he recovered.

'Shit!'

The lady in the scarf looked concerned. 'I was going to tell you about the dogs.'

'Dogs? There's more than one?'

'There's two of them. They're usually quiet and stay in the back room. I've never seen them behave like this before. I suppose they're only protecting their master.'

Another glance through the window revealed the black-haired beast in all his fearsome glory. He was staring intently at the door with his head cocked slightly to one side, ready to launch himself into battle at the next hint of trouble. My immediate impression was that he must have been a cross between a Labrador and a horse. His companion, on the other hand, couldn't have been more diminutive. He wasn't much bigger than a Chihuahua, but what he lacked in stature he made up for in attitude. He was trotting back and forth like a guardsman, and a very camp one at that, tail and head held high, yapping every now and again at nothing in particular.

'I don't fancy yours much,' Larry said as we considered them.

'I suppose we'll have to get a police dog-handler out,' I said.

'I suppose so.' There wasn't much conviction in Larry's voice. 'We could be waiting ages, though, and that bloke might be in a bad way.' He watched the little dog strutting about for a moment, then seemed to come to a decision. 'I've got this theory.'

'Oh yes,' I said. 'And what's that?'

'Deep down all dogs are cowards unless they're mob-handed. I reckon that if we just charge in and make a lot of noise, they'll leg it.'

'Are you serious?'

'Yeah. I reckon it's worth a go.'

'Supposing your theory is wrong? That big one doesn't look like a coward to me. He'll tear chunks out of you.'

'Us,' Larry corrected. 'Chunks out of us. If we take an oxygen bottle or something to hit him with, we'll be OK.'

And so, with the seventies risk assessment completed, we prepared ourselves. Taking a deep breath, we charged into the shop yelling like a couple of riot policemen. The big dog's eyes widened and, with his own risk assessment completed in not much more than a millisecond, he turned and fled behind the counter, yelping as if a swarm of bees was after him. He carried on into the back room and then thundered up the stairs. Larry didn't have time to look pleased with himself. The little dog, red-eyed with rage and distinctly unimpressed by our terror tactics, launched himself at Larry. Larry wasn't quick enough. Before he knew it, the little bundle of fury had latched on to the material of his trousers just below the crotch. Larry spun in a circle and batted him away with the palm of his hand.

'Gerroff, you little bastard!' The little bastard was on his feet in an instant and, his nails scrabbling on the lino, flew at Larry's legs this time. Larry kicked out but, as with all his subsequent defensive actions, he was six inches behind wherever the dog happened to be at the time. He let out a cry as tiny teeth sank into his ankle. Spinning on his good leg in a desperate attempt to shake off his assailant, he crashed into a carousel of greetings cards. Thinking it about time I did something to help, I opened the door fully in the hope that the little dog might be tempted to make an escape. But it was Larry, dancing and yelping all the way, who eventually fell out on to the pavement. His attacker watched him go and trotted back to the counter, from where he stared at us defiantly.

Larry sat on the pavement, dabbing at his ankle with a hankie while the elderly ladies clucked over him like mother hens.

'It wasn't your fault, love,' one of them said. 'It was very brave of you.'

I didn't think the shift would see it that way when I told them later he'd been chased out of the shop by a creature small enough to have fitted in his pocket. He stood up and, after thanking the ladies for their concern, spoke to me.

'Right, time for plan B. We can't mess about any more. We've got to do something for that bloke on the floor.'

'He's come round,' I said. 'He opened his eyes with all the racket. When you knocked over the greetings cards he actually tried to sit up.'

'Oh, that's good – at least something came out of it all. Anyway, if you fetch a blanket we'll sort out that little monster once and for all.'

I returned with the blanket and handed it to Larry.

'You've got to admit that he's got some bottle for such a little squirt,' I said.

'Yeah, he's a tough little blighter. Thank God the big one didn't take a leaf out of his book.'

Larry's plan B was simple. He would enter the shop

and immobilize the dog by throwing the blanket over it when it attacked.

'Brains over brawn,' I said. 'Never fails.'

He gave me a sideways look before squaring his shoulders and entering the shop like a matador.

The little dog looked almost pleased when he saw Larry come out of his corner for round two. I knew his fate, though, and almost felt a twang of sympathy for him as he leapt forward emitting a canine version of the Bruce Lee squeal. Larry waited for all four paws to be off the ground before throwing the blanket and engulfing the little form in mid-air. He then dropped to his knees, quickly gathered up the loose corners and carried the wriggling mass to the back room, where he shook the angry creature out and closed the door. The patient had regained a measure of alertness and proved to be more concerned about the fate of his dogs than his own welfare. The signs were that he'd probably suffered a mini stroke, or TIA, as it's known. We assumed he wouldn't object to a few dog hairs and carried him out wrapped in the blanket that moments earlier had been a weapon. Larry basked briefly in the admiring looks of his little fan club of elderly ladies before loading our man on to the ambulance. I suppose that waiting for the dog-handler would have been the wiser move, but that wasn't Larry's way. And it has to be said that the patient found himself in hospital a lot sooner than if we had waited for help.

I return, though, to Larry's astute talent as a

communicator by remembering a truly tragic case from my time as a probationer. I was the attendant that day and when the case description of 'child won't wake up' came over the radio, a feeling of dread coursed through me. Larry didn't say anything as he switched on the blue lights and stamped on the accelerator. He didn't need to; his expression said it all as he drove to the location with a controlled determination that I hadn't seen before. We ran up the path and through the front door, which had been left ajar. A woman was sitting in an armchair by the fireplace with a child of about eighteen months on her lap. She looked up at us and then returned her attention to doing up the last of the buttons of the little cardigan. We stopped in our tracks, all sense of urgency dispelled. The child was grey, his lips purple and his limbs flopping one way and the other with each movement his mother made. Larry took a step forward as I took a step back. We both knew I was out of my depth and it was up to him.

The mother reached for the child's anorak and began pulling it over his head.

'We'll be with you in a moment.' Her voice betrayed no emotion. Larry stared at her as he tried to come to a decision. He ran his tongue over his lips and took a step closer as the child's head lolled out of the anorak.

'Do you mind if I hold the baby?'

She kept him closer to her breast.

'No, it's better if I keep hold of him.'

'Please,' Larry said, 'just for a moment.'

She stood up and moved to the wall.

'No! I don't want anyone to touch him. He's OK with me.'

My eyes flicked between the two of them, not knowing how the impasse would be resolved.

'Please,' Larry said again. 'I won't do him any harm. I only want to see if I can do anything to help.'

She held up her free arm as if getting ready to ward him off.

'No.'

Larry sat down on the sofa.

'That's fine. I'll just sit here if that's OK.'

I won't attempt to replicate Larry's words, nor the mother's anguish – there's no way I could begin to do it justice. Suffice to say that watching the way he gently manoeuvred himself into her confidence was like witnessing a master class in the art. When she eventually surrendered the baby, it was of her own volition, and as she walked over and put the limp body in Larry's arms I felt a surge of pride and admiration for him. It had been a truly remarkable demonstration of tact and tenderness. That death had visited the little mite some time earlier wasn't in doubt, but that didn't stop Larry going through all the motions of trying to revive him.

I drove to the hospital while Larry continued his efforts in the back. I don't recall the mother saying anything while she was with us. She remained passive in her shock and made no attempt to retrieve the baby from Larry. He said later that there was stiffening about the child's jaw and neck, indicating the onset of the first stages of rigor mortis, and there was never the slightest hope of reviving him. He'd gone through the resuscitation procedure purely for the mother to have the memory of everything being done for her baby when she came out of her shock. Some say that relatives shouldn't be given false hope, and in general I agree with them. But, in this case, I think Larry did the right thing.

# Chapter Twenty

Shift meals were something to look forward to, but only if someone other than Mike was doing the cooking. His reliance on hot chillies to add 'a bit of bite' to whatever he was preparing left us all in dread. He was in good spirits one particular evening when he wandered into the messroom early for the start of the night shift, armed with a carrier bag full of ingredients. One of the afternoon shift noticed him as he put down the emergency phone and came over with an expectant look. He held out a piece of paper.

'This job's just come through. You'll do it for us, won't you?'

'Er, yes, of course.' Mike took the crumpled note.

'Great! Thanks. I've got an appointment with a pint before they put the towels over.' With that he was gone, leaving Mike to drop his carrier bag in the kitchen while I went out to the garage, grumbling to myself that it would have been nice to have a cup of tea before getting started. I was adjusting the driver's seat when Mike joined me and smoothed out the piece of paper. He stared at it for a moment.

'Great – "sixty-year-old woman unwell". Now we know everything.'

As job descriptions go, it wasn't one designed to send the pulse racing. It was also irritating. Surely it wasn't asking too much that the caller give us a clue by coming up with at least one symptom? Vague job descriptions were common enough, and even though I'd been caught out by them in the past, on this occasion I decided it couldn't be too serious. I was wrong in that assumption – quite spectacularly wrong, as it happened.

The caller was the patient's husband and he was in a bit of a state when he let us in.

'She's just collapsed! We were talking and then she just fell backwards on to the bed.' He started making his way up the stairs. 'She's in the bedroom. I think you'd better take a look at her.'

'Was she complaining of anything before she collapsed?' Mike asked as we followed him upstairs.

'She was short of breath and panicky. I was trying to calm her.' He beckoned us to precede him into the front bedroom and shouted through to his wife. 'Marion, it's the ambulance men. They're going to sort you out.'

She was sprawled on her back across the bed, mouth agape and not breathing. I moved forward and felt her neck for a carotid pulse without any success.

'How long since she last spoke to you?' Mike asked her husband, as he broke open the resuscitation bag.

'Just before I went down to let you in. Is she going to be all right?'

Mike side-stepped the question.

'Could you go and gather together all her medications for us, please.'

He left the room, eager to do anything that might help, and we quickly slid the woman off the bed and on to the floor. I still couldn't find a pulse. Mike double-checked and then we fell into the resuscitation routine. Mike was doing cardiac compressions while I used the bag and mask in an effort to get her oxygenated. After two cycles we stopped and I checked again for a carotid pulse. It was as if I had received an electric shock when my fingers picked up on it immediately, strong and unmistakable.

Despite what public perception might be, pulling someone back from the brink when they've gone into cardiac arrest is not an everyday occurrence; in fact, it hardly happens at all. I continued working with the bag and mask with a feeling of elation, determined that she shouldn't slip away again. Her husband popped his head round the door a few seconds later.

'How is she?'

Mike stood up and guided him out on to the landing.

'I'm not going to beat about the bush with you: she's not at all well. We're going to get her on the ambulance in a minute. Gather everything you'll need because we won't be hanging around once we get moving.' We had his wife downstairs and into the ambulance in the blink of an eye. She still needed assistance with her breathing, but her pulse remained strong on the journey to hospital. The last I heard she was stable in intensive care.

We were pleased with the way things had gone and felt set up for the night. If bad things often come along in threes, I wondered to myself, then why shouldn't good things follow the same pattern? This might be the start of a little run of saving lives. I was only kidding myself, little imagining that another life was destined to be saved on the very next job, albeit in a way I couldn't have imagined. The case came over as 'man fallen off a stepladder at home'. Mike looked at his watch.

'Half eleven. What possesses someone to climb up ladders at this time of night?'

The patient's wife was able to answer that. Her husband had noticed a light bulb had blown out when he got home from the pub and insisted on changing it there and then. He'd made it to the third step when everything began to wobble and he tipped backwards, hitting the back of his head hard on the tiled floor. He was unconscious and snoring when we got to him. The back of the skull is poorly protected in comparison with the rest of the head and a blow of any significance can often lead to a fracture. With this in mind, we immobilized him on our scoop-stretcher and made for the hospital with a sense of urgency. We were led straight into the resuscitation room and, after handing over to the staff, Mike wheeled out our stretcher as I washed my hands in a nearby basin. When I turned round it was to find that I was alone in the room with the patient. I waited for a few seconds, expecting a nurse to come in and carry on her work, but nobody came.

Patients strapped on to a scoop-stretcher or similar devices should never be left alone, the great danger being that they might vomit. If they do, they have no way of positioning themselves to avoid inhaling some of it. And it doesn't take much acidity in the lungs to do a lot of damage. If the patient is unconscious, it's even worse. I wandered over and stood beside him, wondering how long I would have to keep vigil. Then his stomach began moving rhythmically in time with choking noises coming from his throat. He was going to be sick. I acted instinctively by grabbing the far side of the stretcher frame and pulling it towards me in an effort to raise it perpendicular to the trolley it was resting on. I had almost made it when there was a thunderous whoosh and a couple of pints of vomit flew past my waist and splattered on the floor behind me. Relief that I'd managed to get him upright just in time gave way to the beginnings of panic as the stretcher frame started to slide towards the edge of the trolley on the sheet covering the rubber mattress. The harder I tried to get him completely upright and arrest the slide, the worse things got. He was still vomiting, albeit at a reduced level, which meant I couldn't lay him flat again. He wasn't a small man, and when my hips were all there was between his staying on the trolley and crashing to the floor, I began shouting. It went against the grain, but I had no choice. Staff came running and the situation was soon under control. It was noticeable that no one made reference to the fact that the patient had been left alone. It was all tight-lipped efficiency. They may have held an inquest amongst themselves later but, if they did, I wasn't privy to the outcome.

Mike whistled when I told him.

'That's terrible.' He was silent for a few seconds. 'What were they playing at? If you hadn't stayed to wash your hands he'd be a dead man.'

'I would say so. God knows how long it would have been before someone came in and found him,' I said.

'Apart from anything else, can you imagine the kick up the arse the hospital would have got?' Mike added.

It's hard to make excuses for the staff; all I can think is that there was a misunderstanding and each thought that the other was with the patient. It was a bad business but, if nothing else, I could at least clock it up as another life saved. And if everything I'd said about things coming along in threes was correct, then there was someone else out there just waiting for us to happen along.

Much to Mike's annoyance, we were given an inter-hospital transfer over the radio while on the way back to the Street. We had to go to the General, which was an adult-only hospital, and transfer an unresponsive baby to the Children's Hospital.

'What's going on? It's bloody Tuesday, isn't it? If this takes too long then we can forget the grub,' Mike said despondently. 'I need at least three-quarters of an hour in the kitchen.'

I didn't feel despondent. In fact, I drove to the General

in an altogether happier frame of mind at the news. A sister showed us to the cubicle where the baby and mother were before going off to find a nurse to travel with us. After saying our hellos, Mike inspected the nine-month-old on the couch and asked her mother the reason for bringing her into hospital in the first place.

'She's been niggly all day and off her food. Tonight she wouldn't settle and once she started crying she wouldn't stop. I thought it best to get her checked over. I didn't realize that this place was just for adults. We'd been here about half an hour when she became unresponsive and started to worry the doctor.'

Mike looked again at the child and pulled away the mask supplying her with a trickle of oxygen.

'She looks fit enough to me. What do they think is wrong?'

'They don't know, other than she's unresponsive.'

Mike reached out and gently tweaked one of the little earlobes. The baby didn't react at first, but when he increased the pressure she gurned slightly and smacked her lips. Mike looked at me with a raised eyebrow and repeated the process. He kept the pressure on this time until the baby launched into a sustained and high-pitched wail. The mother was out of her seat in a flash with a look of unsuppressed relief.

'Oh, thank God. What did you do?'

'I woke her up. She was fast asleep. Hardly surprising if she's been awake all day.'

Presumably alerted by the noise, the sister came into

the cubicle with a young female doctor and ushered us out. Two minutes later she stuck her head round the curtain.

'The doctor's cancelling the transfer. We won't be needing you now.'

Mike didn't grin often, but he was grinning all the way out to the ambulance.

The others were all sitting around when we got back to the Street. It seems they'd had a busy start to the night too. Larry and Jack had been out to a young man hit by a car outside the Deaf and Dumb Club in Ladywood. (I think they have probably changed its name since then.)

'He didn't seem to be badly hurt,' Larry explained. 'The trouble was that I didn't realize he was deaf – I just thought he was foreign and couldn't speak English. It was only when he started using sign language that the penny dropped. Then people began coming out of the club and got themselves quite worked up when they saw him lying there in the road. Before I knew it, I was pushed out of the way and he was out of sight behind five or six people all signing away at the same time. When one of them tried to tell me what the patient was saying, he did it in sign language, and a fat lot of use that was to me. And this girl kept pulling at me wanting to lip-read what I was saying. In fact, they were all trying to read my lips, which meant they had to stick their faces in front of mine. It was daft because I had nothing to say and it was dark anyway.'

'Shame they don't cover that kind of thing in training school,' Steve said.

Larry agreed. 'Yes, maybe I'll see if I can get it put on the syllabus. And it got worse as more and more people came out of the club and joined in. Don't get me wrong, it's not like it was their fault, but in the end we were surrounded by about twenty people looking like they were trying to guide a plane on to an aircraft carrier. There wasn't much else we could do but treat the poor kid as if he were unconscious and whip him off to the Accident Hospital with all his mates following behind in taxis.'

A delectable aroma was starting to drift through from the kitchen. If what Mike put on our plates tasted half as good as it smelled, then it would have been a banquet indeed. The sad thing was that past experience told us it *wouldn't* taste half as good as it smelled – nowhere near, in fact. Any delicate blend of herbs and spices he'd worked so hard to create was blown apart by the half pound of chillies he'd dropped in to 'liven it up'. Twenty minutes later he was pushing loaded plates across the serving hatch along with two fresh loaves. Hunks of bread, we'd discovered from bitter experience, were more effective than rice in diffusing the heat. We stared at our plates in silent contemplation until Mike came round to join us. He scooped up a spoonful and chewed away happily.

'It's just a vegetable dish this time – you lot eat too much meat for my liking. This is better for you. It'll get your insides working properly.' I'm not sure what he meant by *properly*, but it was noticeable that no one felt

the need to contradict him. Jack, despite the veiled warning, bravely popped half a spoonful into his mouth, taking
care not to allow it to come into contact with his lips.
Mike watched with interest, and when Jack spluttered
and reached for the bread, he smiled approvingly and
addressed the rest of us.

'Come on, then! Don't let it go cold.'

'Go cold?' Jack managed to say. 'You've got to be
joking. This wouldn't go cold if you left it at the North
Pole for a month!'

Mike's cooking always stimulated conversation, for no
other reason than if you were talking, you weren't eating.
As we pushed the food about our plates to a background
noise of sniffs and hiccups, I related the two life-saving
cases Mike and I had been on earlier. The others had been
busy too, and as we got talking the general consensus was
that we all found it hard to believe that it was a Tuesday,
usually the quietest night of the week. Howard leaned
back and fanned himself with a magazine.

'Maybe it's a full moon tonight. It's either that, or no
one's told them out there that it's Tuesday.'

'I think it is a full moon,' Larry said. (I should perhaps
mention that all ambulance crews, without exception,
believe that a full moon heralds nothing but trouble.)

'Well, maybe that explains the daft job Steve and I had
earlier. You won't believe it, but a couple of old biddies
went for a swim in the canal at Brindley Wharf.'

'All Saints patients?' Jack asked as he nibbled something green off the end of his fork. All Saints was

purpose-built in 1850 as a 'pauper lunatic asylum'. Designed in the Tudor style, the elegant façade belied a gloomy, not to say creepy, interior encompassing miles of echoing corridors and stairwells leading to dingy wards and miscellaneous rooms, the original purpose of which I wouldn't care to guess at. I doubt even the Addams Family would have cared to spend a night there, despite numerous modernization programmes. Attitudes and treatments concerning mental health may have changed over the years, but All Saints, with Winson Green Prison to its rear and the remains of what had been the work-house half a mile away, remained a dark testament to bygone days. Jack asking if the ladies had originated from there was understandable; at the time, the bodies of inmates were fished out of local canals with monotonous regularity. Howard was able to put him right.

'No, they had nothing to do with All Saints. They'd been to see a play at the Rep and then decided to go for a walk. When they got to the edge of the canal they looked right and left and, with no traffic coming, they stepped out into the water arm in arm, splosh, splosh.'

Larry squinted at him. 'What? You mean they thought it was a road?'

'Yep,' H said. 'If it wasn't the effect of the full moon, then I don't know what it was.'

'Were they OK?' Larry asked.

'As far as I could see, they were. Passers-by had dragged them out before we got there, but they must have swallowed a bellyful of canal water.'

The stories were beginning to run thin and the food was still piled high on the plates. Howard made an effort to stall for time in the hope of a job coming through.

'I don't think you can blame the moon, but we had a strange woman before getting that pair from the canal. She was staying at the Grand Hotel in town and dislocated her shoulder tripping over a rug.'

'This sounds like it's going to be fascinating,' Larry interrupted.

'I don't suppose it is. It's just that when we got talking she said she was staying at the Grand for a two-week holiday. Now that's a strange concept from the start. I don't think I've heard of anyone spending a fortnight in Birmingham for pleasure before. But she said that she comes every year because it's somewhere she knows and feels comfortable with.'

'So?' Larry said.

'So, when I got round to asking her for her home address, it turns out she lives in Digbeth.'

'What?' Larry said. 'Our Digbeth? The Digbeth less than two miles from the Grand Hotel?'

'Yeah, she shuts up her house every year and spends her summer holiday in a hotel just down the road. I told you she was strange.'

Larry shook his head. 'That's weird all right. I wonder if she sends her friends postcards.'

Mike seemed to be losing patience.

'Why don't you all just shut up and get this food down you before that bloody phone starts ringing again?'

Then the bloody phone rang. Larry picked it up with undisguised enthusiasm and a minute later he and Jack were on their way to a road traffic accident near Erdington.

Mike looked at the two half-finished plates in annoyance.

'I knew that would happen. Didn't I say to do less talking and more eating? Oh well, all the more for us, I suppose.'

Howard and I looked at each other ruefully and resumed our task with dogged determination. Five minutes later we were basking in a sense of accomplishment as we pushed away our empty plates and chewed on the last of the bread. Then the phone rang again, five minutes too late from our point of view. Steve answered it and, after jotting down a few details, turned to Howard.

'That's us. Larry wants a second ambulance at that RTA.'

They had barely left the room when the phone rang again. Mike got up from the table and picked it up.

'Don't you lot know that it's Tuesday? Right, right. OK.' He replaced the receiver and grabbed his coat. 'They're asking for a third ambulance at that crash. Sounds like it could be a nasty one.'

The blue lights of Steve's ambulance were visible in the distance as we sped along empty streets and past the Aston Villa ground. A mile or so further on, we pulled up at the accident at what during the day was a busy junction controlled by traffic lights. Three police cars and a fire engine effectively blocked off the approach roads and in the centre of the junction were the two ambulances. Their revolving blue lights, intermingling with the constantly working traffic lights, bathed the two crashed cars in a ghostly wash of colour. We parked beside them and Larry came over to give us a quick update.

'We've got the one out of that car on board.' He pointed at a saloon car with considerable frontal damage. 'He's in a bad way, so we're leaving now for the Accident Hospital. Steve and Howard are going to take the driver of the other car to the General. He's unconscious and badly hurt as well. Your patient is his front-seat passenger. You'll be going to the mortuary with her, I'm afraid.'

I looked round at the car in question. It had obviously been hit broadside, with the passenger door taking the full force of the impact.

'Bloody hell!'

'Yeah, sorry about that. I've got to go.'

He trotted to his ambulance and moments later was speeding off into the dark.

Steve and Howard were busily extracting their patient by way of the driver's door. They were taking great care with his neck and back, but that he was unconscious with a serious head injury took priority over everything else. His passenger, our patient, was obviously deceased, with extensive injuries to her head and body. Both were in their mid-fifties and dressed for a night out. We helped Steve with the driver and then turned our attention to the woman. Reconstructing the accident, it seemed that the driver of our car was turning right across the junction when the other vehicle came across and piled into the side of him. It could be that the second car came over on amber, or maybe even red. What wasn't in doubt was that he was travelling fast. Our patient had been flung sideways into the steering wheel and, from what Steve told me later, her head had ended up down by the driver's feet. Her injuries were appalling and left me in no doubt that she'd died instantly.

We extracted her as carefully as we could and headed off for the General to have her certified by a doctor before carrying on to the city mortuary just round the corner. The mortician was on call during the night, which meant we had to park up at the gates and wait half an hour or so for him to arrive. As always, it was a miserable wait. We sat in hunched silence, trying to pretend that the heater rattling and whirring away in the cab was actually giving out a bit of warmth. Mike eventually found something to say.

'I was just remembering a time when I was sitting here like this waiting for the mortician with a bloke on the back.'

'Oh yes?' I said, not feeling much in the mood for any more stories.

'Yeah, he'd dropped dead at a social club dance. We took him to the General and ended up hanging about here at half past midnight. After quarter of an hour or so there was a tap on my window and a woman was asking if we had Mr So-and-So on the back. She had the right name, and said she was his wife and wanted to see him before he was taken inside . . .'

I was trying to concentrate on what he was saying, but found myself thinking of the broken body just three feet behind me. She was probably a mother, a grandmother even. If the car had taken a different route, or started the journey a minute later than it did, she would now be home in bed with the rest of her life in front of her. Instead she was lying still and cold in a darkened ambulance, waiting to be taken into the mortuary by two strangers. The fragility of life couldn't have been laid out more starkly. I became aware of Mike staring at me.

'You're not listening to a word, are you?'

'Of course I am. You were saying that his wife wanted to see him.'

'Yes. Nothing like that's ever happened before and I wasn't very comfortable about it, especially when I discovered she had her teenage son with her. In the end I decided that saying goodbye on the back of the ambulance was a hell of a better option than in the mortuary, so I let them on board and stood in the corner like an undertaker while they got on with it. I was expecting the floodgates to open, but instead she just stared at him for a bit and then said something I'll never forget. You'd never guess in a million years what it was.'

'Well, no, I don't suppose I would. But we've only got about ten minutes anyway,' I said in response to his questioning glance. He gave me one of those looks over the top of his glasses before continuing.

'She stared at him and said, "You dirty, rotten, fucking bastard!" She said it twice, and it really sounded like she meant it. Then the next thing I know she's off the motor and marching away to her car. I was dumbfounded, and for a horrible moment thought I'd been conned by some weirdo who got a kick out of looking at dead people.'

'But she had her son with her,' I said.

'It was him who told me the whole story. It seems his father had been at the function with his mistress when he dropped dead. A friend phoned his wife from the club and not only told her that her husband had stopped breathing and was on his way to the General, but also mentioned that he'd had his girlfriend with him at the time.' Mike gave a humourless little laugh. 'You don't need enemies with friends like that, do you?'

'No,' I said. 'That's bloody awful.'

'It's hard to imagine anyone could behave like that,' Mike agreed. 'You can understand her being a bit upset by it all.'

The mortician turned up a few minutes later and, while we unloaded the stretcher, he opened up and switched on the lights. There isn't a good time to visit a mortuary, but there are better times than the middle of the night. Of all the things that surprised, confused or shocked me in my first few years on the ambulance service, the city mortuary came top of the list by a long margin. It was archaic. It was a Hammer horror-film idea of what a Dickensian mortuary should look like, with a bit extra thrown in. Even the trolley we had to transfer the patient on to must have been a hundred years old. It had a huge spoked wheel on each side and a caster at each end. To the right as you walked in there were wooden racks where the bodies were stored under sheets. The feet were exposed, with a luggage label tied to a big toe inscribed with each person's details. If an autopsy had been performed, then a plastic bag of giblets nestled between the feet. When trade was brisk, bodies were placed on top of each other and not always separated by sheets. Even the floor was used at times. The autopsy room was off to the left, imbuing the place with a smell beyond description. I could say a lot more, but won't. Suffice to say that the place appalled me at the time and, when I force myself to think back on it, it still appals me.

I left gallows humour at the door along with any pretence that I was cut out for this kind of thing. All I wanted was to get out of the place. We couldn't escape that easily though; we usually had to wait for the body to be stripped of clothes and valuables. Everything had to be witnessed and signed for to forestall any accusations should some personal item not be accounted for. In this particular case the rules were stretched. Her clothing had no pockets and it was highly unlikely that anything was concealed beneath. After removing her necklace and watch, the mortuary attendant turned his attention to her wedding and eternity rings. The struggle for the rings ended with his giving up and marking on his form that two gold-coloured rings were left on the body. Mike and I signed and escaped into the fresh air.

We expected to be sent back to the Street, but this particular Tuesday night hadn't finished with us yet. Neither of us saw the funny side when the radio crackled into life and gave us a maternity case. Mike tried to wriggle out of it by asking if there wasn't another crew available, as we wanted to get rid of the soiled linen we had on board. The Control girl apologized and said all the other vehicles were busy, adding, with a certain amount of relish, that Larry was on the M6 where a lorry had overturned and shed its load of sheep's heads. Mike gave a grim laugh.

'That bloke's a walking disaster area.' He found first gear and, as he pulled out on to the deserted street, gave me a word of warning. 'And I want no nonsense from you. We're going to put this woman in the ambulance and then drop her off at Dudley Road – you got that? Don't go encouraging her to deliver.'

'No. OK, got it.'

And I had got it. The last thing I wanted was any funny business. I was feeling tired and drained, and was starting to develop indigestion as I always did after one of Mike's chillies. All I could think of was the prospect of going home and collapsing into bed. That's why I didn't see what happened fifteen minutes later as being my fault. I had as much reason as Mike to get the case over with quickly. A milkman was delivering in the street when we arrived and, as Mike rang the bell, I bought a pint and felt the acid in my stomach dissolve as I drained it. I was wiping the last traces from my mouth and wondering what to do with the bottle as the door opened. They were an Indian couple, and to say she was beautiful hardly paid her justice. I held the bottle behind my back and basked in her smile, which was so radiant it drove the weariness from my bones. With her husband carrying the overnight bag, we walked to the ambulance. On the way I took the opportunity to ask her the usual questions. Her waters had broken earlier and the contractions were coming every three minutes: a bit close, but nothing to worry about. I thrust the milk bottle at Mike as he was closing the back doors and settled back in my seat.

They were a pleasant couple and, as we casually chatted, it was difficult not to be seduced by their natural charm. So many Indians seem to be endowed with it, and it had the effect of almost making me forget the reason we were sitting together at five in the morning. I casually timed her first contraction while listening to her husband talking about the three restaurants he owned. I knew two of them and both had a good reputation. She looked over from the stretcher when her husband had finished talking.

'I almost wanted to push with that one.'

Restaurants were wiped from my mind.

'Almost? You didn't, did you?'

'No, but I think I wanted to.'

The hospital was still ten minutes away and with that in mind I glanced towards the driver's cab, wondering if Mike had overheard. He had. His eyes were boring accusingly into mine via the interior mirror and the ambulance started moving noticeably quicker. The extra speed was of no avail. The puffed-up cheeks and faraway look I've come to fear accompanied the next contraction and a minute later I was hovering over the stretcher steering a baby boy into the world. The whole business went without a hitch and Mike had barely brought us to a halt by the time I was wrapping up the little mite. The baby's father, moist-eyed and too excited to speak, kissed his wife and child in turn.

Five minutes later I flopped into a seat outside the labour ward and waited for my heart rate to fall back to normal. It wasn't lost on me that a new life had come into being on the very stretcher that an hour earlier had supported the remains of the woman so cruelly snatched from this world. I felt there was something to be taken from that, and was still mulling it over as we steered the empty stretcher back to the ambulance. Perhaps Mike was having similar thoughts? It became pretty clear that he wasn't when I put it to him.

'Never mind all that claptrap. Did you get us an invite to one of his restaurants?'

I stopped in my tracks.

'Bloody hell! No, I didn't.'

Mike, a man who revered curries above all else, looked at me scornfully.

'You're bloody useless! Why didn't you drop a hint or something?'

'It never crossed my mind, and I suppose he was thinking of other things too.'

'Honestly, I despair . . . haven't I taught you anything?'

He was prevented from expanding on my shortcomings by the sound of clattering shoes from behind.

'Excuse me, gentlemen. I'm glad I caught you.' The newly created father, with the same grin pinned to his face that he'd had since the birth, held out a hand for us to shake. 'I wanted to thank you properly and ask you to be my guests for a slap-up meal. Here is my card.'

Mike took it and seemed embarrassed.

'Really, there's no need for this . . .'

'No, no, please. I can't say how grateful I am to you both. Just tell the manager who you are and he will look after you.' With that he made his way back up the corridor at a trot.

Mike studied the card and then dropped it in his pocket with a satisfied smile.

'You know, it's times like this that make you realize that this job isn't such a bad one after all.'

# Epilogue

The seventies dissolved into the eighties without much fanfare. Margaret Thatcher was tightening her grip on the country, the Rubik's cube was on its way in, and the six-penny coin was on its way out. *Dallas* was riding high on the BBC, Abba and Blondie ruled the charts, and John Lennon began his last year on earth. Bombs were going off in Ireland, strikes plagued the UK, inflation peaked at 18 per cent and the interest on a mortgage was something in the region of 15 per cent. Taking everything into account, it was as good a time as any for my son, John, to enter the world, which he duly did on 3 January 1980. As all new parents will testify, nothing changes your life quite as dramatically as an addition to the family. And when a further addition came along less than two years later in the form of my daughter, Claire, my life became a curious blend of nappies and round-the-clock shifts. I had two families now, the one at home and the one at Henrietta Street.

It seems that I submerged in 1980 and when I eventually came up for air it was to find that ten years had passed. My memories of the eighties are of standing on windswept touchlines watching seven-year-olds chasing after a ball, or trying to keep a straight face at school nativity plays, or putting my fingers in my ears at the sound of Kylie warbling from Claire's bedroom. Most other things that might have been going on in the world outside simply passed me by. The decade belonged almost exclusively to our little home, the children and Marie-Madeleine.

Changes were also afoot in the ambulance service. Shamed by the advances being made by services abroad, the powers that held sway over our set-up were forced reluctantly to enter the twentieth century. The initial pressure for improved equipment and an increase in the range of skills we were allowed to practise came from the road staff, but boy, it was painfully slow and met a lot of resistance from the top.

Now my son is a father. Esmee, my granddaughter, is living testament to the passing of the years, as are the youngsters filling Henrietta Street with new blood and enthusiasm. These young men and women are a great bunch and worthy of carrying on a tradition which has, and will, continue to unfold at the Street. Of course, there are plenty of things for someone like me to moan about regarding the modern workplace. Twenty-four-hour television and mobile phones, for a start. Of all the unpleasant things I have been subjected to in my career, being forced to sit and watch a bunch of misfits fast asleep in the Big Brother House at four in the morning must come near the top. Or – and this really gets me – after uttering words laden with wit and wisdom for the benefit of a young colleague, to turn round and find her with her tongue between her teeth busily texting.

Some things never change, though. Walking into the Street for the first time is as difficult now as it ever was, and when a new face appears I know exactly how he or she is feeling. I can remember struggling in the same boat as if it were yesterday. So it was that I recently watched with a mixture of sympathy and amusement a new lad slip into the messroom. He was about twenty-two and looked as comfortable as a Mormon who had accidentally wandered into a bar mitzvah. After nervously scanning the room a couple of times, he gave up on finding a friendly face, made for the notice board and immersed himself in the blizzard of directives. I had to smile at the sight of him standing there, jingling the loose change in his pockets, reading and re-reading a list of instructions for the disposal of soiled linen. When it became too painful to watch, I strolled over to introduce myself.

'Hello, I'm Les. You must be Ben. It looks like we're crewed together for the night.'

He looked at me through a taut smile.

'Hello, yes, that's right. I wasn't sure if I was expected.'

'Of course you were. Do you fancy a cup of tea before we start?'

His smile relaxed. 'Thanks, a cup of tea would be great.'

'Good. You'll find everything in the kitchen. Why don't you put the kettle on and we'll all have one.'

Leaving him to find his own way, I wandered out to the garage.

It hasn't changed much over the years. It's still the same shabby, cavernous space it always was. I'm happy about that. If the mood takes me, I can stand out here and be transported back to those early days at the Street. It's not something I do often, but watching young Ben nervously reading the same notice board I'd stood in front of all those years earlier struck a melancholy chord in me. He and his generation are the future, just as mine once was. Though I doubt if he would have seen it that way at the time; I certainly hadn't entertained such grand thoughts as I crept about Henrietta Street in my youth, trying not to be noticed. The idea that the likes of Mike and all the other wonderful characters would be gone one day was inconceivable at the time. But go they did. It's the way it has to be, of course, but to watch them walk out the door, taking with them all their stories and knowledge, was painful. There is, however, consolation in knowing that these people, and all those who went before them, were the foundations on which the ambulance service of today is built. Sure, their training and equipment wasn't as sophisticated as it might be now, but the ethos that drove them was identical.

The passing of time doesn't stop me taking pleasure in conjuring up 'C' shift in my mind's eye, even if I am resurrecting ghosts. I can see Jack doggedly trying to finish his crossword while Larry did his best to distract him by banging the snooker balls about the table. Poor Jack. He became one of my best friends for a few short years until succumbing to alcoholism and dying with only empty vodka bottles for company. Mike and Steve eventually retired, but sadly Mike didn't have long to enjoy his hard-earned rest. Howard was forced out with a back injury and Larry left to drive a coach shuttling the sick and chronically ill to and from Lourdes. Heaven only knows how the poor souls in his care coped with him. Of course there were many other men and women who came and went from Henrietta Street over the years. Their names are unknown to the newer generations, but I remember them all, these people from my past.

'Here's your tea, Les.'

Ben was at my elbow holding out a mug. I took it with a grunt of thanks, hoping he'd make himself scarce, but he didn't seem inclined to go back inside. Perhaps the reception was even frostier in there. I had to make the effort for his sake.

'So, what made you want to join the ambulance service?' I'd no real interest in what he had to say. He rambled on for a while and ended by asking how long I'd been doing the job. It's a question I hate. When I'd notched up ten years I'd been as proud as punch, but as time moved on I started to become reticent and oddly embarrassed by my length of service. Maybe because I knew I'd been here too long.

'Thirty years.'

He was impressed.

'Wow, that means you joined eight years before I was born.' I really didn't like the way the exchange was going and wished I had inherited Mike's ability to kill a conversation with one menacing look. I did try, but Ben didn't seem to notice and came back with the most predictable question of all. 'You must have seen a lot of things. What's the worst job you've been out to?'

I suddenly felt tired and looked across the garage wondering if I'd put the same silly question to Mike all those years ago. Ben had no idea just how impossible a question it was to answer. What did he expect from me? Did he want to hear about the lad we found mangled under the rear wheels of a bus? That might do, but maybe not. Perhaps if I described how it felt to lift the limp body of a young man from his car after he'd been hit by four bullets in a drive-by killing? Doubtless that would satisfy him, but it wouldn't be fair because it wasn't the worst job. The worst jobs are the ones that sneak under your defences, the ones that get to you emotionally. I thought of the little girl electrocuted in the park. If she'd lived she'd now be in her thirties with a family of her own. Perhaps that was the worst job.

But what of the best job? Why doesn't anyone ever ask me what my best job was? After all, it's the best jobs that allow you to come to terms with the worst. And not only that, the best moments far outnumber the worst. And I really do mean that. If the highs didn't outweigh the lows, then joining the ambulance service would have been a miserable career choice indeed. For a moment I tried to conjure up my *best* job and it quickly came to me that there was probably no such thing. How could there be? So much of our work is rewarding, and those rewards come in such a variety of guises that trying to set one case above another is little short of facile. As if trying to prove the point to myself, I allowed a procession of past cases to flit through my mind again before giving up on the whole business. Trying to give marks out of ten was just plain daft.

I returned my attention to Ben, who was patiently waiting for an answer to his question. Well, he wasn't going to get one; you don't unburden yourself to kids straight out of training school.

'Oh, I don't know,' I said, in an admirably grumpy voice. 'That's something you're going to have to let me think about.' I made a show of looking at my watch. 'Have you checked the truck?'

'No. I was just going to.'

'It's the first thing you should do. You don't want to get into bad habits.' I watched him scurry off and then made my way back to the messroom. He'd be busy for a while and I might as well find myself a comfortable chair. It was going to be another long night.

# Blue Lights and Long Nights

## Les Pringle

---

'A great read. I loved every page'
JACK SHEFFIELD, AUTHOR OF *TEACHER, TEACHER!*

Card-playing corpses, unfaithful husbands and 'flying' ladies – life as an ambulance driver in the 1970s was certainly varied . . .

At the age of twenty-three, Les Pringle decided to escape from office life, broaden his horizons and become an ambulance driver. Little did he realize how broad those horizons would turn out to be.

Filled with warmth and humour, *Blue Lights and Long Nights* takes us back to a time when lonely old ladies could call 999 and have a cup of tea waiting when the drivers turned up for a chat; when learning to drive the ambulance meant going out for one test drive and managing not to hit a pedestrian; and every day brought a glimpse into other people's lives.

Gripping, poignant and darkly funny, *Blue Lights and Long Nights* is an affectionate, warm-hearted look at a world gone by.

'It's the most wonderfully written book . . . I do recommend *Blue Lights and Long Nights*, I really do'
LIBBY PURVES, *MIDWEEK*, RADIO 4

'His fascinating insight will make you laugh [and] cry'
*YOURS*

'Les's writing is so good that, even though I knew the material inside out, I was still drawn to read more – he's a very engaging a writer . . . I cannot recommend it enough'
TOM REYNOLDS, AUTHOR OF *BLOOD, SWEAT AND TEA*

9780552158527